Object

Evolution

Dr. Nirushan Sivanesan

First published in 2019
ISBN 978-1091362901

Contents

Preface

Evolutionary theory is proclaimed as the scientific explanation of how all species came to be from a single source. We are told that there is such overwhelming evidence for the theory that it has become irrefutable. It is taught as fact in most science classrooms in the Western world, and the consensus in the scientific community is that evolution is true beyond doubt. In Western civilisation, if you do not accept it, you are considered unintelligent or uneducated. However, there has been much controversy and debate over the theory since it was first brought into the public domain about 160 years ago. This book attempts to explore this controversy and examine the case against evolution from various perspectives.

It should be noted that this book does *not* try to disprove evolutionary theory, as this would appear to be a futile task, analogous to trying to disprove the existence of God. It only aims to demonstrate the flaws of evolutionary theory and address the pertinent question of whether the theory has been proven to a reasonable degree, such that it can be considered as fact.

The majority of contemporary anti-evolution books are written from a religious point of view. We want to emphasise that this book has a different motive. Rather than promoting religion or God, this book will stick to analysing the evidence for evolutionary theory, in order to demonstrate that it is unproven.

It is important to distinguish the case against evolutionary theory from the case for God. The two are not synonymous. Diminishing the validity of evolutionary theory does not provide evidence of God's existence. "It's either evolution or God" is a false dichotomy. However, we will look at the arguments from a pro-creationism point of view for completeness.

Of course, the existing counter-arguments and the alternative explanations of the existence of life will be mentioned: however, these do not necessarily reflect the views of the author. They are only included for your information so that you have a complete understanding of the whole issue.

All you need to formulate a well-informed opinion on evolutionary theory is a rational mind. You don't need fancy qualifications or PhD's from esteemed institutions to be able to intelligently evaluate a theory such as evolutionary theory. In fact, it could be argued that self-education is the best form of learning, as it promotes independent thinking and minimises the risk of indoctrination. This is why a jury member does not have to have prior knowledge of the subject matter which is involved in a case. In fact, having such prior knowledge is often considered a hindrance for reasons of bias, which we will look at later.

Indeed, most of the greatest thinkers are those who have been able to question what they are taught and not just blindly accept it. Their opinions are not based on the credentials of others. Think about the great scientific discoveries of the world that were initially rejected by the scientific communities of the time: Nicholas Copernicus's Heliocentric Theory, Albert Einstein's Theory of Relativity and Louis Pasteur's Germ Theory were all dismissed by the scientific community when they were first proposed.

Organised education does not promote creativity; it only promotes obedience. Try not to just accept what you are told by others, even if they are described as eminent thinkers or scientists. Think about it for yourself. Otherwise, all you are doing is adopting a faith: a faith in science. This mechanism of accepting and believing is really no different to the psychological mechanisms adopted by religiously indoctrinated people.

My personal opinion (if I have one) on the truth of evolution is not relevant to the conclusion drawn in this book. This book does not deal with the question of whether evolution is true or not, just the question of whether evolution has been proven to a reasonable degree or not.

The two are very different. And the latter may not be a matter of opinion, as we shall see.

Introduction

In order for us to make our case, we first have to explain exactly what evolutionary theory is and the background of the whole debate about it. Obviously, it is not the purpose of this book to describe the whole process of evolution in great detail, as this in itself is a huge topic. However, the fundamental points about evolutionary theory will be mentioned. A basic background knowledge of the theory would be beneficial but is not essential. For your information, Charles Darwin (1809-1882), who was a British naturalist, is credited with the discovery of the theory. By the way, feel free to jump to the next section if you already have a good understanding of what evolutionary theory is.

What is evolutionary theory?

A species is a group of genetically related organisms that can interbreed with each other but not with organisms outside the group. Evolutionary theory states that all species, both past and present, arose from an original common ancestor. This process is known as *common descent*. This original common ancestor is proposed to have been the most primitive form of life that could exist. This is presumed to have been a single-celled prokaryotic cell similar to a bacterium, thought to have originated about 3.8 billion years ago. It is important to note that evolutionary theory does not attempt to explain the cause or origin of this first organism: it only attempts to explain the origin of all species after the initial development of this first organism.* So we are not directly concerned with questions over how the first organism came to be, as this is not relevant to the validity of evolutionary theory.

After this first organism developed, it underwent reproduction, resulting in a group of such organisms. Random mutations in the DNA/RNA (the building blocks of all organisms) of members of this group resulted in new types and species of organisms emerging. This

---

* The mechanism of how the first organism came into existence is known as the process of abiogenesis, which is the development of the first organism from inert matter.

process continued for billions of years, resulting in all the subsequent species that we see in existence today, as well as the multitude of species that have gone extinct. This includes all plants, bacteria, fungi and animals. The exact process by which this happened is disputed between evolutionary biologists, however, one of the most accepted theories is that a process of "natural selection" took place. Natural selection proposes that organisms of a species that are better adapted to their environment are at a selection advantage – they are more likely to survive and reproduce. These "favoured" organisms then reproduce and pass on their genes, ensuring that their traits and characteristics are the ones that are passed on to future generations. This process is known as *descent with modification*.

Macroevolution refers to the major evolutionary change between species. *Microevolution* refers to the smaller intra-species changes that a species undergoes before it evolves into a new species. These changes are the result of random mutations in the DNA/RNA of organisms within a species which result in advantageous changes to these members. These changes are then naturally selected by the environment so that the species as a whole begins to change. These serial microevolutions result in significantly morphologically-different organisms developing within a species. The process of microevolution repeats itself continuously, and the small changes add up over multiple generations to create an overall dramatic change whereby the descendants of a species eventually look, behave and function differently. A point eventually arrives when they are considered to be a completely new species (a process known as *speciation*).

Species are generally considered to have become separated when members of one group are no longer able to successfully reproduce with members of the other group. Speciation occurs very gradually over a large period of time: a good analogy is the way that a boy turns into a man – a 30-year-old man looking at a photo of himself when he was 10 years old can see a huge difference in appearance: however, he is unable to identify a single point in the preceding 20 years when that change happened. Instead it happened gradually over time, and now he looks, behaves and functions very differently. It is also important to note that in order to get the huge biodiversity that we see today, a species will often evolve into more than one new species, causing the total number of species in existence to grow exponentially.

The tree of life, which is known as a phylogenetic tree, has been created to show how all life originated from the original common ancestor, as shown in Figure 1.

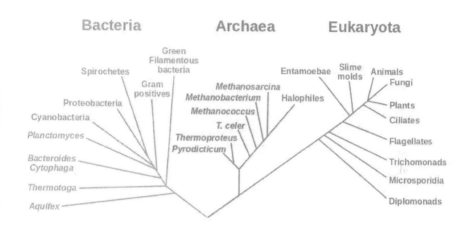

Figure 1. The phylogenetic tree showing the origins of the various kingdoms of organisms from the three original domains.

Figure 1 shows how all life originated from one point that separated into three groups (domains), namely bacteria, archaea and eukaryota. The eukaryota group includes animals, plants and fungi, amongst others. For the purpose of our investigation we are going to focus on the animal group and only use examples from this group, because to analyse the case for evolution of every single group depicted in Figure 1 would be too much. Also, this tends to be the group that interests most of us, as it directly concerns our own species.

Any one of the groups shown in Figure 1 can be opened out to reveal an extensive evolutionary tree of that particular group. It's important to understand that ranks are created in a hierarchical system in order to classify organisms. Organisms that share certain characteristics are grouped together and related through this mechanism. The principal ranks in current use are:

1. Life
2. Domain
3. Kingdom
4. Phylum
5. Class
6. Order
7. Family
8. Genus
9. Species

All living things, and all species, belong to the Life rank. The Domain refers to the bacteria, archaea and eukaryota groups. There are several kingdoms, such as the animal kingdom, the plant kingdom and the fungi kingdom. The animal kingdom is then divided into about 30 groups known as phyla (plural for phylum): one phylum (chordata) groups together all vertebrate species, and the other phyla cover all invertebrate species (over 90% of all living animal species are invertebrates). Examples of the different invertebrate phyla are: sponges; jellyfish and sea anemones; flatworms; roundworms; segmented worms; insects, spiders and crustaceans; snails, clams and squid; starfish and sea urchins. The chordata phylum, which is descended from an invertebrate common ancestor, is then divided into the five main vertebrate animal groups of fishes, amphibians, mammals, reptiles and birds, as depicted in Figure 2.

Human beings (known as Homo sapiens) belong to the Homo (human) genus, which also includes Homo habilis, Homo naledi, Homo erectus, Homo ergaster, Homo antecessor, Homo heidelbergensis, Homo rhodesiensis, Homo floresiensis and Homo neanderthalensis (Neanderthals): however, none of these species exist today. Humans belong to the Hominidae family (also known as the Great Apes), and the order that they belong to is Primates. Primates include all monkeys and apes.

We will expand on certain elements of the theory throughout the book, as and when required. However, for now, this basic understanding should be sufficient.

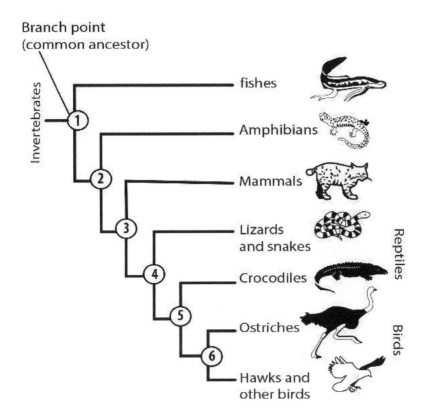

Figure 2. A simplified section of the phylogenetic tree showing the development of the animal groups from the original invertebrate animal group.

The controversy surrounding evolutionary theory

When evolutionary theory was first proposed, it caused huge controversy and uproar. Many people refused to believe that they could be related to or, even worse, descended from apes, let alone more primitive forms of life. Most people previously believed that God was responsible for the creation of all species and had created all animal groups independently. Now evolutionary theory provided an alternative theory for explaining all life on Earth. As a result, the Church and many religious institutions refused to accept the theory, and ever since, there has been an ongoing debate over evolutionary theory versus the theory of creation by God or some kind of supernatural intelligence.

This debate is often known as evolution versus creationism, or evolution versus Intelligent Design. Intelligent Design is a version of creationism which states that the world and all species in it are deliberately designed and created by God (mostly considered to be the Christian God). There are other versions of creationism, but all of them suggest the creation of at least some species through supernatural processes that cannot be explained by the known laws of science and nature. Most people who adhere to and promote creationism belong to a religious belief system and believe in God or gods. By contrast, most informed atheists support evolutionary theory and argue that it is incompatible with traditional religious belief. As a result, the debate over evolution often becomes a proxy for the argument between atheism and theism, which is one reason why it has become such a contentious and hard-fought affair.

However, many pro-evolutionists would argue that their religious faith or belief in God, or lack of either, has nothing to do with their support of evolutionary theory. They argue that evolutionary theory is a purely scientific question and should be evaluated as such. These are points which we will explore in some detail throughout the book.

There are also people who accept evolutionary theory while retaining a belief in God. They argue that the two are not incompatible, and that one can logically support both God and evolution. We will also explore the reasoning and logic of this later.

The question at hand

The principal question that is being addressed in this book is:

"Has evolutionary theory been proven to a reasonable degree?"

The "reasonable degree" element of the question refers to whether the theory has met the burden of proof so that it can be taught as scientific truth to children in science classrooms. The burden of proof refers to the expected threshold required for accepting something as true. Of course, everything in the world can be questioned, and there will always be some sceptics and conspiracists out there, but there is generally considered to be a threshold for accepting something as true. For example, the theory that the Earth is round and not flat, would appear to have met this threshold and can be considered as true. Conversely, the existence of aliens in the universe has not met this threshold and cannot be considered as true.

To answer this question, we need to keep in mind the main claim of evolutionary theory, which is that all species evolved from an original common ancestor (common descent). So it would be useful to have a "default hypothesis" which captures this idea so that we are able to conceive of what evolutionary theory is fundamentally proposing.

This default hypothesis will be:

"Human beings evolved from a single-cell organism through a series of random mutations".

This is essentially what evolutionary theory proposes. On first sight, it does seem quite extreme, but you should keep this proposition at the back of your mind when analysing the case for evolutionary theory.

Charles Darwin's theory of evolution explains the origin of *species*. Reproduction explains the origin of all organisms within a species. Charles Darwin based his theory on the observation that there is a biological similarity between all species. This led him to conclude that there is a biological relationship between all species. As we cannot theoretically have *direct* evidence for the origin of all species, a presumption was made by Charles Darwin that all species arose through evolution, thus this presumption indirectly incorporated the idea that all individual organisms arose through reproduction. So his theory was founded on the naturalistic philosophy that *all* life is related.

For purposes of this investigation, our definition of evolutionary theory asserts that *all* species arose through common descent, descent with modification and speciation, and that *all* organisms, bar the original common ancestor, arose through reproduction. That is to say, all species evolved, and all organisms are related. The theory will be tested against these assertions.

To appreciate the arguments brought forward in this book, you need to completely clear your mind of pre-conceived beliefs. Think of yourself as a jury member in a court case where you are expected to set aside any bias that may influence your decision or prevent you from assessing whether or not the burden of proof has been met.

Chapter 1 – The scientific approach

This chapter addresses the question of whether evolutionary theory is a scientific theory, and whether the evidence given for it constitutes scientific evidence.

Science is a concept, and its definition and methodology are somewhat disputed amongst philosophers of science. However, we will test evolutionary theory against the currently accepted understanding of what science is and how it should be practised.

What is science?

Science is the study of the natural world through observation and experimentation. The process of science uses the "scientific method" to answer a question or hypothesis. Through this process the initial question or hypothesis may become a "scientific theory". A scientific theory explains an aspect of nature in a way that is widely accepted as the truth. This is because it has been repeatedly scrutinised, tested and verified in accordance with the scientific method. It should be observable and testable through experimentation. A scientific theory is sometimes proven wrong and replaced by a new one: for instance, the heliocentric model replaced the geocentric model. A scientific theory can be modified to fit in new findings, but if the theory cannot accommodate new findings, it will ultimately be rejected. It is recognised in science that no scientific hypothesis or theory is ever proven to be certain, as it is always possible that future data might contradict it. Hence, a scientific theory can only be disproved and not proved. However, a scientific theory is expected to have a high degree of certainty and to be the best available explanation for the phenomena which it seeks to explain.

The scientific method is the way that observations lead to scientific theory. It starts with a general observation about nature which then leads to a question about this observation, for example, my toaster is not working; why is this? From this, a hypothesis is made with various predictions, for example, the toaster is not working because there is a power failure, and therefore all appliances relying on the same power supply will fail to work. The hypothesis is then repeatedly tested through study, controlled observation or experimentation until it is either accepted or rejected. Observation in science is the process of using the senses to collect empirical data. The scientific method relies on empirical evidence or data. Science can make predictions and theories based on what is observable and reproducible through experimentation.

Karl Popper, the 20th Century Austrian-British philosopher of science, established that a scientific theory must be falsifiable – it must be possible to create tests which *could* disprove the theory. This is now widely accepted as an essential feature of a scientific theory. Theories that are not falsifiable are considered unscientific. For example, the question of whether God exists is not falsifiable, and therefore it is not a scientific question. Evolutionary theory must have falsifiability for it to be considered a scientific theory.

Reproducibility in science is the principle that it should be possible to replicate an experiment under the same conditions and obtain the same results. While reproducibility is considered an important part of the scientific method, it is not essential to the scientific method. This is because it is not feasible to repeat certain experiments due to factors such as time and cost. However, what is considered essential to the scientific method is *testability* and *retestability* of the hypothesis. A testable hypothesis is one that can be proved or disproved through study, observation or experimentation. Only testable hypotheses are subject to the scientific method. *Retestability* is the principle that it should be possible to retest a hypothesis.

A solid theory of causality should be provided when explaining any phenomena through scientific means. For example, science has established that certain bacteria can be killed through the use of the antibiotic penicillin. A specific mechanism of action has been shown for this: the antibiotic inhibits bacterial cell wall synthesis, resulting in water leaking into the cell, thus causing it to burst and die. This process can be observed and can be reproduced in the laboratory. Also, science has been able to show how a rainbow is produced by reflection, refraction, and dispersion of light in water droplets, which results in a spectrum of light appearing in the sky in the formation of a rainbow – again, scientific experimentation can reproduce this phenomenon.

The falsifiability of evolutionary theory

Evolutionary theory proposes that it is falsifiable. The most well-known argument for falsifiability of evolutionary theory was proposed by John Haldane, a famed British evolutionist. He stated that finding "fossil rabbits in the Pre-Cambrian era" would immediately disprove evolutionary theory, as, according to current scientific thought, mammals did not emerge until approximately 40 million years ago, whereas the Pre-Cambrian era ended approximately 570 million years ago.*

It is important to note that some falsification tests are not the same as others. For example, if I hypothesise that there is an elephant in your house, you could easily falsify this hypothesis by walking through your house and seeing for yourself that there is no elephant. This is known as "evidence of absence", in other words the evidence that something is absent. But if I say to you that there is a ladybird in your house, it might not be so easy (or practical) for you to falsify this theory by checking the whole house for a ladybird, and a search is likely to result in the "absence of evidence" whereby a ladybird cannot be found. In the case of the elephant, the absence of the elephant acts as evidence to disprove the theory, whereas in the case of the ladybird, the absence of the ladybird does not disprove the theory. This essentially is the difference between the "evidence of absence" and the "absence of evidence".

Conversely, if I was to say that there are no ladybirds in your house and then challenge you to prove me wrong by finding a ladybird in your house, it may not be so easy for you to find a ladybird and falsify my theory. Of course, your inability to find a ladybird in your house would not actually do much to prove my hypothesis that there are none, because you could not be expected to have simultaneously searched every iota of the whole house in great detail in order to falsify my theory. Falsification challenges have to be achievable in theory but also practically feasible to be used as evidence to support a theory.

Considering this, it is clear that there are significant problems with evolutionary theory's falsification challenge of finding "fossil rabbits in the Pre-Cambrian era". According to the theory, animals rarely fossilise so we only have a very small selection of fossils. So the challenge of finding fossil rabbits in the Pre-Cambrian era could be likened to the challenge of finding the ladybird in your house.

There is also an element of hypocrisy in the pro-evolutionists' position here. Transitional fossils are crucial for proving evolutionary theory, and they defend the lack of transitional fossils on the grounds that fossils are very scarce. Yet they are happy to interpret the lack of certain fossils to mean that evolutionary theory passes falsification

---

* The Cambrian is a geological period from about 500 million years ago.

tests, and then use this as support for the theory. The absence of evidence (of a fossil in the wrong place or wrong era) cannot be used to add any weight to evolutionary theory, much in the same way that your inability to find a ladybird in your house does not add weight to the hypothesis that there are none there.

Of course, scientists should try to disprove a theory as well as trying to prove it. However, the inability to disprove a theory does not *necessarily* act as proof for the theory. This idea can be understood well through the "sensitivity and specificity" measurements used in determining the performance and suitability of certain tests. These measurements are used in modern medicine to determine the success rates of certain diagnostic procedures. Let's digress for a moment and expand on this point, as it will help with critiquing the tests that are used in evolutionary theory...

Sensitivity measures the probability of detection, and a sensitive test is one which won't miss the disease in question and is therefore able to collect all of the "true positives" in one group. By contrast, a specific test is one which will not misdiagnose a fit person as having the disease and therefore is able to collect all of the "true negatives" in one group. There is often a trade-off between these measures, meaning the more sensitive a test is, the less specific it will be, and vice versa.

Generally speaking, sensitive tests will have low specificity, and specific tests will have low sensitivity. This results in "false positives" and "false negatives" respectively, as demonstrated in Figures 3a and 3b. So in a 100% sensitive test, a positive result means that you may have the disease, whereas a negative result means that you definitely do not have the disease. In a 100% specific test, a positive result means that you definitely have the disease, whereas a negative result means that you may still have the disease but the test has not detected it. This means that in a sensitive test, a passed test result does not give a conclusive outcome, whereas a failed test result does give a conclusive outcome (that the person definitely doesn't have the disease). Conversely, in a specific test, a failed test result does not give you a conclusive outcome, whereas a passed test result does give you a conclusive outcome (that the person definitely does have the disease).

A good example is the test used in an airport security scanner which detects metal and potential weapons. The test is designed to not miss potential weapons that pose a threat, but the cost is that the test will detect a lot of harmless objects, such as keys and belts. The test therefore has high sensitivity but low specificity – potential weapons are not missed but at the cost of many non-weapons (false positives) being detected.

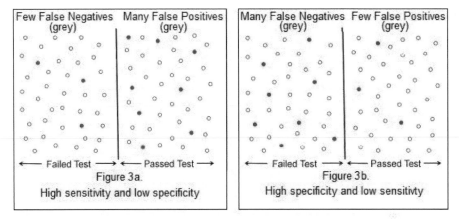

Figure 3a. Outcomes for a test with high sensitivity and low specificity.
Figure 3b. Outcomes for a test with high specificity and low sensitivity.

The challenge of finding fossil rabbits from the Pre-Cambrian could be considered a specific test because, if the test was passed, it could disprove evolutionary theory. However, the test would have a low sensitivity, as a failed test (not finding a fossil rabbit from the Pre-Cambrian) would tell us nothing about the presence of evolution, so could not be taken as proof of evolutionary theory. A failed test in this case is likely to produce a false negative, meaning that the failed test cannot correctly identify the presence of evolutionary theory. A negative result (or failed test) in a low sensitivity test does not tell us whether a person is fit or whether they have the disease. Just because the test cannot prove the disease, this does not equate to fitness. For that, we would require a sensitive test which could prove fitness or in this case evolutionary theory.

The earlier mentioned hypothesis of the toaster not working due to a power failure can be falsified by demonstrating other items relying on the same power supply are working, for instance the kitchen light. A passed test of getting light by flicking the kitchen light-switch on tells us our hypothesis is wrong. But a failed test of getting no light when we switch the light-switch on gives us useful information to support our hypothesis. So this test also has a high sensitivity. (Although note that it is not 100% sensitive, as the light bulb could have coincidentally burned out at the same time a malfunction occurred in the kettle).

Evolutionary theory has not been able to provide a similarly suitable test – all of the theory's falsification tests appear to have high specificity and *low* sensitivity. This is because a passed test result gives you a conclusive outcome (evolution is not true) but a failed test result tells you nothing about whether evolution is true or not. For example, failing to find a fossil rabbit in the Pre-Cambrian layer could be easily due to multiple other reasons and not just evolution: the reported scarcity of fossils, rabbits not fossilising, searching in the wrong areas, and so on. Trying to find a fossil rabbit in the Pre-Cambrian is thus not a viable practical test for evolutionary theory.

The fact that no test so far has been able to successfully disprove evolutionary theory does not equate to evolutionary theory being true: it merely highlights the inadequacy of the tests being used. There is no gold-standard test for disproving evolutionary theory. The fact that we can't come up with a viable, sensitive test which could disprove its validity is not proof to suggest its validity. This is much in the same way that an inability to devise a medical test to detect a specific disease, is not evidence to suggest the absence of that disease.

Is evolutionary theory scientific?

Anti-evolutionists assert that evolution is at best a poor scientific theory, as it is not falsifiable. They state the theory is too flexible and no test could be devised to decisively reject its key tenets. Henry Morris, an American engineer and anti-evolutionist, argues that almost any observation of the natural world can be accommodated within the overall evolutionary framework, and that this renders evolutionary theory unscientific. It is proposed that even finding fossil rabbits from the Pre-Cambrian would not necessarily result in evolutionary theory being dismissed in entirety. This finding could be accommodated into evolutionary theory by making the necessary revisions to the theory, for example by suggesting a second genesis with multiple descents. While this would negate common descent, it would still allow for the other major tenet of evolutionary theory, which is that species evolve into new species (speciation). Fossilised specimens can never falsify this tenet of evolutionary theory. In fact, there is no test that can.

The common descent component of evolutionary theory could be falsified by finding organisms that were not made of DNA. However, this would not disprove evolution outright. The theory could incorporate this new finding and modify itself. It could suggest a second genesis and separate evolutionary pathway of these new organisms without having to forgo the idea that all other species evolved. Evolution and descent with modification would still be viable, only now there would be more than one common ancestor. It would now be a theory of multiple descent and evolution, but the suggestion that man evolved from a single cell organism would still be viable.

The fundamental premise of evolutionary theory is that species evolve into new species. This is not falsifiable. Finding fossil rabbits in the Pre-Cambrian or organisms without DNA does not falsify this. So while certain *aspects* of evolutionary theory may be falsifiable, the fundamental premise is not. This makes evolutionary theory unfalsifiable. Therefore, according to Karl Popper's criteria, it cannot be considered a *scientific* theory.

Of course, scientific theories are expected to incorporate new findings and modify to some degree. Evolutionary theory has already done this. A good example of this is evolutionary theory's position on birds and dinosaurs, which were previously thought to be evolutionary cousins. Some dinosaurs were recently found to have feathers which made them more likely to be direct ancestors of birds rather than cousins, so evolutionary theory changed the phylogenetic tree to accommodate this new finding.*

The periodic table is an example of a vague hypothesis which became a proven scientific theory through a gradual accumulation of evidence. It was initially built mainly on guesswork and speculation, but through a succession of guesswork, new discoveries and experimentation, it was proven. The periodic table was rewritten numerous times to accommodate new discoveries. However, there has to be a limit to *how* "flexible" a theory can be. Evolutionary theory appears far too flexible to be considered a serious scientific theory.

Karl Popper said: *"Darwinism is not a testable scientific theory, but a metaphysical [religious] research programme..."* Granted, as pro-evolutionists are quick to point out, he later said, *"I have changed my*

---

* The reason why dinosaurs having feathers makes them more likely to have been direct ancestors of birds rather than cousins is explained through lineage and inheritance of traits – the random mutation resulting in feathers is predicted by evolutionary theory to have only happened once, as it is a specific anatomical trait. Therefore, we would not expect this trait to appear in two species not belonging to the same lineage, as this would mean that they developed feathers independently of one another.

mind about the testability and logical status of the theory of natural selection, and I am glad to have the opportunity to make a recantation." However, it is interesting to note he was only referring to *natural selection* and not evolution. Natural selection is *not* evolution. It is just one aspect of evolutionary theory. Natural selection is a proposed mechanism of *how* certain features can be selected by nature. It does not account for how new features originate, nor does it explain the exact process of a how a species becomes another species.

There is no *empirical* evidence to support common descent with species evolving into new species, which is the fundamental tenet of evolutionary theory. In fact, there is not even any evidence (scientific or non-scientific) to suggest that one species can evolve into another. Pro-evolutionists argue that all the separate pieces of "evidence" for evolutionary theory may seem insufficient when looked at in isolation, but when put together they form a very strong (or even indisputable) case for the theory. They argue that all the pieces of evidence, such as the DNA sequencing, the geographical distribution, and the transitional fossils work together and complement each other. This may be true, but it still does not constitute a scientific method, as the combination of this evidence does not provide observations or experiments for establishing the evolution of all species from a single-cell common ancestor.

Science is not about providing lots of little pieces of historical evidence and then building up a circumstantial but unverifiable case. Science is about establishing specific processes based on study, observation or experimentation which go towards proving an initial hypothesis. It is true that certain *aspects* of evolutionary theory may be scientific, for example the process of natural selection which has been shown to be reproducible to some extent. However, one cannot scientifically extrapolate this to scientifically judge the whole of evolutionary theory (i.e. that all life descended from a single-cell organism). The inference is too great. Furthermore, even though natural selection has been shown to be a viable scientific theory, it has not been shown to be the cause of all life (bar the original common ancestor) on the planet and is not unequivocally thought to be even amongst evolutionary biologists.

Obviously, for an initial hypothesis to become a scientific theory or law, there is a scientific threshold which needs to be met. There are, of course, scientific theories and laws which are indisputable, for example the atomic theory of matter, the cell theory of life, the theory of relativity and the periodic table of elements. All of these theories have met the scientific threshold. Also, the theory that the Earth is round and not flat has been observed to be true – people can fly out into space and actually see the evidence, so this is a case of a hypothesis being scientifically proven through observation and empirical data. Evolutionary theory has not met this threshold.

The evidence that is used to support evolutionary theory, such as DNA similarity, geographical distribution and transitional fossils, does support the theory and does not contradict it. But there is a significant difference between not contradicting a theory and scientifically proving a theory. There are alternative explanations for the observations made by evolutionary theory (as we will see in later chapters), and to say "God did it" is no less scientific than to say "random mutations did it", as we are unable to scientifically prove either. Both are presumptions which are not based on observation or testable scientific principles. Of course, biology has made very interesting observations about the biodiversity of the natural world, but this is all they are – observations. No-one has provided any actual scientific evidence to substantiate any explanation about how these observations came about. All we can say is that there *is* DNA similarity between all species, there *is* geographical distribution of species, there *are* fossils of species that look like they are a cross between one species and another, and so on. We cannot scientifically deduce anything more from these observations, and we certainly cannot scientifically deduce that man evolved from a single-cell organism based on these observations.

Past events cannot be studied through the scientific method. Firstly, it is not possible to observe the past. Observation is an activity that utilises the senses to collect data in the present. We cannot use the senses to collect empirical data about past events. Of course, we can examine past events in the present, but a degree of interpretation and inference will always be required to establish *how* these past events occurred. Secondly, it is not possible to design experiments to determine what happened in the past. Controlled observations or experiments may determine whether an event is possible in a specific situation, but the *exact* conditions that existed in a past moment, which will often be unknown, can never be replicated. Thirdly, it is not possible to predict the past. Science predicts future events arising from certain situations based on current observations of nature. It is not used to make predictions of what happened in the past based on current observations of nature. Nor can it be used to establish the past events that led to the current observations.

Observable findings can be predicted from events. But science cannot retrodict events from observable findings. For example, science can predict that a person shot in the head at close range is going to have a gaping gunshot wound in his skull. But the scientific method cannot be used to establish that a gaping gunshot wound in the skull of a person was caused by a shot in the head at close range. Science may establish that event *A* always results in observation *B*, but this does not mean that observation *B* is always caused by event *A*. While science can predict event *A* will result in observation *B*, this is something which can be repeatedly tested, and it can be proven wrong by finding a test in which event *A* does not result in observation *B*. But a hypothesis of observation *B* being caused by a *past* event *A* is not something which can be tested. There may be other unknown causes of observation *B* which are yet to be discovered. A gaping gunshot wound in the skull of a person may have been made by a device that mimics a gun but is not a gun. There may be numerous scenarios for this past event, and determining which scenario is most fitting is achieved through a non-scientific enquiry.

Determining what happened in a past moment is not the remit of scientific inquiry. This is why a forensic scientist uses the non-scientific term "consistent with" to describe the link between an observation and a past event. Evidence can make a solid case for a past event having occurred, but this is done using a non-scientific method. When a prediction is made by a scientific theory, it should be possible to check the prediction and see whether it is proven to be correct or not. This is done through observation. It is not possible to check a prediction of a past event through observation. The past event causing a gaping gunshot wound in the skull of a person cannot be observed and verified. As it can never be verified, it cannot be a scientific prediction.

A scientific theory is falsifiable if an event in the present can lead to an observation which contradicts a prediction made by the theory. On the contrary, a prediction of what happened in the past can never be falsified. For example, an alibi may exonerate a suspect from a crime, but the alibi does not *scientifically* falsify (disprove with certainty) the hypothesis/prediction that the suspect committed the crime – the alibi could be fake or be erroneous in other ways. As mentioned earlier, a scientific theory must be falsifiable, and falsifying a scientific theory is disproving it with certainty. A prediction of the past can never be disproved with certainty.

Evolutionary theory is a hypothesis about the past. It is a question about how biodiversity arose historically. It is not a hypothesis about how nature behaves in the present, as it does not make any meaningful predictions about how nature will change, and, unlike most scientific theories, it cannot be turned into technology. And the hypothesis is so vast that it covers a timescale that we are unable to retest in the present.

Evolutionary theory does not make predictions about the future. It is an assessment of the past. It tells us what happened, not what will happen. Some pro-evolutionists argue that evolutionary theory does make predictions about the past, for example predicting the previous existence of a specific transitional species. However, this is not what is meant by a scientific theory making predictions. A prediction about the past is made with an end-event in mind: in the case of evolutionary theory the end-event is the biodiversity of life today. So predictions made about the past are made with knowledge of how the process ends, and thus the "prediction" simply attempts to fill in the gaps and explain this process. It is not the same as making a prediction about what is going to happen based on specific mechanisms.

For example, evolutionary theory may predict that an ape-man turned into a human being through a series of intermediate ape-men, but this prediction is only made because we know that human beings exist today. Evolutionary theory cannot and does not make a prediction about what a human being is going to evolve into. This is because it has no theory about the specific mechanisms of mutations and features arising, so it cannot predict what mutations are going to happen and what new features will arise from these. While the smaller components of evolutionary theory may be able to make limited predictions under artificial conditions, for example predicting antibiotic resistance, the theory as a whole cannot make meaningful predictions about the future.

Of course, aspects of evolutionary theory are scientific and subject to the scientific method, such as natural selection, DNA similarity, molecular genetics and antibiotic resistance, as these are testable components of the theory. However, the assumption that these components are the result of common descent with evolution of all species is not testable. It is not possible to observe, test or repeat the process of the original single-cell common ancestor evolving into all the extinct and extant species. It is not viable to create experiments to reproduce this supposition, as it occurred over a period of reportedly

3.8 billion years and in conditions which are unknown and non-replicable.

In certain circumstances a theory is not amenable to experimental testing, and in such cases, it is accepted that "abductive reasoning" can be used to evaluate the theory. Abductive reasoning uses logical inference to explain an observation through the simplest and most probable explanation. While it gives a plausible conclusion, there will always be an element of uncertainty with abductive conclusions, and they are generally considered the "best available" rather than empirically true. For example, you notice your driveway is wet and *abduce* that it must have rained, as this is the best explanation in your mind, even though there are other possibilities, such as someone hosed your driveway down. Clinicians in medical practice will often use abductive reasoning – examination findings will lead them to conclude on the likelihood of a disease. Abductive reasoning may be applied to evolutionary theory since it cannot be empirically tested. However, abduction on its own only leads to the most likely hypothesis: it cannot complete the scientific method and convert a hypothesis to a scientific theory. This is because testability is integral to the scientific method. A doctor may hypothesise that a patient's cough is due to asthma, but this can only be confirmed to be a scientific theory through further investigations and tests. Similarly, abductive reasoning *may* conclude that evolutionary theory is the most likely cause of biodiversity, but experimental testing would be required to convert this hypothesis into a scientific theory.

Evolutionary theory is not reproducible and not retestable. While certain *aspects* of the theory can be tested, such as natural selection, the fundamental tenet of common descent with evolution of all species cannot be tested. This is because these events are historical, and we do not know the circumstances in which they occurred. It is not possible to reconstruct the exact same conditions that were present when the first common ancestor began to evolve, nor when any other species evolved into another. For instance, speciation in nature is proposed to be a process which takes place over thousands, if not millions, of years. It has never been observed to happen in the present, nor has it been reproduced. Experiments have been done on bacteria and fruit flies which have shown natural selection, and possibly the *process* of evolution, taking place, but these studies have not decisively resulted in speciation. Therefore, they do not confirm speciation could happen and did happen. In fact, the idea of speciation is conceptual. No scientist has ever proposed an *exact* method of change from one species to another and how this could occur. By this we mean a detailed hypothesis of specific changes in DNA leading to specific changes in the organism leading to specific selection leading to specific evolution.

You may say that using the lines of argument that have been used here to dismiss the scientific case for evolutionary theory, the theory can never be scientifically proved. Because, of course, it is not possible to travel back in time to observe the process having taken place, and we do not live long enough to observe it happening in the present either. This is true, however, this cannot be used as an excuse. It goes to show that evolutionary theory is *not* a scientific question; it seems to be more a question of history. The same way that the existence of God is not a scientific question, evolutionary theory is not a scientific question. Some may even see evolutionary theory as more a question of philosophy or faith rather than science or history, and this is something we will explore later.

If there is no *scientific* evidence to support evolutionary theory, then why do the majority of scientists agree with it? This is an interesting question which we will investigate in Chapter 8, as it is a point of curiosity. However, a scientist's opinion is not synonymous with truth. And it is not synonymous with scientific evidence either. Just because the majority of the scientific community agree with evolutionary theory, this does not constitute scientific evidence for the theory (although, this may be used as a non-scientific argument to promote and support the theory).

In short, there seems nothing in evolutionary theory which could be called serious scientific theory. It is not falsifiable, there is no empirical evidence to support it, it is not testable, and it cannot make any meaningful predictions. David Berlinski, the American mathematician and philosopher, has commented that he could never discern any scientific theory in evolutionary theory, and there is nothing in it that would be recognisable by a physicist or a mathematician. Regarding evolutionary theory: he said: "*[It is not] a solid theory that a physicist could recognise or an engineer could implement.*"

But even though we can see that there is no scientific case for evolutionary theory, this does not mean that evolutionary theory is untrue. There are many questions in life that are not scientifically testable but can be proved through other means. A murder conviction can be made without any scientific evidence at all through other means, such as a confession, eye-witness testimony or even through a lack of alternative explanation. As evolutionary theory is not a scientific hypothesis but rather a non-scientific hypothesis, it can only be evaluated using a non-scientific enquiry. Therefore, understanding how non-scientific enquiry works will assist us in assessing the strength of the non-scientific case for evolutionary theory.

Non-scientific enquiry

The scientific method eliminates certain hypotheses from scientific enquiry. If a hypothesis is not testable and falsifiable, and is not conducive to repeatable experiments and observations, then it cannot be established through the scientific process. However, there are alternative methods of enquiry used to answer questions in life.

The historical method is used to answer questions about history. It uses archaeology, relics, narratives, eyewitness evidence and second-hand testimony. Knowledge in history is generally not obtained using the means that scientific knowledge uses. It is developed through a whole array of techniques which uses evidence, just not *scientific* evidence. Science can often be turned into technology. History cannot. However, history does help with other aspects of civilisation, for example our laws, ethics, morality, social norms and religious faith. These are not scientifically determined. There are also other methods of obtaining knowledge non-scientifically, such as through experience, logic, tradition and intuition. Non-scientific enquiry is not necessarily weaker than scientific enquiry: indeed, in some situations, it can be more compelling. Sometimes witnesses can provide more detailed and reliable evidence than scientists. History can trump science, especially where multiple reliable sources corroborate evidence.

Certain theories can be proven to a reasonable degree without any scientific evidence at all. A legal case is a classic example of this. The criminal justice system deals with crimes which have occurred in the past. Even though criminal evidence is interpreted in the present, it regards historical events. A witness does not describe what they are currently seeing but what they *saw*. Blood from a suspect may be analysed in the present, but it is the correlation with historical blood found at the crime scene that makes it relevant as evidence.

Non-scientific evidence can be either direct or circumstantial. Direct evidence is that which supports a theory directly with no inference required, for example an eye-witness who directly saw Mr X murder Mrs E. Circumstantial evidence, on the other hand, is that in which an inference is required in order to establish causality, for example an eye-witness who saw Mr X threaten Mrs E and then follow her home but did not witness him murdering her – as the actual murder was not witnessed, an inference has to be made to conclude that he was the murderer. Of course, direct evidence does not prove a theory beyond any doubt, as it could have been manipulated or mistakes may have been made, such as perjury in the case of an eye-witness testimony or coercion in the case of a confession. However, for the non-scientific case of evolutionary theory, we would only expect to prove the theory to a reasonable degree, which is beyond reasonable doubt. This would be sufficient to accept it as true.

It is obvious that there is no direct evidence to support evolutionary theory, and that all the evidence requires inference, so would be considered circumstantial. Hypothetically, the strongest evidence would be eye-witness testimonial accounts from organisms that had lived through millions of years and witnessed the process of evolution happening in action. However, of course, this is not available.

Non-scientific evidence can be derived from scientific methods. For example, a DNA test which confirms that the blood sample found on Mrs E's corpse belongs to Mr. X is a scientific piece of evidence which establishes the blood is from Mr. X. However, it is not a scientific piece of evidence for establishing Mr. X murdered Mrs. E. It is only a scientific piece of evidence for establishing the blood comes from Mr X, and to conclude anything else requires a degree of inference. Similarly, with evolutionary theory we have lots of pieces of evidence which have used scientific methods: however, this evidence does not scientifically prove the theory. Therefore, it cannot be considered as scientific evidence *for* evolutionary theory but rather should be considered as scientific evidence which is being used to support a non-scientific case for evolutionary theory. A scientist's observations of an experiment are considered scientific evidence for proving or disproving a hypothesis. An eye-witness testimony of a past event may be persuasive, but it is not scientific evidence for proving or disproving a hypothesis. This is because, unlike the scientist's observations, an eye-witness testimony of a past event is not a controlled observation and is not retestable.

In certain questions, non-scientific evidence can be more potent than evidence derived from scientific methods. As with our murder case, an eye-witness testimonial may be given more weight than DNA tests that reveal matching blood samples on the suspect and murder victim (especially if we have no way of dating the blood samples and confirming they originated from the actual act of murder).

The sudden collapse and virtual disappearance of the once successful Mayan civilisation of Central America is considered a puzzling historical mystery. There are several hypotheses about what happened to them and why they died out. Some say that it was disease brought by European travellers which the Mayans had no immunity to, some say that it was excessive farming and deforestation, some say that it was drought and famine, and some say that it was harsh weather. These are all hypotheses based on evidence derived from scientific methods, but they are still only hypotheses at best. The fact that there are several tells us that no one knows for sure, and most of the proponents of these hypotheses would agree with this. But if we were to find diary accounts from Mayan people who had lived through, witnessed and recorded the events that had led to their demise, then this would probably act as the most convincing piece of evidence. No amount of soil sampling, mathematics or DNA sampling could probably match this.

A non-scientific enquiry into a historical event should not start with a hypothesis. For instance, a detective or forensic examiner investigating a crime scene does not, or at least should not, form a hypothesis of what happened and then attempt to prove or disprove the hypothesis. Instead they enter the crime scene and allow the evidence to establish the cause of the crime. Similarly, if you return home to find your house an unexpected mess, then you may try to work out what happened. Robbery, an earthquake or naughty children are all possibilities. The prediction you choose to go with about which past event has occurred is likely to be based upon initial evidence that you obtain and analyse. You do not start with a hypothesis and *then* look for evidence to support it. Eventually you make a best-fit analysis which is consistent with the evidence. This is what Charles Darwin did. He observed biodiversity and made a prediction of the past events that led to the current observations of biodiversity. Then he engaged in a non-scientific enquiry to try to establish these past events.

Helen Longino, an American philosopher of science, proposed that an individual's assumptions about the relationship between observations and a hypothesis will determine whether that individual considers the observations as evidence for the hypothesis. The same observations that were available to Charles Darwin when he proposed evolutionary theory were available to other naturalists and scientists at the time, yet they did not draw the same conclusions as he did from those observations. Darwin observed similarity of organisms, vestigial structures and the geographical distribution of species, and concluded that this was all evidence for evolutionary theory. These were not new observations. Other naturalists and scientists were aware of these observations too, yet they did not interpret them to be suggestive of evolutionary theory. So the hypothesis of evolutionary theory would appear to impact the way in which an individual interprets observations as evidence for the hypothesis. This is an important consideration which we will consider in more detail later.

A lack of alternative explanation is not a scientific argument. However, it could be a viable non-scientific argument, and it is used in legal cases. Providing an alternative explanation as to how an offence might have occurred is seen as a crucial part of a defence team's case. Without it, the burden of proof may be lowered. However, we will not get stuck on this point in this chapter, as we are going to look at the alternative theories and explanations for the biodiversity of life in Chapter 6. For now, it is enough to assume that there are alternative explanations, and therefore the "lack of alternative theories" point should not be used as evidence to support evolutionary theory or lower the burden of proof – the reasons for this will be expounded in Chapter 6. But it is important in the meantime to remember that just because there is no other naturalistic explanation possible, that does not make something true. Past events should remain a mystery, or be classified as "cause unknown", until there is adequate evidence to suggest otherwise.

Chapter 2 – The evidence

We have established that there is no scientific case for evolutionary theory. So now let's look in more detail at the non-scientific case for it (including any scientific evidence which is used in an attempt to support that non-scientific case). This chapter will focus purely on establishing whether the evidence for evolutionary theory makes a solid case for it. It will not debate the authenticity of the evidence: some do make the claim that the evidence itself is not authentic (as we will see later), but for now let us presume that it is genuine. Also, we will not propose alternative theories but just evaluate the current theory based on the evidence alone. The debate between evolution and creationism and other suggestions for how life originated and/or developed on Planet Earth are not relevant here.

The explanation of biodiversity is a unique question which cannot be compared to any other, as life on Earth is the only life that we know of. We do not know of foreign or alien life that would offer us a template of how life should function and be. So most of our analogies and comparisons will have to be with inanimate examples. However, the purpose of the analogies is not to form a platform of evidence but to demonstrate the mechanisms of thinking that are being used in evolutionary theory.

There are several pieces of evidence that are given for the theory. Some are considered to be stronger than others. We will examine each of the main pieces of evidence one-by-one. We will categorise them as follows:

1. Biochemical evidence – The similarity of life
2. Phylogenetic evidence – The tree of life
3. Palaeontological evidence – Transitional fossils
4. Anatomical evidence:
    4.1 Vestigial Structures
    4.2 Atavisms
    4.3 Comparative anatomy
    4.4 Embryology
    4.5 Imperfectness of design
5. Biogeographical evidence:
    5.1 Geographical distribution

1. The similarity of life

It is argued that because all life shares similar characteristics –
metabolism, catalysis, replication and hereditability – then all life
must be related. In addition, all life uses the same building blocks
(DNA and RNA) to achieve these characteristics. On this basis, the
presumption is made that all life is biologically related. The conclusion
made by evolutionary theory is that all species must have evolved from
simpler species, and that all species arose through common descent.

There are three parts of this argument. The first part *presumes* that
as all life shares similar characteristics, then all life must be related.
Now, this is a big presumption for evolutionary theory to make.
Consider an analogy applying the same reasoning to cars. Cars use the
same mechanisms as each other to convert fuel into energy which then
creates motion. All cars share fundamental characteristics with each
other, such as a combustion engine burning fuel to create energy which
then turns pistons which then turn wheels to create motion. There are
many other similarities too: they require an operator, they have four
wheels, they have a steering wheel to control direction and so on.

Now, we cannot simply presume that because all cars share many
traits, all cars must have been made by the same company. To
presume so is pure speculation. Using a scientific approach, if you
were to examine two cars of different make with no information
available to you other than the cars themselves, all you could
scientifically conclude is that the same processes are used to power
both cars, and both cars share many traits. You cannot scientifically
deduce any more than that. You might presume that it shows all cars
must have originated from the initial design and manufacture of one
car, but you could not scientifically deduce this from simply examining
the two different cars with no other information available (even though
in this example we know this to be true). It would be a theoretical
assumption rather than an empirical observation.

Think about it; the first cars could have been designed and built completely independently of one another on different sides of the planet by the chance that two independent inventors came up with the design at more or less the same time. Even if you were to examine every single car on the planet at one given time, without the necessary historical facts you could not deduce the origins of the car, its ancestors, or prove relatedness to other cars. Similarly, with evolutionary theory, all current life can be examined today and interesting similarities between all species can be observed, but this tells us nothing about how these species originated, how they are related or whether they share a common ancestor. Subsequently, this information does not tell us anything about *how* evolution happened.

The second part of this argument suggests that because all life is made of the same core material (namely DNA and RNA), then all life must be physically related. This again sounds like a gross presumption. It is analogous to suggesting that because all clay pots are made of clay, they must all be made by the same potter. Simply saying that all things made of the same material must have a common ancestor, is nothing but speculation. Now, you may wonder "how else could it have happened", and we will consider this in later chapters. But remember, we are only looking at whether the current evidence used to support evolutionary theory meets the burden of proof. An alternative theory does not need to be given at this stage.

The fact that all life shares the same essential characteristics and uses the same building blocks (DNA and RNA) to do this is, according to pro-evolutionists, highly suggestive of relatedness. In addition, the more closely related species are, the more similar their DNA make-up is. For example, the DNA similarity between a gorilla and a chimpanzee is much greater than that between a dolphin and a parrot. Now, of course, relatedness can still not be proved here, and an inference is required to establish that DNA similarities are the result of common descent and evolution. So the question really is, how big of an inference is this?

Without looking at other pieces of evidence, this is clearly a big inference. As said earlier, just because two items are made from the same material, it does not mean that one originated from the other. Surely it is reasonable to presume that in order to make life, the core ingredient DNA (or RNA) is required, and that the more similar species are, the more similar their DNA make-up will be. This tells us nothing about how the various species came to be or whether they are all derived from a common ancestor. Many advocates of evolutionary theory state that the fact that animals such as a mouse share 90% of the same DNA as humans do proves relatedness. As interesting a fact as this is, it goes nowhere to proving evolutionary theory; it can only prove that all life is made up of the same stuff. To go from this to saying that a single-cell organism evolved into a human being through a multitude of random mutations (our default hypothesis) is grossly speculative. Just because all life is made of DNA and RNA, that offers us no insight into *how* the various species came to be.

Because of the presumption that all life is related, a third and final presumption is made: complex organisms have evolved from simpler organisms. "Complexity starts with simplicity" is the concept which evolutionary theory is founded on: that is why the tree starts with a single-cell organism and gradually evolves into more complex organisms. This may initially sound logical but is it really? Why does complexity have to come from simplicity? There is no scientific law that says it should be so. In fact, the second law of thermodynamics is the law of increasing entropy, which actually means that systems get more disorganised with time. So again, it seems like we are in the land of speculative presumption.

Stating that complexity starts with simplicity appears to be the greatest trick evolutionary theory has pulled: this concept is essential for the theory to be viable, yet the theory brushes over this concept and uses no scientific method whatsoever to support it. Remember, life on Earth is the only known life in existence, so no other life forms can be studied to establish this idea. We may consider natural structures, such as mountains and rivers, or think of man-made structures, such as buildings and bridges, and think that these are complex structures that developed gradually. A building is built brick by brick and therefore goes from a simple structure to an increasingly complex one. However, these are inert structures and it would be irrational to use such comparisons to draw solid conclusions about life.

A species changing into another has never been observed or demonstrated, and simple organisms becoming more complex has never been observed or proved. Certainly, "complexity arising from simplicity" cannot be determined through the scientific method, as it is not testable or observable. Given this, any evidence used to support evolutionary theory which relies on this principle is a circular argument, and certainly unscientific. As we shall see, this appears to be most of the evidence currently used to support the theory. We will discuss the logical aspects of this principle in more detail in Chapter 3, but in the meantime let us beware of any argument that relies on this principle.

2. The tree of life

Evolutionary theory has proposed a phylogenetic tree or evolutionary tree to show the origins and the relationships of all species. This tree has multiple branches and nests which show a hierarchical system of all the organisms that have ever lived, starting from one individual single-cell organism. Now, the tree itself is the product of evolutionary theory so needs to be proved. This means that any information or presumptions which are derived from the tree cannot be used as evidence for evolutionary theory. To do so would again be considered a circular argument. Firstly, the tree is composed on presumptions such as "complexity starts with simplicity" – it presumes progression rather than regression. But remember, there is no scientific evidence for this. So dating and placing species on the tree based on the complexity of their DNA or morphological characteristics is redundant. But the tree *has* been created from the principles of evolutionary theory, such as DNA sequence analysis and cladistic morphological analysis.* For example, it *presumes* that morphological features that look more advanced are more recent, despite not having any empirical evidence to support this.

Supporters of the phylogenetic tree state that the tree is based on the ages of species. However, we know that dating fossils and species is very difficult. Some of the current methods used rely on theoretical presumptions (from evolutionary theory itself) rather than scientific principles. For example, it is presumed that more complex or advanced DNA must have come from simpler DNA, even though there is no actual proof of this. Also, of course, a fossil only tells you when a specific member of a species was living – it does not tell you when that species first existed and when it went extinct (that is if it has gone extinct). What's more, some dating techniques for dating fossils will actually use direct information from the phylogenetic tree itself in order to date them! For example, if a new fossil (let's call it fossil *a*) is found together with a fossil of a species already allocated a place on the phylogenetic tree (fossil *b* belonging to species *b*), then fossil *a* is

---

* "Cladistics" is the method of *presuming* that organisms which share morphological similarities must be relatives - the more similarity they share, the more closely they are related.

given a similar date of existence to species *b*. The obvious problem with this is that a presumption is being made that the creature of fossil *b* must have lived and died in the time zone already allocated for species *b* by the phylogenetic tree. There is no accommodation for the possibility that the phylogenetic tree may be wrong and fossil *b* may actually represent species *b* pre-dating or surviving longer than initially thought. So clearly this is a form of circular reasoning.

There are some species that were thought to have gone extinct millions of years ago that have been found to be living today, such as the coelacanth.* Now, if a coelacanth fossil had been found before the discovery of the first found living coelacanth, which was only a few decades ago, then evolutionists would have presumed this fossil to have been millions of years old. This could have resulted in huge errors for the rest of evolutionary theory and the phylogenetic tree, and possibly even for other branches of science, such as rock dating, which sometimes uses fossilised specimens to determine the age of rocks.

You may have heard that fossils can be dated based on the rocks in which they are found and the subsequent dating of these rocks. However, while there are accurate scientific methods for dating rocks and minerals found within a rock, dating fossils purely because they are found in certain rock layers is much more complicated and requires non-scientific presumptions. In order to follow this point, a quick explanation of rock dating may be helpful...

Fossils are mostly found in sedimentary rock rather than igneous rock. Sedimentary rock can be dated using radiometric dating techniques involving the element carbon. But carbon decays relatively quickly, meaning that dating of sedimentary rock can only go as far back as about 70,000 years. That's 70,000 years out of a 3.8-billion-year history of life, which is about 0.0018%. So this method can only be used to cover 0.0018% of the timeline in which life has reportedly existed, which is clearly insufficient for proof of the whole of the phylogenetic tree. In order to date older fossils, a technique called "bracketing" is used. Here the rock layers above and below the fossil (typically igneous rock or volcanic ash) are dated using radiometric methods involving other elements found in these rocks. Consequently, a date range or bracket can be created for the fossil, as it must have been laid down at a time in between the layers of rock above and below. The problem with this method is that it is subject to a lot of

---

* A coelacanth is an ancient fish.

errors, such as contamination and geological events like erosion and mixing up of layers through folding of the layers.

Dating a species based on rock dating also only tells you the date of that individual fossilised specimen. As already mentioned, there are species like the coelacanth which were thought to have gone extinct millions of years ago but have been found to be living today, so clearly rock dating does not *prove* the age of a species. It only addresses the question of the age of that one fossil. The phylogenetic tree is designed on the principle that species went extinct when evolutionary theory says that they went extinct, but as shown, it is scientifically impossible to prove extinction dates. While dating rocks and minerals is a scientific process, dating species is not. Therefore, the age of species and the phylogenetic tree do not constitute good evidence for supporting evolutionary theory.

Now, evolutionists will tell you that a combination of all the above factors (fossil dating, DNA analysis, morphological similarities as well as others, such as geographical location) go into making the phylogenetic tree, and that together they constitute solid evidence for the factual correctness of the tree. While this may be true, the method relies on presumptions, convergence of different information from different sources and the subjective interpretation of these. There is no standard for testing this.

It is worth mentioning that even if the dating methods are exactly correct, and even if newly discovered extinct species fit perfectly into slots on the phylogenetic tree, this still does not *scientifically* prove relatedness or common descent. Different species arising at different times consistent with the phylogenetic tree does not prove *evolution* of one species to another. It does not prove ancestry or relatedness. Neither does it *scientifically* prove that complexity arises from simplicity; it would only show that this is what is *suggested* in the relatively few examples of fossils in existence.

One of the most compelling arguments that you may hear from pro-evolutionists is the claim that all new fossils that are found fit perfectly into the phylogenetic tree where it has been predicted that they will. This is a statement based on circular reasoning, as the phylogenetic tree has been created on the premise that evolution is true. So this statement does not offer proof to support the default hypothesis.

Pro-evolutionists also argue that the phylogenetic tree provides a basis for evolutionary theory to be disproved. For example, if a fossil can be found where it should not be found or in a time zone when it should not have existed or is a mixture of two animal classes that is not possible according to the tree, then evolutionary theory could immediately be disproved. These are the falsification arguments to which we previously alluded and which we dismissed on the grounds of unreasonableness and inability to falsify the key tenet of evolutionary theory. So the absence of contradictory examples to the phylogenetic tree does not constitute good evidence for evolutionary theory.

In short, the phylogenetic tree is unsound in its origins. It is based on presumptions and circular reasoning. It is theoretical. The tree depicts evolution of one species to another, but remember, this is only a depiction. There is no *empirical* evidence for speciation. Anyone can draw a picture of what they think is true, but this does not act as evidence for what actually *is* true.

3. Transitional fossils

A transitional fossil is any fossilised remains of a life form that has traits common to both its presumed ancestral group and its presumed descendant group. Transitional fossils are used to demonstrate the gradual transition from one species to another and thus to support evolutionary theory. It is important to note that the majority of the fossils of extinct species are not considered to be transitional species, and instead represent species that have gone extinct without evolving into a new species. These are the majority of the well-known extinct species, such as the woolly mammoth and the sabre tooth tiger. In fact, it is fair to say that most people would not be able to name a transitional species off the top of their head, as they don't come with the same glamour and reputation as the non-evolved extinct species.

In essence, the transitional fossils are the remains of extinct species who have borne descendant species. These extinct transitional species are represented on the phylogenetic tree. Technically speaking, these species have not really gone "extinct" as such: instead they have evolved into the descendant species. However, this is just semantics, as either way, the species effectively goes out of existence. So please don't get caught up in the terminology. It makes no practical difference if we refer to them as extinct.

Evolutionary theory states that most species go extinct.* Finding fossilised remains of an extinct transitional species is virtually the only way of proving its past existence, as human records do not go that

---

* This is a curious statement. We will explore it more in a moment.

far back. However, according to evolutionary theory, only a very tiny fraction of extinct species have fossilised and can be found in fossil form.* This means that only a tiny minority of the extinct transitional species on the phylogenetic tree can be *proved* to have existed. So the vast majority of the extinct species on the phylogenetic tree are just presumptions or theoretical species. Of course, these species are not depicted on the tree as such, but their past existence is presumed and is essential to the validity of the tree (they are represented as bifurcation points as well as unmarked points on every branch/line of the phylogenetic tree). They are the so-called "missing links"... You may have cottoned on to a bizarre paradox which is emerging here, but if not, don't worry; we're going to elaborate on this point later.

Transitional fossils do not constitute scientific proof of evolutionary theory. As we have just said, transitional fossils are very hard to come by and that is the reason we have so few of them. But would the situation be different if we had fossils showing the existence of every single proposed intermediate species on the phylogenetic tree? It is natural to think it would, but, in actual fact, this would still not constitute *scientific* or *empirical* evidence to support evolutionary theory. The reason is that evolutionary theory proposes common descent with *evolution* of one species to another. In order to *scientifically* prove evolution, this evolution needs to be observable and reproducible. We would also need a scientific model for *how* one species evolved into the other, for instance a specific genetic pathway detailing the genetic changes that occurred resulting in the specific morphological changes in the descendant species. If all we can demonstrate is the existence of a full series of species with minor differences between adjacent ones, then all we can *scientifically* conclude from this is that every species is accompanied by other species with very similar features and traits. Even if we could accurately date them so that we were able to show that the timeline perfectly fits in with evolutionary theory's model of the change from species to species, we could still not *scientifically* conclude that one species evolved into another – this still wouldn't prove *evolution*, as we have not actually observed one species evolving into another. It is only evolutionary theory which proposes that fossils of extinct species are transitional fossils. In fact, we have no reason whatsoever to believe

---

* It is only a tiny fraction of extinct species that have fossilised *if* evolutionary theory is correct about its assertion that a vast number of species have gone extinct.

that any particular fossil actually represents a species that is in transition from one species to another. To conclude so is using presumptions based on evolutionary theory itself, and this again, of course, is a form of circular reasoning.

That being said, if we did have a complete fossil record with compatible dating which precisely fitted in with evolutionary theory and the phylogenetic tree, then we would admittedly have a strong non-scientific case for evolutionary theory. But, as it stands, we only have a very limited supply of transitional fossils. So it seems that even a non-scientific case cannot be made based on this evidence alone. Just because the current transitional fossils fit in with the current model of evolutionary theory/phylogenetic tree and do not contradict it, this is not good evidence *for* evolutionary theory. As we have established, finding information that does not contradict a theory is very different from finding information that supports a theory.

Some transitional series are better than others, although importantly, no series is fully complete, so a degree of inference is always required. Many, many branches and even whole sections of the phylogenetic tree are lacking the transitional fossils to confirm their accuracy. And what's more, there are significant problems with using any of the transitional fossils as evidence for evolutionary theory...

It is widely accepted that the majority of mutations in genes are harmful or not beneficial, and only a minority of mutations result in a beneficial outcome for a creature. It therefore seems logical to deduce that when species change, each new characteristic would have to develop independently of the other. For example, for a cow-like creature to have changed into a whale, as proposed by evolutionary theory, it would not be a simple case of one mutation occurring and then all of a sudden a cow gives birth to a whale. A series of changes would have to happen – the nostrils would need to fuse together and move back over the head to form a blowhole, the teeth would need to become simpler and peg-like, the snout would have to elongate, the neck shrink, the back become more flexible to aid swimming, the hands become flipper-like, the legs and pelvis reduce and disappear, and the bones become denser. This is just to name a few. Now, not only is it likely that each positive change is happening independently, but also that each change is gradual, in other words the neck shrinks in stages, the nostrils move back gradually and so on. So there are multiple steps of microevolution happening before the macroevolution occurs. This means that there should be multiple significantly morphologically-different creatures between a cow-like creature and a whale with several being termed new species (due to the differences being considered significant enough to deem them so). "Significantly morphologically-different" implies that it is not the normal minor variations or differences within most species that we see, for example with features like eye colour, skin tone or nose shape. Instead it would need to be a gross difference that is immediately appreciable, for example the difference between a tiger and a lion, or even the difference between a Great Dane dog and a Chihuahua dog (note these two dogs do belong to the same species: we will explore this later).

Transitional fossils are presumed to act as evidence for evolutionary theory but they are grossly sparse. Take the transitional series of the above mentioned land mammal to whale. Pro-evolutionists boast that this series is one of the best for supporting evolutionary theory: however, the transitional fossils of only about ten intermediate species have been found. That's ten out of what would presumably be hundreds, if not thousands, of intermediate creatures (significantly morphologically-different creatures) that should have existed in order for the cow-like creature to turn into the whale. That's hardly solid evidence is it? Just looking at Figure 4, which shows the only intermediate species that have been discovered, one cannot conclude that there is a complete enough series to support the *evolution* of the first species to the last.

The vast majority of intermediate creatures/species between each of the species depicted in Figure 4 are only *presumed* to have existed and not *proved* to have existed. Therefore, the few intermediate species that are shown cannot act as strong evidence in supporting evolutionary theory. The same applies for all proposals on the phylogenetic tree, not just cow-like creatures turning into whales. Even for the proposed "evolution" of monkeys to humans, there are only a few fossils of the proposed intermediate creatures/species. In order to get from a monkey to a human, there are hundreds of significant morphological changes that are required just to allow the human to walk upright – the spine, hip joints, the knee joints and the whole musculature make-up all have to change. That's hundreds of gene mutations creating hundreds of morphologically independent creatures/species between a monkey and a human, and yet we only have a few fossils of such proposed creatures/species. This cannot rationally be considered as decent evidence.

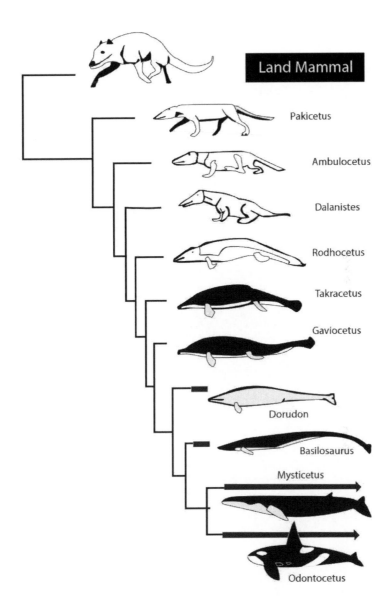

Figure 4. The reported evolution of land mammals to whales.

Another series that evolutionary theory boasts about is the series of transitional fossils of the horse series. This is considered to be one of the best examples for demonstrating evolution. Figure 5 illustrates this.

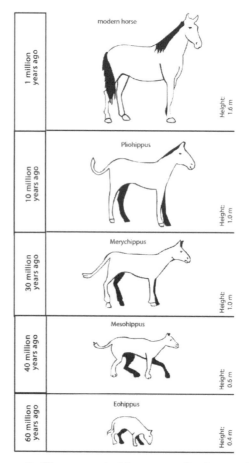

Figure 5. The reported horse evolution series.

As with the whale series, the majority of intermediate fossils are missing for the transition from the first creature/species on this proposed change to the last. Even though any two adjacent species on Figure 5 do not look too far apart, there are significant morphological differences between them, such as their limb bones and teeth. This proposed series requires multiple transitional creatures/species in between any two of the adjacent species. However, fossils for these are not present, so the existence of such animals are not proved. Evolutionary theory claims that the fossils that are present for this proposed series are sufficient to prove the transition, but common sense says that this is not adequate. Assumptions are made based on the fossil record that species in between two transitional fossils must have existed, but, of course, there is no actual evidence for this. It is purely speculation.

It is also worth noting that evolutionary theory's examples of transitional fossils only account for evolution within a specific order, such as mammals, and usually just within a specific family or genus. There is very weak fossil evidence to support evolution from one class (such as reptiles) to another class (such as mammals), let alone from one phylum to another. Most evolutionary biologists will concede that the current transitional fossil evidence does not strongly support one class evolving into another and they rely on the other pieces of "evidence" to corroborate this and promote evolutionary theory. This means that even if it could somehow be proved that the changes depicted in Figure 5 did actually occur, and "mesohippus" turned into the modern horse that we see today, then this would still not offer any meaningful evidence to support our default hypothesis, which states that *all* life came from a single-cell organism. So what if a horse-like creature can turn into a bigger and stronger horse? One cannot extrapolate that to mean that human beings descended from a single-cell organism.

You may hear some evolutionary biologists say that the reptiles-to-mammals transition is actually well documented, and that late reptilian to mammalian transition is well shown by the fossil record such that evolutionists cannot draw the line of where one class ends and the other begins. However, the reality is that this is not nearly as well demonstrated as would be expected to meet the burden of proof to establish even this one component of evolutionary theory. Yes, the transition is better represented by fossil evidence than other class-to-class transitions but this doesn't mean that it is adequate: of course, 5% is better than 1%, but it is still only 5%. And just because you have a species that appears to straddle the line between the two classes, such as the platypus, this does still not get us anywhere near our default hypothesis.*

---

* A platypus has features of both a reptile (egg-laying) and a mammal (fur), and so is thought to represent a close descendant of a species in transition from reptile to mammal. However, it is still morphologically very different from any other known (extant or extinct) mammal-like reptile or reptile-like mammal. We will discuss the platypus in more detail in Chapter 4.

What about Archaeopteryx, some of you may say. For those who don't know, Archaeopteryx is a fossil which has received iconic status, as it is believed to represent the "missing link" between reptiles (or dinosaurs) and birds, at least it was initially – some palaeontologists are now beginning to rethink this. Let's consider that this species does have some features of a bird and some of a reptile or dinosaur that makes it a "missing link". Unfortunately for evolutionary theory this still does not prove that reptiles or dinosaurs *evolved* into birds through a series of random mutations. It is just the fossil of one species that shares characteristics of both groups of animals. There would still have to be many, many unfound and unproven intermediate species between Archaeopteryx and its nearest known ancestor and nearest known descendant (both of which are, of course, only presumed to be the ancestor and descendant and not proven to be so).

There are hardly any transitional fossils of invertebrate animals, and very little is known about the evolution of this group of animals. Of course, this is a hugely missing piece of information, as the theory of common descent only works if every single species on the planet can be accounted for. To have hardly any transitional fossils for the group of animals that accounts for over 90% of all extant animal species should be seen as a major problem for the theory. Also, there are no fossils which represent the transition from single-celled organisms to complex invertebrates. Nor are there fossils demonstrating the transition from invertebrates to the first vertebrates (thought to be fish). Analysis of rock strata for fossils in the Cambrian period instead suggests the sudden appearance of complex invertebrate species with no suggestion of evolution from single-celled organisms. This is termed as the Cambrian explosion.* Several eminent evolutionists, such as Stephen Jay Gould, who have studied the appearance and distribution of fossils, conclude that the fossil evidence suggests stasis and sudden appearance rather than evolution.

In evolutionary theory's defence, it is reportedly very hard to find transitional fossils as most organisms do not fossilise, and that is why the evidence is lacking. Fair enough. But this is a very significant missing piece of the jigsaw so to speak. If we hypothesise that everybody likes chocolate, we should not use the observation that

---

* The Cambrian explosion was the relatively short event in the Cambrian period where many animals suddenly appeared, as demonstrated by the fossils of such animals in the rock strata relating to this period.

people refuse to admit this to us as an excuse for being unable to prove our theory – this is a crucial piece of evidence in determining the theory; if it cannot be obtained, the theory is significantly weakened. Similarly, in a court case a prosecutor will have a really hard time convicting a murder suspect without the victim's body – they may use the excuse that it is very difficult to find, which may be true, but it means that a significant piece of evidence will be missing.

This brings us on to the most intriguing issue about transitional species and their fossils…

Evolutionary theory claims that 99.9% of species that have ever existed have gone extinct. Now, do you know what the evidence is for such a claim? It is the phylogenetic tree based on the theory of evolution!

Once evolutionary theory has been proposed, the theory has to account for all the species that *should* have existed to turn a single-cell organism into all the species in existence today as well as all the discovered extinct species. This is estimated to be over 5 billion species. Evolutionists and biologists estimate that there are around 10 million species in existence today (although only about 1.2 million are actually known and documented). Thus, according to evolutionary theory, the bulk of the 5 billion species ever to have supposedly graced Planet Earth with their presence are now extinct. But it is estimated that only about 250,000 of these 5 billion extinct species have been identified in fossil form. That's about 0.005% (or 1 in 20,000). So of course, the theory has to state that "most species go extinct" to remain viable. And then it has to further justify this by saying "most species don't fossilise", as we have no actual evidence of these "unfossilised species" having ever existed. Once again, this is circular reasoning. This can be understood better by examining the following sequence of deduction which is used by evolutionary theory:

a. There is life on Planet Earth.
b. Evolutionary theory explains how all life arose from an original common ancestor.
c. Evolutionary theory states that there are around 5 billion extinct species.
d. Transitional fossils of about 0.005% of these extinct species have been discovered.
e. The fact that only a tiny proportion of these extinct fossils have been found in fossil form means that most species don't fossilise.

Of course, the illogicality of the above sequence is plain to see. Statement *b* has not been proven and is the very question that needs to be answered. Statement *c*, which is directly derived from statement *b*, is pure speculation and is only true if evolutionary theory is true. Thus, statements *b* and *c* rely on each other in a circular fashion. The subsequent statements that follow are also dependent on statement *b* and *c* being true and are therefore redundant in argument. Claiming that there are around 5 billion extinct species is sheer folly! It is not founded on any *actual* evidence or good reasoning. Pro-evolutionists have to *assume* that innumerable species existed in the transitional gaps in order for their theory to work, but there is no *actual* proof that these species did exist. Think about it. How can you prove, or even be confident, that something existed when there is no way of being able to establish that it existed? Remember, the only way of proving an ancient extinct species existed is by having a fossil of it, which demonstrates its past existence.

There is clearly no factual ground to establish that "most species go extinct" or "most species don't fossilise". However, these are both regular mantras of evolutionary theory. Pro-evolutionists frequently refer to them when they are questioned on the lack of transitional fossils. It is nonsensical. "Most species go extinct" is only true if there have been 5 billion species in existence. But the only things that we actually *know* (to a reasonable degree) are that there are about 10 million species in existence today and about 250,000 extinct species. So actually, only 2.5% of species that we *know of* have gone extinct, which contradicts the idea that "most species go extinct". And the presumption that most extinct species have not fossilised is only true if close to 5 billion species have gone extinct, which has not been proven. If, for example, only 300,000 species have become extinct, which *scientifically* is equally as likely as the 5 billion number proposed by evolutionary theory, then actually most extinct species *have* fossilised!

The only *facts* that can actually be stated are that there are about 1.2 million species in existence today, and there have been around 250,000 species not known to exist today identified from fossils. To make the leap from these facts to the theory of common descent through a series of random chance mutations is extraordinary when you think about it. Granted, evolutionists do say that it is the combination and amalgamation of all the pieces of evidence that makes evolutionary theory viable. But to presume the existence of 4.99975 billion species out of 5 billion species without any *actual* evidence of them having ever existed is grossly speculative.

It is certainly *possible* that most species do go extinct. But there is no evidence to make a claim one way or the other. One can't just *presume* that most species go extinct because that fits in with their theory. And it's not possible to prove a negative: we cannot prove that these unknown and unfound extinct species have never existed. It would be like trying to prove that fairies never existed – it's just not possible. So evolutionary theory has created these species, which cannot be disproved, much the same way that God cannot be disproved. We could call them the species of the gaps.

4. Anatomical evidence

4.1 Vestigial structures
4.2 Atavisms
4.3 Comparative anatomy
4.4 Embryology
4.5 Imperfectness of design

4.1 Vestigial structures

Vestigial structures are anatomical features of a species that have little or no purpose. According to evolutionary theory, such features would have previously served a purpose in the ancestors of the species. Evolutionists propose that these features became redundant through evolution, as new species no longer required them, resulting in these features losing their original purpose and function. Evolutionists consider the presence of such futile structures as strong evidence for evolution. Charles Darwin described such structures as "rudimentary, atrophied and aborted organs", and he claimed that there were several such structures in man, including the appendix, the coccyx, body hair, wisdom teeth and ear muscles.

If you observe such structures and then propose evolution as a possible explanation for them, then the structures themselves cannot be used as proof of evolution. To do so would be circular reasoning. Alternatively, if you propose a hypothesis of evolutionary theory which predicts such structures, then the dilemma of observer bias comes in. That is to say that the observation of a futile structure is made, and then it is explained through the hypothesis of evolutionary theory. This can be understood by appreciating that these structures were known to anatomists and biologists *before* Charles Darwin proposed evolutionary theory, but this did not lead anatomists and biologists to conclude that they must have arisen through evolution. So it is only awareness of the evolutionary theory hypothesis that leads one to make such a conclusion.

Pro-evolutionists say that evolutionary theory provides an explanation for these structures, and it would on the surface seem to give a plausible account. But let's once again examine the logic being used in the following sequential analogy:

a. Some animals have futile structures.
b. A hypothesis of evolutionary theory can explain these structures through vestigiality.
c. The presence of these structures is evidence for my hypothesis of evolutionary theory.

It is simple to see the fallacy in the above analogy. It has not been shown that evolutionary theory is correct, so presumptions that come out of the theory are only valid if statement b is first proved. Statement c does not necessarily validate or support statement b. Of course, in this analogy multiple other options are possible – these structures may not actually be futile or they could have arisen through means other than evolution.

It is important to note that so-called vestigial structures are only *seemingly* redundant. Many of these structures have been shown to have some function even though they were previously thought not to have. The appendix in humans is now thought to offer immunity. The flightless wings of ostriches are now thought to aid ground running whereby ostriches reach speeds of above 40 mph. This, of course, nullifies the whole argument from vestigiality for these examples.

Also, most species do not have recognised vestigial structures, but this does not suggest that evolutionary theory is untrue. So the hypothesis of evolutionary theory can work without the presence of any vestigial structures – if no such structures were observed, evolutionary theory would still be viable. Consequently, it seems poor logic to use vestigial structures as evidence for evolutionary theory.

It is not rational to propose evolutionary theory based on vestigial structures alone. You could not expect someone to see the wings of an ostrich as being futile and then suggest from that observation alone that common descent and evolution is true. However, other evidence, such as the biochemical evidence or the transitional fossils, are adequate to hypothesise the theory on their own. This indicates that vestigial structures should not add any significant weight to evolutionary theory.

The vestigial-structures argument appears to be more of an argument against creationism rather than evidence *for* evolutionary theory. The two are not synonymous. Disproving creationism does not necessarily add any weight to evolutionary theory. This can be better understood using the sequential argument below:

a. Some animals have futile structures.
b. An intelligent designer would not create such structures.
c. Therefore, these structures must have arisen through accidental, naturalistic processes.
d. A hypothesis of evolutionary theory can explain these structures through vestigiality.
e. The presence of these structures is evidence for my hypothesis of evolutionary theory.

When vestigial structures are used to argue against creationism, the question put forward is "why would a supernatural intelligence give a species a useless organ or appendage? Surely if the designer is intelligent enough to create life from non-life, they would design species perfectly." The problem with this argument is firstly, we do not know for sure whether these vestigial structures are completely redundant and useless. And secondly, does this argument actually reduce the likelihood of a supernatural intelligence significantly enough to promote evolutionary theory as very likely? It would seem not, but this is something we will explore in Chapter 6.

Vestigial structures are also used to determine the positioning of species on the phylogenetic tree. As we have already said, the composition of the tree is founded on presumptions like "complexity starts with simplicity" – it presumes progression rather than regression. But remember, there is no evidence for this.

Of course, the vestigial structure argument only makes sense if the species with them are on their designated spots on the proposed phylogenetic tree. For example, the flightless birds are placed further down the tree than the first flighted birds, which, according to evolutionary theory, indicates that species with flightless wings evolved from species with flight-able wings. So to use these structures as evidence for evolutionary theory involves yet another layer of circular reasoning.

Pro-evolutionists state that the presence of vestigial structures is what they would expect to find in concordance with the theory – this is understandable. But we should not be focused on findings that validate the presumptions but findings that would actually prove the theory. The only logical deduction that can be made from the presence of vestigial structures is that some species have structures that appear useless. It is not rational to end up with evolutionary theory from this observation.

4.2 Atavisms

Evolutionary theory makes predictions that individual members of a species can at times develop structures or features that are not present in other members of the species but were present in the ancestors of the species. These are known as atavisms and are considered to be the reappearance of a lost trait or characteristic. This is proposed as supporting evidence for evolutionary theory, as it suggests that through some form of mechanism an old developmental pathway may be reactivated causing an old feature or characteristic to reappear.

Now, firstly it is important to note that there are very few examples of actual atavisms. The most cited examples are new-born babies with tails, and whales and dolphins with hind legs. However, even if a large amount of atavisms were present, would this be good evidence for evolutionary theory? The answer is no: this is not evidence at all. It is an interesting observation, and that is all.

It is a presumption to state that these features have arisen due to ancestors having had them previously, as this has never been witnessed, observed or reproduced, and this is not a testable statement. It is therefore an unscientific claim. All we can state from the observation of atavisms is that some members of a species develop strange features that are presumed to have existed on older or extinct species.

Opponents of the atavism argument state that most gene mutations result in very strange *new* features which have nothing to do with evolutionary theory. Often these represent anatomical abnormalities and diseases. Therefore, on what grounds do we consider only *some* gene changes to be the result of evolution? It can only be on the grounds that the changes are explained through the phylogenetic tree, meaning that they resemble traits that the supposed ancestors had and thus can be explained by evolution. If the changes can't be explained by evolution (or the phylogenetic tree), they are not considered to be an atavism. This, of course, is yet another example of circular reasoning.

Humans can be born with extra digits (toes or fingers), but no-one claims that the ancestors of humans had six fingers or six toes – we know that the fossilised specimens do not support this. However, if a human is born with a tail, pro-evolutionists argue that this is evidence for evolution, because our supposed ancestors did have tails. This is the dilemma. It is cart-before-the-horse reasoning. Pro-evolutionists only use the examples that fit in with the theory. And they do not use those examples or observations to formulate a solid theory demonstrating a mechanism of action. Instead they jump on anything that remotely fits in with their existing model on the biodiversity of life.

There are cases of humans being born with two heads, but, understandably, this is not claimed by pro-evolutionists to be anything to do with evolution. There are also conditions which may appear like an evolutionary regression or reactivation of an old pathway but are not considered to be so. One such example is congenital generalised hypertrichosis (previously known as Werewolf Syndrome): in this condition human beings are born with excessive body hair, similar to the amount of hair found on monkeys. However, this condition appears to be caused by loss of genetic information in the form of gene deletions, which is obviously incompatible with the idea that the hair excess is a true atavism and the result of evolution.

One of the most cited atavisms is tails in humans, but there are only about 100 reported cases. Of these, only about two-thirds have been shown to be true bony tails as supposed to pseudo-tails, which are actually soft tissue abnormalities and not linked to any evolutionary hypothesis.

The fact that bony tails occur in humans is an interesting observation, but it is still only an observation. A presumption is made by pro-evolutionists that this is the result of a reactivation of an underlying developmental pathway inherited from ancestors who had tails, but this is only a presumption with no scientific mechanism to back it up. Opponents of the idea that these tails represent ancestral inheritance argue that the occurrence of such tails only proves morphological similarity between species and not inheritance. For example, monkeys and humans both have arms and legs, but this in itself cannot be used to prove evolution – it only proves they have similar morphology. The existence of something does not provide evidence of its origin. In fact, no specific scientific pathway or causal mechanism of DNA/gene changes has been established for any of the proposed atavisms. Therefore, to claim that they are true atavisms is a gross presumption. And opponents claim that all such features are the result of new gene mutations, which is a viable alternative theory. So once again, it appears that the argument of atavisms does not meet the threshold to be considered as decent evidence to support evolutionary theory.

4.3 Comparative anatomy

Morphological study has shown that species next to each other on the phylogenetic tree, or species that are presumed to be ancestor and descendant, have very similar anatomy. Now obviously, the various species have been placed next to each other on the phylogenetic tree partly for this reason, so it seems irrational to claim this as a piece of evidence for evolutionary theory, as it would be circular reasoning. But there are other problems with using anatomical similarity to support evolutionary theory...

Anatomical variation within a species can be great, as can be seen with various dog breeds which all belong to the same species – the difference between the Great Dane and the Chihuahua appears significantly greater than that between many organisms which belong to different species. So the degree of anatomical similarity between two organisms does not *necessarily* correlate to the degree of evolutionary relationship between them. But the phylogenetic tree has been largely based on the degree of anatomical similarity, especially regarding extinct and transitional fossils where usually DNA is absent. Using comparative anatomy to establish the evolutionary relationship between a fossil and a species is not an exact science – anatomical variations in the fossil could represent a variant type of the species rather than a distinct transitional form. What's more, most fossils form very incomplete skeletons, and are often just a few fragmented pieces of bone, so establishing the degree of anatomical similarity to other species is in itself a big challenge. Other factors like age of the fossil and geographical location can play a part in determining the evolutionary relationship of the fossil to other species, but these are weaker determinates for reasons already mentioned. Geographical distribution is limited in establishing the evolutionary relationships of fossils belonging to migratory animals like birds and sea-animals, and it doesn't establish exclusivity for the area in which the fossil is found.

Also, as we have mentioned, Charles Darwin's observations of anatomical similarity were available to other naturalists and scientists at the time, yet they did not draw the same conclusions as he did from those observations. They did not interpret them to be suggestive of evolutionary theory. It is only observer bias that leads one scientist to conclude so while another doesn't, so such observations should not act as evidence for evolutionary theory.

Falsification arguments are once again used with regards to comparative anatomy – we are asked to find creatures which contradict proposed models of anatomical change. However, we have already dismissed such arguments on the grounds that they are unreasonable and do not add significant evidential weight to the case for evolutionary theory.

Evolutionary theory proposes that the anatomical structures of different classes of species suggest relatedness. One of the commonly cited examples of this has to do with the jaw and ear bones of reptiles and mammals. Mammals are theorised to have evolved from reptiles. Reptiles have at least four bones in their lower jaw (known as the dentary, articular, quadrate, angular, surangular, and coronoid bones), whereas mammals only have one (the dentary bone) – see Figure 6.

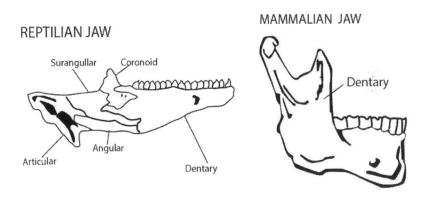

Figure 6. An example of reptilian and mammalian jaw anatomy.

Reptiles have only one bone in the middle ear (the stapes), whereas mammals have three (the stapes, anvil and hammer). Embryological studies have shown that in the reptilian foetus, two developing bones from the head go on to form two of the bones in the reptilian lower jaw (the quadrate and the articular bones). By contrast, in the mammalian foetus these two bones go on to form the bones of the mammalian middle ear (the anvil and hammer – also known as the incus and malleus respectively). Evolutionists suggest that this shows that the anvil and hammer bones have evolved from these reptilian jawbones. They say that the bones which make up our middle ears developed through random mutations resulting in these bones going on to form middle ear bones rather than lower jaw bones – these bones were supposedly extensively modified and scaled down gradually over time to form the mammalian middle ear bones. Transitional fossils have been found for intermediary species which have shown a gradual change in the position of these bones from jaw to middle ear so as to substantiate this theory. Obviously, the dating of these transitional fossils fits in suitably with the timeline of this evolution, otherwise this part of the theory would be disproved. Pro-evolutionists cite this as further evidence for evolutionary theory.

Fascinatingly, in some of the known intermediate creatures/species, the bones of the jaw/middle ear have overlapping functions, meaning that one bone can be called both an ear bone and a jaw bone, in other words these bones serve two functions. This is given by pro-evolutionists as the main reason why we do not require transitional forms with an intermediate number of jaw bones or ear bones (note that we don't really have these). So the transition is thought to be a process whereby the ear bones, which are initially located in the lower jaw, eventually detach from the lower jaw and move closer to the inner ear and become more specialised in the function of sound transmission.

Evolutionary theory and the phylogenetic tree makes significant predictions about the morphology of the intermediary creatures/species which no longer exist and which have yet to be discovered. Each predicted intermediary creature or species should have clearly specified morphological characteristics, which are based on the characteristics of its descendants and based upon the transitions that must have occurred to transform the last known ancestor into the descendant (in this case the reptile into the mammal). The discoveries of the transitional fossils for the series of late reptiles to early mammals have shown that no creature/species found further down the line of time contradicts the theory of jaw bones changing into middle ear bones, for example we have not found creatures between a reptile and a mammal who have four middle ear bones and one jaw bone.

Now, this all sounds very enchanting and technical and even perhaps scientific, but does it actually help us with our default hypothesis, and does it actually constitute evidence for evolutionary theory? What has been demonstrated in this example is a very technical hypothesis of how jaw bones changed into middle ear bones, with none of the fossil evidence (both before and after the creation of this hypothesis) contradicting the hypothesis. There are two parts to its argument, the first being the actual hypothesis. While this is certainly plausible, it is only a hypothesis, and it has not been proven to a reasonable degree. No mechanism of action has been established to demonstrate mutations leading to gene changes leading to feature changes. Furthermore, no change has actually been observed or reproduced. The different bone make-up of jaws and ears in reptiles and mammals are observations alone: while they may be *suggestive* of change from one to the other, they do not *prove* this change. The second part of this argument is the idea that no fossils contradict the hypothesis. This is a falsification argument, and, as we established in Chapter 1, this is a specific test and not a sensitive one and therefore should not add significant weight to evolutionary theory. So the suggestion that mammals descended from reptiles based on this piece of evidence is grossly speculative.

This is a similar situation with all the cited anatomical examples that pro-evolutionists use to suggest evolution – they are speculative, and do not offer direct evidence of *change* or *evolution* from one type to another. All that these examples show is that similarities exist between species. It would be ambitious to say that these observations significantly support the default hypothesis.

4.4 Embryology

It has been observed that the embryos of different species have similar characteristics and may look very similar during particular stages of development. Evolutionists conclude that these embryonic similarities are suggestive of homology (similarity of characteristics due to shared ancestry) and consequently support common descent and evolution. However, such similarities have been shown to be incongruous with evolution. For example, vertebrate forelimbs were previously cited as an example of such homology and considered very supportive evidence for evolutionary theory. But recent embryological studies have shown that vertebrate forelimbs develop from different body segments in different species and are not developmentally homologous. The kidneys have also been shown to have different developmental origins in certain animal classes.

In fact, embryonic similarities are only observations, and they offer no meaningful evidence to support evolutionary theory. All they show is that embryos of different species have similar characteristics which then go on to develop into more specific derivations, which are distinct and unique to the species that they belong to. So what if embryos are even exactly the same?! This would not prove that human beings descended from a single-cell organism. To jump to that conclusion would require a huge inference.

If you take a step back and think about it, there is no logical way that the study of embryology could offer any meaningful evidence to support evolutionary theory, as such study cannot demonstrate *evolution* of one species to another. This is much in the same way that comparative anatomy and morphological similarities between species cannot establish biological relationships between species.

4.5 Imperfectness of design

Another anatomical argument that you may hear from pro-evolutionists relates to the way that species are imperfectly designed. Because many species have features which could have been designed better in terms of safety and efficiency, pro-evolutionists argue that this makes it less likely that a supernatural intelligence created them. Instead they are more likely to have developed through evolution and inert nature, which uses no intelligence or conscious preference in the development of species.* One of the most cited examples of this is the left recurrent laryngeal nerve in mammals, including humans. The argument is as follows:

> The nerve takes a very long-winded and seemingly unnecessary route from the neck all the way down to the heart and back up to the neck only to end up supplying the larynx (voice box) in the neck. Why does it take this unnecessary route? There is no practical purpose or benefit of it doing so. Surely a supernatural intelligence would not have created it in such a way and would have had the intelligence to fix this and make it more efficient and practical?

Evolutionary theory does give a viable explanation for this. It states that the route this nerve would have taken in our fish ancestors would have been more direct. But through evolution of fish to mammals, a

---

* We are using the term "inert nature" to refer to naturalistic processes which are not driven by a conscious intellect or supernatural intelligence. The term incorporates all non-living matter in the universe, such as astronomical structures and chemical elements, and incorporates all non-living phenomena and processes in the universe, such as gravity, weather and physical geography.

neck developed and elongated. This resulted in the nerve getting caught on the wrong side of the heart, meaning it had no choice but to adapt and take this extended route.

Now, while this may be true, it obviously does not constitute solid evidence for evolutionary theory, as there is no evidence to show that this *is* what happened. It is only speculation. Once again, this seems to be more of an argument against creationism rather than evidence for evolution. But remember, disproving creationism does not necessarily act as evidence for evolutionary theory. So once again, anatomical arguments based on imperfectness of design cannot be considered good evidence for evolutionary theory.

5. *Biogeographical evidence*

5.1 Geographical distribution
5.2 Finch beaks

5.1 Geographical distribution

The geographical distribution of species across the world is thought to support evolutionary theory and was instrumental in the development of the theory. There are a couple of points to this argument. Firstly, the features and characteristics of a species appear to be related to the geographical location in which it exists. Species are generally found in the environments which best suit their attributes and where they will have a survival advantage over other species that could theoretically occupy the same niches.* Sometimes the differences between species in different locations are very subtle, but they confer a significant, and sometimes vital, survival advantage. Many species are only found in specific areas, for example the Gelada is only found in Ethiopia and the Pink Iguana is only found on one of the Galapagos Islands. The specificity of species to their environment is thought by pro-evolutionists to represent adaptation and change and subsequently evolution itself. To support this idea, transitional fossils are found in locations which are consistent with gradual evolution of transitional forms into the extant species. Apart from cases of excessive migration, such as with humans, flying animals, sea animals and artificially-introduced species, extant species are found close to their ancestor species.

---

* A niche is the habitat and ecosystem that a particular organism occupies.

The second point of this argument is that evolutionary theory fits in perfectly with the theory of continental drift.* This is because continental separation has resulted in species not being found in some environments where they should thrive, and where one would expect to find them – land-animal species that evolved after continental separation are confined to the land mass in which they arose, as they cannot cross oceans to access different lands. For example, placental mammals evolved outside of Australia and thus are not indigenous to Australia, even though they would flourish there: many placental mammals have been introduced to Australia and are now feral. Pro-evolutionists say that this is huge supporting evidence for evolutionary theory, as there is no other logical explanation for why species would not *naturally* exist in environments suitable to their characteristics. Continental separation also fits in perfectly with the dating of species, giving a perfect explanation for why species are found where they are, and why they are not found where they are not. Interestingly, the knowledge and acceptance of continental separation came into play only after Darwin's death, so it is unlikely to have influenced his formulation of evolutionary theory.

Looking at the first part of this argument, the geographical distribution of species is only an observation, and it offers us no proof of *how* this variation and distribution came about. Pro-evolutionists argue that fossil records are smoothly connected geographically and intermediates are found close to their fossil ancestors, which is consistent with the theory and what they would expect to find. Once again, this argument only fits in with the theory rather than getting anywhere close to proving it. It also depends on the phylogenetic tree for its validity (as it is only evolutionary theory that states that these fossils *are* ancestors or intermediates) and therefore should be considered redundant due to its reliance on circular reasoning. The proximity of extant species to fossils which *may* be transitional or ancestral to that species, is not proof of *evolution* of one species to another – it is simply an observation that extant species exist in areas where the fossils of similar looking organisms are found. Even though the geographical distribution of species across the planet matches what evolutionary theory predicts, this is meaningless if evolutionary theory is based on the geographical distribution. So using examples of

---

* The theory of continental drift was proposed by Alfred Wegener in 1912. It proposes that all the continents were previously one land mass but separated (or drifted apart) over 200 million years ago.

geographical distribution to support evolutionary theory is circular reasoning, and such examples only *fit in* with the proposed model of evolutionary theory and go nowhere to actually *proving* it. Consequently, this cannot be used as a *solid* argument for evolutionary theory. We will explore this in more detail in the next section with the finch beaks example.

Regarding the second part of the argument, certain observations of geographical distribution are thought to be only explainable through continental separation and evolutionary theory...

The Earth's continents were previously connected and formed a supercontinent known as Pangaea. Reportedly, sometime between 280 million to 230 million years ago, continental separation occurred, resulting in these continents becoming separated by vast tracts of ocean. The continents of South America, Antarctica, Africa, India and Australia remained connected to form a supercontinent known as Gondwana, which is thought to have begun separating about 170 million years ago – South America, Antarctica and Australia remained connected 65 million years ago and finally separated after this, with South America and North America eventually reconnecting. Because of this, it is argued that evolutionary theory is the only viable theory that can account for the following:

1. Extant marsupial species living only in Australia and the Americas, and fossils of extinct marsupial species being found in Antarctica despite marsupials not living there today.
2. Lungfish and ratite bird species living only in South America, Africa and Australia.*

These examples are used as supporting pieces of evidence for evolutionary theory. However, if the above observations were not present, evolutionary theory would still be viable. For example, if marsupials were exclusive to Australia, this would hold as much evidentiary weight for evolutionary theory as the observation of marsupials existing on both Australia and the Americas. So it seems poor logic to use this observation as evidence for the theory. In fact, the lack of lungfish and ratite bird fossils in Antarctica contradicts the use of these observations to support evolutionary theory – for these species to exist in Australia and the Americas means that, from evolutionary

---

* Ratites are (mostly) large flightless birds – ostriches, emus, cassowaries, rheas and kiwis.

theory's point of view, they must have existed in Antarctica too. Although granted, the theory can recite its "most species don't fossilise" mantra to explain this problem away. Also, once again, these arguments are reliant on the phylogenetic tree for their validity: it is only the phylogenetic tree that supposes that marsupial fossils in Antarctica represent ancient ancestor species to modern marsupials, and that similar species (whether geographically close or not) must descend from a common ancestor.

Importantly, the phylogenetic tree is partly based on continental separation and geographical distribution. For example, because each ratite species is localised to the continent in which it naturally exists, the phylogenetic tree supposes that each extant ratite species evolved *after* the separation of these continents. Otherwise, problems arise in explaining the separation of ratite species on different continents *if* they previously coexisted on Gondwana. Of course, though, there is no way of proving that these species did not exist prior to this continental separation, as most organisms do not fossilise and thereby we cannot know for sure when a species came into existence.

Similarly, apart from humans, all land-animal species are naturally endemic to a specific land mass – they are all presumed to have evolved *after* continental separation. If an extant land-animal species existed prior to continental separation, evolutionary theory would struggle to explain why there are no fossils or living organisms of it on different land masses, especially considering the theory's own argument that many land-animal species would thrive on different land masses.

Furthermore, dating of continental separation is largely based on fossils and the phylogenetic tree. So the phylogenetic tree partly relies on continental separation, and continental separation partly relies on the phylogenetic tree. There is clear circularity here which renders any argument based on continental separation a form of circular reasoning, as exemplified below:

a. Extant land-animal species are endemic to a land mass.
b. These land-animal species must have evolved after separation of the continents, as otherwise they should exist on separated land masses.
c. Evolutionary theory dates the oldest extant land-animal species to be around 200 million years old.
d. Thus, continental separation occurred before 200 million years ago.

e. So newly discovered land-animal species that are endemic to a land mass will be dated after 200 million years ago, based on dating of continental separation.

f. If an extant land-animal species is found to naturally exist on two or more separated continents, it must have evolved over 200 million years ago (before continental separation occurred).

g. If new evidence finds that an extant land-animal species is, for instance, 500 million years old and endemic to a land mass, the dating of continental separation will be revised to *over* 500 million years ago.

The above sequence of deduction is illogical. Dating species and dating continental separation are both precarious, yet they use each other to substantiate themselves. And they can both adapt to new observations brought forward by the other, as demonstrated by statements *f* and *g*.

Coming back to Australia; bats, rats and mice were the only placental mammals that were native to Australia prior to human-mediated introduction of other placental mammals. These rodents evolved outside of Australia. Bats can fly so their presence in Australia is easy to explain. But the presence of non-human-introduced rats and mice in Australia is unexpected. To propose that such rodents evolved independently in Australia would be a stretch too far, so evolutionary theory instead proposes that these rodents migrated to Australia from Asia millions of years ago by clinging to floating foliage. But this suggestion renders arguments from continental separation somewhat redundant, as it supposes that any species can float to any place.

The discovery of fossils of the same species on different continents was instrumental in formulating and substantiating the theory of continental drift. But only three animal species have been found to have existed on different continents – *Lystrosaurus*, *Cynognathus* and *Mesosaurus* (all small, ancient, extinct reptile species). Firstly, it seems possible that these hundreds-of-millions-of-years-old fossil specimens may not be preserved and extensive enough to definitively conclude that they come from the same species, considering different species can share remarkably similar anatomy. Secondly, for fossils to strongly support continental drift theory, we would expect fossil evidence of *many* species existing on different continents. Thirdly, we cannot rule out "clinging to floating foliage" as an explanation for these fossils on distant continents, as evolutionary theory itself uses this to explain other unexpected geographical distribution – also, note that *Mesosaurus* was a sea-dwelling creature, so it is not inconceivable that it crossed oceans. And finally, even if there were multiple land-animal species found on different continents, this would still not on its own be sufficient to prove continental drift theory, as it is only the unproven hypothesis of evolutionary theory that proposes that a species has only one point of origin. Thus, it seems presumptuous to use fossils and geographical distribution to support continental drift theory.

Even if the dates of continental separation are correct, continental exclusivity of extant land-animal species does not suggest evolutionary theory anymore than if these land-animal species existed on multiple continents – both observations can be fitted into the theory's framework. In fact, having some extant land-animal species that existed on Gondwana and then on multiple continents would be more supportive of evolutionary theory than the current observation of having none. So using continental separation to provide evidence for evolutionary theory does not make much sense.

In fact, we have several examples of extant sea animals that evolved prior to continental separation and that have undergone hardly any evolution. So theoretically, some pre-continental-separation land-animal species could also have survived to now without evolving – this would result in an extant land-animal species existing on separated land masses. But this phenomenon, unexpectedly, is not observed. So, for purposes of self-preservation, evolutionary theory is forced to propose the idea that all extant land-animal species evolved after continental separation, and that all pre-continental-separation land-animal species either evolved into new species or went extinct.

Pro-evolutionists also argue that continental separation and geographical distribution offers great falsification tests for the theory by, for instance, finding species in locations where they should not be. Such falsification arguments are, of course, more practically reasonable than previously mentioned ones, as it is more feasible to examine living species than it is to find fossil rabbits in the Pre-Cambrian era. However, they are still problematic: they would appear to lack sensitivity – a negative test result does not offer any meaningful proof of evolutionary theory.

Also, there are other flaws with these falsification arguments. Evolutionary theory predicts that we won't find particular animals in certain areas. For example, we should not find elephants on the Pacific Islands (despite the conditions being ideal for them), due to continental separation prior to elephants evolving. Consequently, pro-evolutionists claim that finding indigenous elephants on the Pacific Islands would falsify evolutionary theory. But such falsification tests cannot actually disprove evolutionary theory. Such findings, should they occur, could be accommodated into the evolutionary theory model, as is the case with the Borneo elephant...

This (sub)species of Asian elephant only exists in a small region of the Southeast Asian Island of Borneo, and how this happened is a mystery. But evolutionary theory is not falsified by this: instead the theory proposes two possible explanations – either these elephants were introduced to Borneo by human beings, or they diverged from Asian elephants a few hundred thousand years ago and crossed low sea levels to arrive there.

In a similar manner, any finding of a modern species in an unexpected region can be explained by human introduction or remarkable migration. If the theory can find a way to explain rats in Australia and elephants in Borneo, it seems that it can explain any observation of geographical distribution, rendering any falsification test related to geographical distribution unfit for purpose.

In summary, we can say that geographical distribution is only an observation about the here and now. It tells us nothing about how this geographical distribution came to be. Of course, hypotheses and speculation can be made, but this is very different to having actual evidence or scientific methods to determine the causality of this distribution.

5.2 Finch beaks

Many of you will have heard of the finch beaks of the Galapagos Islands which are famously associated with Charles Darwin and his formulation of the theory of evolution by natural selection. The story is that Darwin was on a voyage around the Galapagos Islands during which he observed various different species of finch birds over the separated islands. He identified differences in the beak sizes and shapes in the variant species of finches, and he found that the variant species were located on different islands. He also observed that the beaks that were found on each island were the most suitable for that island in terms of the food supply available, in other words one group had beaks more suitable for digging worms, another for cracking nuts, and so on. From these observations he came up with theory of natural selection through a survival of the fittest mechanism, and from this, the theory of evolution soon followed.

Now, no-one would disagree with the statement that different finch beaks were found on different islands. But does this really prove evolutionary theory, or even just add any decent weight to it? No, it just tells us that species with the best features suited to a particular environment seem to exist in greater numbers in that particular environment. It does not provide any evidence for how those species came into existence, and it certainly goes nowhere to helping us with our default hypothesis. Darwin simply took a simple observation of finch beak distribution over the Galapagos Islands and *assumed* that this observation arose through a mechanism of natural selection and evolution without any actual evidence to support this assumption.

Even *if* we can demonstrate a finch species changing, this tells us nothing about evolutionary theory and common descent. So what if a certain characteristic or two can be favoured and selected? A huge inference is required to go from this to the suggestion that one finch species evolved into another.

There is variation of beak size and shape *within* a finch species as well. This variation *can* be explained through natural selection. But *intra*-species variation is very different from *inter*-species variation. Natural selection has not been proven to be the cause of variation *between* finch species, or any species for that matter.

In order to prove *evolution* of one finch species to another, one would have to observe the finch population evolving (incidentally this has been attempted, as we will see later in Chapter 6). But even *if*, very generously, we were to concede that all finch beaks have come from one ancestor beak, this only demonstrates evolution within one similar group of animals. It is still, obviously, a far stretch to go from this to stating that *all* life is physically related and evolved from an original single-cell common ancestor.

Natural selection only means that a certain feature, or variation of a feature, is favoured and subsequently becomes more prevalent in a given population. It has never been shown to result in the formation of a new species. Natural selection and "survival of the fittest" can certainly exist without common descent and speciation. In fact, natural selection seems logical, even if it is unproven and disputed as being the mechanism for evolutionary theory. It is funny to think that scientists and evolutionary biologists claim that there is no doubt, argument or debate over whether evolutionary theory is true or not, and the only debate is over the actual mechanism of how it happened, with some saying it was natural selection and others saying it was not. This is odd because actually it seems that there is probably more evidence for natural selection than there is for common descent and evolution!

6. Experimental/observational evidence

6.1 Experimental evolution
6.2 Antibiotic resistance

6.1 Experimental evolution

Experimental evolution is the process of using experiments to study and reproduce evolution. Of course, there are significant limitations to this as macroevolution of larger species happens over the course of thousands or millions of years, making it impractical to observe or reproduce in the laboratory setting. However, studies have been carried out on smaller organisms, such as microorganisms like bacteria, to observe evolution taking place. These studies have shown that bacteria do adopt a natural selection process resulting in certain bacteria types changing (or "evolving"). No-one disputes this: it is a well-recognised observation which has practical benefits, such as in the use of antibiotics, but it doesn't prove speciation (as we will explain in a moment).

Furthermore, even though laboratory studies with foxes and rodents have apparently shown adaptations occurring in as few as 10-20 generations, this still does not get us anywhere close to predicting that either of these species can evolve into a new species. From a logical point of view, all it shows is that a natural selection process can be induced in a species by imposing the relevant external pressures. (Note that it does not show us that natural selection *has* happened in the real world, although one may be able to reasonably *presume* this).

The same is true of the infamous fruit flies that you may have heard of. Experiments have been going on with fruit flies for over a hundred years. Again, these show that fruit flies can adapt and change, but none of them have evolved into a new species as such. Deliberate manipulation of genes has been able to artificially produce new and beneficial adaptations in the fruit flies, such as an ability to survive in low oxygen concentrations. However, as interesting as this is, once again it does not get us close to our default hypothesis. For starters, artificially inducing such changes through scientific methods and gene isolation procedures does not tell us whether the same processes could happen naturally in the real world and did happen in the real world. Even if scientific experiments could show that the fruit flies, or any other species for that matter, could evolve into a completely new species, it would still not provide solid evidence for our default hypothesis. Remember, evolutionary theory states that *all* life evolved from a single-cell organism. So demonstrating change from one species to another within a genus is a long way from proving this. It would, of course, represent a small starting point at least, but evolutionary theory is yet to even reproduce *this* on a scientific level.

Humans have been artificially breeding domestic animals such as dogs for decades, and this is also argued to have shown evolution in practice. All dogs reportedly descend from a wolf. Through artificial breeding, many varieties of dog have been created. The argument is that artificial breeding has shown how it is possible to select and choose certain members of a species to reproduce with each other so that certain features and characteristics are created or preserved. This process can be repeated indefinitely, and eventually descendants may look very different to their ancestors. Artificial breeding is done by humans; natural selection is done by nature (through a survival of the fittest mechanism). Both result in certain members of a species being chosen and favoured over others. However, artificial breeding has not been able to create a new species. All the different dogs created through this process, from a Great Dane all the way down in size to a Chihuahua, are still dogs belonging to the same species. This is because technically they can still interbreed to produce fertile offspring. So all dogs are part of the same species, along with the wolf variant from which they are descended – a wolf and a dog can still interbreed to produce fertile offspring. While it is argued that a Great Dane and a Chihuahua do not mate and reproduce, this is due to mechanical reasons with the size and shape of the animals making it impractical or rather difficult to naturally mate. Technically speaking however, if artificial insemination methods were used, the two animals could produce live offspring.

Pro-evolutionists argue that artificial breeding has only been going on for decades or a few centuries at most, whereas evolution has been going on for millions of years. If artificial breeding were to continue, they argue that the changes that eventually occurred would result in new species arising: in other words the Great Dane's and the Chihuahua's descendants may no longer be able to technically reproduce with each other and would be determined new and distinct species.

This may be true, but at present it is just a presumption. The fact is that all artificial breeding has *definitively* shown so far is that through selection, new variations within a species can be created, thus increasing the diversity within that species. Artificial breeding has not been able to create a *new* species, therefore it has not shown that members of a species can evolve into another species. We want to know if a single-cell organism can evolve into a human being, not whether certain traits of a species can be deliberately created or preserved.

It seems likely that knowledge of heredity would have existed before evolutionary theory and artificial breeding, as people could see that offspring typically resemble a combination of both their parents. Tall parents are more likely to give rise to tall children, so humans too can select certain characteristics and features by selecting their partner. If a dark-skinned individual reproduces with a very fair-skinned individual, it's no great secret that their child is likely to have a mixed complexion which is dissimilar to both its parents.

Also, is the variation seen within the dog species that remarkable? A Great Dane and Chihuahua might look miles apart but technically they are much more similar to each other than a human being is to a chimpanzee. The basic anatomical make-up of both the Great Dane and Chihuahua is one and the same. In fact, if you think about it, is the difference between a Great Dane and Chihuahua actually significantly more than the difference that can exist between two people from different ethnic backgrounds? They too can look very different to each other. But it seems extreme to suggest that they are likely to evolve into new and distinct species. So the whole argument from artificial breeding seems irrational and certainly does not add any significant weight to proving evolutionary theory.

6.2 Antibiotic resistance

Antibiotics are artificially made drugs which are designed to kill bacteria for the purpose of combatting diseases. The advent and use of antibiotics has led to new strains of bacteria "evolving" and becoming more prevalent. The mechanisms of this are disputed. Some think that mutant bacteria, which already exist in the bacterial population as a minority, have immunity to the antibiotic and therefore survive and reproduce at a higher rate, creating an increase in their population size and percentage – this previous minority group of bacteria are naturally selected due to having a beneficial trait for survival. Others say that different genetic processes are used to confer immunity to certain bacteria. Either way, it does not matter. The question is; does this act as evidence for evolutionary theory?

Unfortunately, all this shows is that a certain type of bacteria can be selected over another type through the constraints of the external environment in which it exists. The bacteria are changing but not necessarily *evolving* into another species. They are still bacteria. You cannot extrapolate this change into evolution of one species to another, and you certainly cannot state that this change shows that it is likely (or even possible) that a bacterium can continue to "evolve" like this so that one day it turns into a human being: it may at most be considered a form of microevolution but certainly not as evidence for macroevolution of distinct species arising from one another.

Also, antibiotic resistance certainly does not demonstrate complexity deriving from simplicity. It just shows a different type of bacteria emerging – one could not conclude that this new type of bacteria is more complex than the previous type. The new type simply has unique traits which are more suitable for the environment in which they exist. So variations in bacteria populations offer no meaningful value to our default hypothesis.

No experimental or observational evidence has shown evolution of one species to another. In addition, note that, even if such experiments had not yielded the results that they have, evolutionary theory would still not be disproved. Because, the tests that have been used are very specific to just minuscule elements of evolutionary theory rather than establishing the main postulations. A negative result in any of these experiments does not disprove evolutionary theory any more than a positive result proves it.

7. Theoretical evidence

7.1 The age of the Earth
7.2 Sub-theories

7.1 The age of the Earth

This is a contentious issue. As we will see later, there are some people who argue that the evidence for the world being billions of years old is lacking and the planet is not as old as the consensus says that it is. We will look at this argument later (in Chapter 5). However, as we said earlier, let us not question the validity of the evidence that evolutionary theory uses. Let us presume that the world is as old as the consensus says that it is and ask ourselves the question; how does this impact on the argument for evolutionary theory?

Pro-evolutionists argue that because the world is billions of years old and life started over a billion years ago, common descent and evolution are mathematically possible. This is because with time it is feasible that random mutations to organisms of a species will result in beneficial characteristics, and there is plenty of time for these species to evolve into more complex species. It would be too complicated to go into the mathematics of the exact probability of this, but let us presume that it is possible. It still does not *prove* the theory. It just shows that the theory is plausible. "Could happen" and "did happen" are two very different things. Time makes the theory feasible, but it does not prove it. And it is certainly not a strong argument to support evolutionary theory. In fact, a clever distraction technique is being used here. The focus of the debate is being switched from evolutionary theory to the age of the Earth. As soon as evidence suggests that the world is billions of years old, people wrongly accept this as evidence for evolutionary theory. They wrongly conclude that if the world is billions of years old, evolution must be true, whereas if the world is only thousands of years old, evolution must be false. Only the latter presumption is correct.

Think about it. If the world is as old as we are told it is, then, of course, the proposed model of evolutionary theory is plausible. But obviously, the age of the Earth tells us nothing in itself about evolutionary theory. A test that could show the Earth to be only a few thousand years old would be considered a specific test for disproving evolutionary theory. Because, if it could be proven that the Earth is only a few thousand years old, evolutionary theory is automatically disproved, as the theory is not feasible. However, the test has low sensitivity, as failing to prove the Earth is only a few thousand years old does not tell us anything about whether evolutionary theory is true or not; it just makes evolutionary theory possible. Similarly, a test that shows the Earth definitely is billions of years old does not tell us anything about evolutionary theory – this test would have both low sensitivity *and* low specificity for proving or disproving evolutionary theory. As, a passed test result would only prove that versions of creationism which state the Earth to be only a few thousand years old are wrong – the test has a high specificity for disproving young Earth creationism.[*]

As we have already mentioned, "plausible" is not the same as "actual". But also, "plausible" is not the same as *probable*. The reported age of the earth only means that evolutionary theory is *plausible*. But the question we need to ask is, how *probable* is evolutionary theory? Of course, this is almost impossible to determine with mathematics alone. This is because the proposed mutations that

---

[*] Young Earth creationism is the idea that the universe and all life in it were created only a few thousand years ago.

result in new favourable features in a species are random, and not based on any specific law or conscious or unconscious adaptation to the environment. So they are completely unpredictable. Asking whether a single-cell organism can evolve into a human being if it is given 3.8 billion years to do so is not a question that we are likely to get an answer to. Of course, the burden of proof is to prove evolutionary theory to a reasonable degree. Bearing this in mind, it seems unreasonable to use the age of the Earth as active evidence to support evolutionary theory, as it only shows the theory is possible but does not help us with whether the theory is probable or not.

7.2 Sub-theories

Another interesting thing that evolutionary theory does is to appeal to technical mechanisms, mathematics and complex scientific processes as a form of self-justification. You may have heard of mechanisms such as "Genetic Drift", and laws such as "Mendelian Inheritance" and the "Hardy-Weinberg Law". Such sub-theories and laws may show that parts of evolutionary theory are possible, but none of them go anywhere to showing that evolution actually happened. Also, none of these technical-sounding sub-theories or laws can give a solid scientific theory that a physicist or mathematician would recognise or be able to implement to demonstrate how evolution could actually occur. For example, none of these laws or theories can actually tell you *how* to go from a monkey to a man or from a cow-like creature to a whale: no genetic pathways or specific DNA changes are proposed that might explain this.

These sub-theories and laws make evolutionary theory sound scientific and appear technical, and that is all. But they can lead to intelligent people who know nothing about evolutionary theory being misled into believing evolutionary theory is scientifically sound. These sub-theories and laws make the extravagant claim of a single-cell organism evolving into all species *appear* more plausible.

Consider this analogy: describing how carbon changes to carbon dioxide is one tiny, albeit very important, step in the combustion engine, but it does not complete the explanation of how motion in a car is produced. There are many other processes involved which result in the car moving. Demonstrating this one tiny step does not prove a moving car has ever been produced.

The issue with these technical sub-theories and laws is that they cannot and do not provide causality for all the biodiversity we have on

Planet Earth. They do not actually demonstrate evolution happening. They only examine some of the minute mechanisms involved. Speculating about how a missing person has been murdered seems irrelevant if there is no good evidence to suggest that the person is even dead. A few traces of blood in the bathroom sink tell us nothing about whether a person has been murdered or not, let alone methods of murder, such as being shot, stabbed or beaten to death. Analysing the blood to see what type it is and who it belongs to may be of some interest and use, but it goes nowhere to telling us about a potential murder. And that is all these technical sub-theories and laws are; they focus on the minutia of evolutionary theory and are more interested in establishing whether aspects of evolutionary theory are feasible rather than whether evolutionary theory is actually true.

Of course, the specific mechanisms detailed in these sub-theories may be true, but this still has no relevance on the matter in question. In the same way, it may come to light that the few traces of blood in the bathroom sink come from the missing person in question, but this does not prove the hypothesis that the missing person has been murdered. Similarly, natural selection resulting in a specific characteristic becoming more prevalent in a given species may be shown to be true, but this does not prove that one species has evolved into another species. The two are significantly different. Using these technical sub-theories and laws as evidence for the case of evolutionary theory could be likened to saying, "I've built a car, and to prove it I will demonstrate carbon changing to carbon dioxide".

The circumstantial case for evolutionary theory

We have shown that none of the aforementioned pieces of evidence on their own provide a solid case for evolutionary theory. We have no smoking gun. None of the pieces of evidence when looked at on their own can directly lead one to a rational conclusion that evolutionary theory is true beyond reasonable doubt. However, most pro-evolutionists state that it is the convergence of all the evidence that proves evolutionary theory. So the question we need to ask is whether all the evidence above collectively provides a strong circumstantial case for evolutionary theory?

There is no doubt that all the evidence does seem to complement each other. The fossil record (although grossly incomplete), the chemical and anatomical similarities of species, and the geographical distribution of species, would appear to be the strongest pieces of evidence. But do they simply fit in with the theory and not contradict it rather than proving it? This is the vital question that needs to be considered.

The problem with the evolutionary theory hypothesis is that no detailed mechanism from start to end is provided. Pro-evolutionists say that they know for sure evolution is true, but they're just not sure exactly how it happened. This weakens the whole case for evolutionary theory. Claiming that X evolved into Y because X looks like Y and lives near Y, seems inadequate. One would need a detailed methodology of *how* X evolved into Y before accepting this as true, in the same way that one would need a detailed account of the events surrounding a murder in order to convict a suspect of the murder.

The circumstantial case for evolutionary theory is very difficult to assess, and it seems likely that there is a huge element of subjectivity involved in determining the strength of this. Establishing whether the separate pieces of evidence combine to form a probability that evolution actually happened is very complex. In a murder case, we can clearly understand, rationalise and visualise the various pieces of evidence, as we are probably going to have a prior understanding of the fabric of this evidence. Also, we can draw comparisons and refer back to our own personal experiences of life to help us make our deductions on the likelihood of the said event having happened. The suspect's finger-prints and blood at the scene of the crime, CCTV footage of him entering the victim's house at the time of the murder, an eye-witness over-hearing the suspect plotting to kill the victim are all pieces of evidence which are relatively easy to interpret, understand and form a conclusion on.

Contrast this to evolutionary theory's evidence of geographical distribution, transitional fossils, DNA analysis and morphological comparisons, and you can see the problem. It is difficult to extrapolate from this information to a decision on evolutionary theory. Also, evolutionary theory is a question about how inert nature works. Obviously, it is not possible to guess or rely on instincts when it comes to this, as inert nature does not purposefully make any decision. It's not the same as trying to establish what a person may do in a given situation. If we are asked to determine the guilt of a conscious man, we can use our own experience and understanding of human nature to help us make this determination. We know that there are certain traits and situations that are likely to increase the chance of someone committing murder. However, we have no prior examples or experience of inert nature determining the progression of life to compare evolutionary theory to.

It is interesting to question why evolutionary theory has gone so far with its hypothesis. It seems that it would have been more reasonable to suggest descent with modification within a specific family or genus of life forms. It could provide a good circumstantial case for this using some of the demonstrations that it has, such as horse evolution. The evidence for this is much stronger than it is for common descent with complete relatedness of all species. But the evolutionary theory movement seems very keen to extrapolate the latter from the former. As we will see later, there does appear to be a plausible reason (or motive) for this.

Pro-evolutionists say that all the evidence fits in perfectly with their proposed model of evolutionary theory, and therefore it must be correct. However, as we have demonstrated, they mostly use circular reasoning to establish this, using proposals based on their own model to substantiate the evidence that they do find. Much of the supporting evidence seems to rely on an assumption made on the grounds of other evidence, and therefore is redundant. This is a significant problem with the circumstantial case for evolutionary theory.

With any circumstantial case, there is an expectation that there should be no other logical conclusion inferable from the evidence provided, and there should be no other reasonable explanation for the matter in question. Otherwise, enough reasonable doubt would have been created. Now, this is where it gets complicated. To a religious person who strongly believes in the Biblical version of creation, there is a viable alternative explanation. By contrast, for the staunch atheist, this version is simply illogical. Of course, it is not the aim of this book to examine the case for creationism. To critique evolutionary theory from an unbiased perspective, we need only to accept (but not necessarily believe) that there are alternative theories out there which might explain the biodiversity that we see in existence today, and, as we have briefly touched on, not just creationism by God.

It is clear that the burden of proof is not a clear-cut target that one can reach with certainty. Of course, there is a degree of subjectivity involved in determining this, hence the long jury deliberations that can often follow a court case based on circumstantial evidence. However, it seems that the inference required to get from the evidence available to evolutionary theory is just too great, and this opens the door for much more than just reasonable doubt.

Chapter 3 – Is it logical?

The probability of evolution

Evolutionary theory essentially states that all species on Earth originated from a single-cell organism via a process of random mutations in genes creating favourable organisms which are then selected by nature and become more prevalent. Essentially, this is to say that through a series of accidents, a single-cell organism has evolved into all extinct and extant species, having gone through a multitude of intermediate species in between. This, of course, includes human beings. Forgetting the science and the scientific theory proposed for a moment, let us just think about this as a concept...

The idea of a human being evolving from a single-cell organism like a bacterium, which you are unable to even see with your naked eye, is a very difficult concept to comprehend and accept with an unbiased and unconditioned mind. Even if you start many steps further through the process and consider the change from one of the proposed intermediate species, such as Juramaia Sinensis (an extinct mammal resembling a modern rat), it is still very hard to comprehend. The idea of a rat-like-creature turning into a human being through a series of accidents would be hard for anyone with reasonable intelligence to just blindly accept.

This can be better understood by considering an intelligent mind which has not been conditioned by the typical Western education – perhaps the mind of an individual living in a lost tribe in the Amazon rainforest.* Presumably, they have no prior knowledge of the theory of evolution. Let us also, for the purpose of this thought experiment, presume that they have no religious or spiritual beliefs. Now give them the two prevalent theories of how they came into existence (evolutionary theory and creationism). It seems likely that they would think it absurd that a human being came from a single-cell organism (or even a tiny amphibian creature) through a series of accidents, and

---

* A "lost tribe" is synonymous with the terms "uncontacted people" and "isolated people". The terms refer to people who live in isolated groups that have never had contact with the "civilised world". Thus, they have no knowledge of different peoples and different civilisations. There are thought to be very few such groups in existence today.

that they would thus find evolutionary theory more preposterous and unbelievable than the theory of creationism.

Regarding evolutionary theory, Sir Fred Hoyle, the renowned British astronomer, said the probability of "higher life forms" arising from non-living matter can be likened to the probability of a tornado sweeping through a junkyard and by chance assembling a fully functional Boeing 747 aeroplane from the materials therein. There is some confusion about whether he was referring to the process of abiogenesis, evolution or both combined, as he appears to conflate the origin of life with the higher forms of life. However, Hoyle was opposed to evolutionary theory, so it seems fair to presume that he thought the mathematical probability of higher life forms evolving from an original single-cell common ancestor to be *extremely* unlikely.

The smallest known genome of a living organism has 525 genes. A man has about 20,000 genes. So while the jump from 0 to 525 genes is remarkable, the jump from 525 genes to 20,000 genes is still significant. Many anti-evolutionists equate the "junkyard tornado" probability to the *evolution* of complex species, and not abiogenesis. Critics of this comparison dismiss it on the grounds that evolution is a slow process that occurs over millions of years, so it is more plausible than it seems on the surface. But even if the tornado is given 3.8 billion years to assemble the aeroplane (the same time the single-cell common ancestor was given to evolve into a man), it still seems unfathomable. Pro-evolutionists argue that evolution is a gradual process, one step at a time. Okay, the tornado does not have to complete the job in one go – it can assemble the aeroplane piece by piece over a series of different and separate evolutions (such as with evolutionary theory). For example, it can assemble the engine first, then the outside body of the aeroplane, then the cockpit, then come back for the cabin and so on. But even with this freedom, it still seems unfathomable. Even if mathematicians tell us it is possible, logic and our own intuition tells us it is not.

We can use another analogy to demonstrate the implausibility of evolutionary theory. The infinite monkey theorem was devised by the French mathematician Emile Borel. In this theorem the question of time does not come into play as we assume an infinite timespan. It states that if a monkey was to hit keys at random on a typewriter keyboard, eventually the monkey will reproduce the entire works of a great writer such as William Shakespeare. Now, this may be true, but ask yourself this; if someone was to tell you that a monkey had written great literature through random typing of a keyboard through complete chance, with no direction or design, would you believe them? What about if they told you that a tornado had assembled a fully functional aeroplane through complete chance and with no direction or design; would you believe that? Almost certainly you would find it hard to believe either of these claims. And you would at least question them to determine whether they were true or not. But people do not seem to question evolutionary theory in the same manner. One of the reasons is that a time factor of billions of years is difficult to comprehend and conceive of. Many people simply accept the theory as they are coerced into believing that it's possible for anything to happen in such a time-frame. Of course, the mathematics of the probability of evolutionary theory happening is too difficult for most people to work out – some mathematicians say it is possible, some say it is too improbable.

You may have seen the infinite monkey theorem being invoked in support of evolutionary theory, most notably by Richard Dawkins, a famous British evolutionary biologist. Dawkins claims that natural selection is not random, and he used a computer program which demonstrated that a line of Shakespeare could be reproduced by random typing with "non-random cumulative selection" in as little as 43 generations – the program had the set line in target and only selected the correct random letters which went towards producing this target, and incorrect material was disregarded. The obvious error with this comparison, which Dawkins himself concedes, is that without the line set as a target, the chance of the program producing the line is minuscule. If there is no intelligence behind evolution, as Dawkins believes, then there is no set target for a common ancestor to reach. So the chances of the original common ancestor evolving into all known species are still minuscule. This is also because natural selection does *not* make speciation a non-random event, as we will see shortly.

Evolutionary theory is based on the premise that life arose only once and then this original single-cell common ancestor evolved into all other species. There is no scope for multiple descent with more than one original ancestor. The reason evolutionary theory makes this claim is because of the premise that all life is made of up of the same material (DNA and RNA), which results in the claim that all life must be *directly* related. If they assumed multiple descent, they would have to forgo biochemical evidence as evidence for evolutionary theory. This is because the theory would now be claiming that DNA can arise independently in which case the mere presence of DNA would not prove relatedness, and consequently DNA could not be used to promote the idea that any two species are related. This would be a massive blow for evolutionary theory, as the biochemical evidence is considered by many to be the strongest piece of evidence for evolutionary theory.

Now, if one thinks that a monkey, if given enough time, would reproduce Shakespeare, then it seems logical and probable that a single-cell common ancestor made of the same material would arise more than once. If a monkey can reproduce Shakespeare's *Macbeth*, why can the processes that resulted in the original single-cell common ancestor not recur and produce a second common ancestor? Perhaps the first ancestor evolved into all plant life and the second ancestor went on to evolve into all animal life. The Earth is assumed to be 4.5 billion years old, and abiogenesis is assumed to have occurred 3.8 billion years ago. So it only took 15% of the timeline of Earth for this first organism to appear? Why would a similar organism not reappear in the remaining 85% of the Earth's timeline? Why does evolutionary theory insist that the random act of abiogenesis has only occurred once in 4.5 billion years? (For now, we will presume the act of abiogenesis to be random – we will expound on this in Chapter 7). If this random act happened once, surely it is conceivable it could happen again, especially if it is argued that a monkey can randomly reproduce a very complex and masterful *non*-random event. Surely an event that has actually happened before cannot be considered more unlikely than a monkey randomly typing *Macbeth*, which has never happened before? Asserting that abiogenesis can only occur once, yet *Macbeth* can occur twice, does not seem consistent on the surface of it. But if evolutionary theory was to concede this point, the whole theory would break down. This argument is summarised below:

    a. If it is argued that a monkey typing randomly can reproduce *Macbeth* word-for-word, it should be argued that the random process of abiogenesis can also be reproduced, yielding independent, yet (almost) identical, original ancestral organisms.

    b. If there were multiple original ancestral organisms, there would be multiple descents, which would negate the theory of common descent yet result in the same observations of biodiversity seen today.

    c. If present-day observations would be the same with common descent and multiple descent, there is no evidence to support common descent from one original ancestor *over* multiple descents from more than one original ancestor.

   d. Thus, common descent and multiple descent are equally likely, and common descent cannot be assumed.

   e. Multiple descent would imply that DNA similarity between organisms can arise independently.

   f. Thus, DNA similarity and biochemical evidence does not prove relatedness.

   g. Thus, biochemical evidence cannot be used to support evolutionary theory.

   h. Without biochemical evidence, the evidence for speciation is severely weakened.

But natural selection is not random

As we have seen, Dawkins, and many other pro-evolutionists, argue that evolution is not random. They argue that evolution through natural selection is actually not chance at all. The argument is that natural selection is, in simple terms, survival of the fittest. If there is only enough food to sustain 20% of the population of a species, it is the strongest (or rather the most able at obtaining the food) 20% that will get the food and survive and reproduce.* This is not down to chance; this is an expected, logical and predictable outcome.

Now, it does seem reasonable to accept this line of argument from pro-evolutionists – natural selection is not improbable, because it happens gradually over a vast amount of time. But while this all seems logical, we must remember that they are only talking about natural selection, and how nature favours and selects the fittest members of a species. They are only talking about the mechanism of how certain traits and characterises are favoured and selected. They are not talking about the random mutations that allow a creature to develop a new feature in the first place. They are not talking about the mutations that need to occur to turn a cow-like creature into a whale. Remember, a bacterium doesn't gradually evolve into a human being (or any other species for that matter) through natural selection alone. To go from not having hair to having hair is not a gradual process of natural selection; a mutation has to occur to allow for this new feature to develop, and then through a natural selection process, this new feature can perfect itself. A new feature cannot arise from nothing.

---

*This obviously does not account for true altruism whereby a creature may sacrifice their good for the good of another creature. Although, this type of behaviour appears to be an exclusive trait of human beings.

Hair cannot arise from no-hair. Evolutionary theory dictates it comes from a mutation in the DNA. And it is these mutations which are the driving force behind evolution. And they are random. If there is no intellect behind them, it is purely chance that dictates how and when and if they occur.

If there was an intelligence behind evolution, it would not be random – it would be intentional. Later, in Chapter 7, we will explore the idea of whether an intelligence could be implementing these mutations, thus rendering them non-random. But, for now, we are presuming that inert nature is responsible for these mutations, which means that they have to be considered random in the true sense of the word. This is because there is no determinable mechanism for predicting the mutations that lead to the development of new features and characteristics of an organism.

Inert nature cannot intend events to happen. So if evolutionary theory is true *and* there is no supernatural intelligence behind it, all the species that we see in existence today are here by accident. It was a series of accidents that resulted in you, me and every other life form. It is remarkable to think that the complexity you demonstrate is the result of accidents. Your ability to read and understand this is an accident. You, according to evolutionary theory, are essentially an accident.

So even though natural selection is not random, evolution per se is. It is reliant on chance, as the random mutations are the real, original cause of all the various features and characteristics that you see in life. Every single organ, muscle, bone, tendon, nerve and so on, is the result of a random mutation (as remember, the original single-cell common ancestor had none of these). So even if you discount the odds of natural selection occurring, evolutionary theory is still an extremely improbable theory.

Complexity starts with simplicity

In Chapter 1, we said that we would come back to the question of "must complexity start with simplicity?" This would appear to be more of a philosophical question than a scientific one, as there is no law in science that says that complex life forms must arise from simpler life forms. We have already mentioned the law of entropy which contradicts the idea that complexity *must* be preceded by simplicity.

The idea of common descent is thought by some to have originated from Erasmus Darwin, who was a renowned physician, philosopher, poet, botanist, naturalist and grandfather to Charles Darwin. In his book Zoonomia (1794) he wrote:

> *"The great CREATOR of all things has stamped a certain similitude on the features of nature, that demonstrates to us that the whole is one family of one parent... Would it be too bold to imagine, that in the great length of time, since the earth began to exist, perhaps millions of ages before the commencement of the history of mankind, would it be too bold to imagine, that all warm-blooded animals have arisen from one living filament, which THE GREAT FIRST CAUSE endued with animality, with the power of acquiring new parts, attended with new propensities, directed by irritations, sensations, volitions, and associations; and thus possessing the faculty of continuing to improve by its own inherent activity, and of delivering down those improvements by generation to its posterity, world without end!"*

Both Erasmus and Charles Darwin *presumed* progression of species. They did not presume that complex species devolved or regressed into simpler species. But they had no transitional fossils, no knowledge of DNA and no knowledge of dating species, so why would they presume progression rather than regression? Why did they base their hypothesis of common descent on a model of *increasing* complexity from an original single-cell organism? They had no actual evidence to support one hypothesis over the other. "Simpler" species are not necessarily less fit for survival, and therefore could potentially be selected by nature. For example, bacteria can survive in conditions that human beings cannot and so too can rats. So rather than human beings evolving from the rat-type creature Juramaia Sinensis, perhaps Juramaia Sinensis evolved (or devolved) from human beings. In which case, it is either yet to be discovered in living form, or it has gone extinct and been outlived by its ancestor, Homo sapiens. Remember, some ancient species like the coelacanth, were thought to have gone extinct millions of years ago yet have recently been found in living form. Also, fossils cannot *prove* the age of a species, and according to evolutionary theory, most species don't fossilise. So complex species may be much older than thought. (Granted, there is circularity in this argument in that it uses evolutionary theory's own paradoxical mantra in order to support an idea opposed to their own).

Perhaps there is a mixture of both progression and regression with some species devolving into simpler forms which then evolve into different, more complex forms. For example, modern man devolves into Juramaia Sinensis which then evolves into the chimpanzee which then devolves into the bacterium. This model would not necessarily need to start with one common ancestor – there could be multiple ascents and descents. Instead of increasing complexity of DNA, we could, at times, have increasing simplicity of DNA with gene deletions or mutations in DNA accounting for this.

This all sounds far-fetched, but remember, there is no law in science that says that complexity comes from simplicity. You have no reason to *believe* in evolution rather than devolution – you have witnessed neither and therefore cannot presume either. Granted, this hypothesis does seem more complex, and the Darwins' hypothesis is much cleaner and easier to formulate. However, as stated, the Darwins had no observations or evidence to favour one over the other, so it could only have been intuition or a predisposition that led them to select the "progressive" evolution hypothesis. We will explore this idea further in Chapter 8. For now, let's explore the concept that complexity must come from simplicity further. As we have no life forms outside the evolutionary theory hypothesis to make an analogy with, we will use an inert analogy from human history...

The first European visitors to Easter Island were Dutchmen in 1722.* They were impressed and amazed by the sight of the monumental Moai statues.† On seeing them for the first time they may

---

* Easter Island is a small volcanic island situated in the Southeast Pacific Ocean. It is the most remote inhabited island in the world, located about 2,200 miles from the coast of Chile and about 1,200 miles from the closest inhabited island. It is thought to have been home to civilisation for more than 1,600 years. The first inhabitants and subsequent settlers of Easter Island were Polynesians, who were presumed to have migrated there from other islands in the Pacific Ocean. The island is famous for its monumental human statues made of stone.

† Moai is the collective name of the 887 monolithic human statues found on Easter Island. They average 4 metres (13 feet) in height and almost 12,000 kilograms (about 1,900 stones) in weight, with great variation amongst the statues. The largest completed statue is 10 metres (about 33 feet) in height and 82,000 kilograms (about 12,900 stones) in weight, and it was carved from a single block of stone. The smallest is just 1.1 metres (3 feet and 7 inches) in height. It has been a great mystery as to how these monumental statues were constructed and transported. Only relatively recently, and after decades of experimentation, modern-day researchers successfully recreated and

have deduced that the smaller statues preceded the larger ones, and then through evolution of architecture, the largest statues were built. Now, they might be right, but it would be guesswork alone, which is open to debate. They could not have proven anything simply by looking at the statues and making assumptions. Does the largest statue *have* to have been preceded by a gradation of smaller and less complex statues? Likewise, does the complex human being *have* to be the result of the relatively uncomplex bacterium-like organism? Logically speaking, no they don't. The idea, knowledge and architectural skill of creating the largest statue may have arisen in the designer first so that they made the most complex statues before the smaller, less complex ones. This is not inconceivable. However, this argument does require the presence of a conscious intelligence to create and guide the whole process. Does this reasoning apply to inert nature? Well, as mentioned, there is no law in science that says that simplicity must precede complexity.

What about the idea that each statue was carved and developed gradually over time? This may be true (although it cannot be proved on observation alone). However, in this case the statue is an individual structure designed and built with an end goal in target. The human, on the other hand, is reported to have evolved from a single-cell organism by chance without purpose or design.* It is hard to think of any great structure that has been built without a plan, design or methodology in place from the beginning or at least near the beginning.

Some atheists, such as Richard Dawkins, like to use the argument that a supernatural intelligence is not plausible due to the concept of complexity having to arise from simplicity, which makes creationism an illogical position to adopt. This is because the origin and cause of the supernatural creator cannot be explained. However, this line of argument relies on the premise that complexity *must* come from simplicity, which is actually a product of evolutionary theory itself and consequently should be considered as circular reasoning. This can be explained by considering the following sequence of deduction:

---

transported such statues with the tools and resources that would have been available to the pioneers of the Moai statues.

* Some pro-evolutionists think evolution is designed, intended and orchestrated by a supernatural intelligence or God, and we will look at the reasoning and logic behind such a position in Chapter 7.

a. Evolutionary theory is the explanation of all life from an original common ancestor.

b. Evolutionary theory states that complexity starts with simplicity, meaning that complex life forms cannot originate spontaneously and must evolve from simpler life forms.

c. Based on statement *b*, a supernatural creator/intelligence would have to be more complex than any known life form, and therefore could not have existed before the first life form, and therefore cannot be the cause of life or evolution.

It is easy to see the fallacy of this argument. Statement *b* is derived from statement *a*. If statement *a* is untrue, statement *b* has no validity. If statement *b* has no validity, it cannot be used to deduce statement *c*. Evolutionary theory has not been proved true, so pro-evolutionists should not use presumptions derived from evolutionary theory to make a case against a supernatural intelligence.

Irreducible complexity

This is a common point of disagreement between pro-evolutionists and anti-evolutionists. The irreducible complexity argument from anti-evolutionists states that complex structures, like the human eye, cannot arise from the incremental changes associated with natural selection and evolution. This is because if you take parts away from the eye, it fails to function. Therefore, the argument goes, the eye must have been made in a single act of creation by a supernatural intelligence, much in the same way as a watch would have to have been made from start to finish by an intelligent watchmaker with the intention of an end-goal which would be the final watch itself. Half a watch, or three-quarters of a watch would serve no practical purpose.

Pro-evolutionists counter this argument by stating that complex structures are the result of a process of accumulation. Complex structures develop gradually over time through natural selection and evolution, becoming increasingly more complex over time. The eye is used as a classic example to demonstrate this, as described by David Attenborough, the award-winning English broadcaster and naturalist, in the BBC documentary *Charles Darwin and the Tree of Life* (2009):

> Some simple organisms have only light-sensitive spots that enable them to tell the difference between light and dark; such spots evolved and became bigger, forming pit-like structures

that created shadows thus revealing the direction of light, such as those found in flat-worms which enable the flat-worm to detect the shadow of a predator; the pit-like structure then got deeper and began to close, enabling the light to form a blurred image, such as with a snail who's blurry vision is good enough to locate food; light landing on cells led to mucous secretions which, when hardened, formed a lens which transmitted a brighter and clearer image, which is the lens found in any complex eye, such as with an octopus which has an eye with a fully formed lens that enables it to see as much detail as a human eye.

A process of evolution of the eye is given here, with examples of species who have intermediary complex eyes and the functional benefit that they gain from having them. Now, this might sound very impressive, but it is still far from defeating the "irreducible complexity" argument. The main reason is that in order to go from a pit of a few light-sensitive spots to the intricate and exceptionally complex structure that is the human eye, we need more than just a few changes.

The human eye is thought to have around 2 million working parts. So the pit of spots, as described in the sequence above, would have to undergo a multitude of changes with a multitude of intermediary structures in between to get to a human eye. And in order for the process to work, each change would have to incur a significant survival advantage to the recipient creature. Can every single random-mutation-induced change required to get from a pit of spots to a complex eye really offer an additional functional benefit? We certainly don't have enough of a series of intermediary functionalities to account for this, although pro-evolutionists argue that this is because the species displaying these have gone extinct. Also, bear in mind, the brain would have to develop in tandem to the developing eye in order to process the increasingly detailed sensory information being received by the increasingly complex eye. It is no surprise that an octopus with its advanced eye has an advanced brain, and that a flatworm with its basic eye has a relatively simple brain. So focusing on a flat-worm and a snail tells us nothing about how a light-sensitive spot of a single-cell organism evolved into a fully functional, complex eye. Evolutionary theory has simply brushed over this point in a way analogous to saying, "it's simple to turn a bicycle into a car – you just add two extra wheels, a cabin, an engine and a steering wheel."

Let's consider another structure – the wing. Much has been written on the evolution of the wing in order to allow for flight, and how a part wing can actually incur functional benefit to the creature to which it belongs. This is because a part wing can be used for purposes other than flight, such as gliding, which could save the life of a creature falling from a great height. So it is not inconceivable to suggest that a wing stub could, through a process of natural selection, gradually evolve into a fully functional wing. But the problem with this is that it seems highly unlikely that the first random mutation leading to the very beginning of the wing (and by the way we are presuming that the mutation results in wings on both sides of the animal) would incur a functional benefit. Is it not more likely to be a stub that serves no beneficial purpose? And if so, it would have no reason to be selected favourably by natural selection.

To support the idea that structures like wings evolve incrementally, pro-evolutionists cite examples of partial wings on species, such as the flying tree squirrel, the flying lima and the gliding lizard. But all of these wings are actually flaps of skin between the limbs which specifically offer the function of gliding and not flying. And these structures do not appear partial; they appear complete for the purpose they serve. Clearly, these cannot be used as examples for demonstrating how the wings of birds developed. They are completely different structures, offering a completely different function, which anyway would appear to have evolved independently of bird wings and insect wings if evolutionary theory is true. These examples do not tell us about whether a wing stub (or stubs) offer any functional benefit and would have been favoured and selected by natural selection.

Another animal worth mentioning is the bat, the only mammal capable of true flight. Its ability to fly is probably due to its forelimbs forming webbed wings. Even though the bat can fly like a bird and a flying insect, it developed its wings independently of birds and insects, as the bat's ancestors did not have wings. They all developed their wings through independent random mutations resulting in wings. Now, this is a remarkable claim from evolutionary theory. Understandably, evolutionary theory has no choice but to say this, as the wings are structurally different and arise in different lineages. To claim that the function of flying occurs by random mutations and has happened at least thrice in the history of life is extraordinary when you think about it, but that's another discussion, which we will come onto next.* For now, it seems reasonable to conclude that studying bat wings does not help us with the conundrum of how wings enabling flight can develop gradually over time from small wing stubs.

Similar to the wing conundrum is the problem of the backbone. The first vertebrates (animals with a backbone), thought to be fish, are proposed by evolutionary theory to have evolved from invertebrate animals. There is no record of fossils which supports this transition. So it is conjecture only. But anyway, the logic of trying to get from no backbone to a backbone just seems too irrational. A backbone is a complex structure. Clearly, it seems too implausible for a whole backbone to have evolved through one mutation of DNA, or even a few simultaneous mutations. Instead could this be a structure that could have evolved gradually in stages? It's hard to imagine how this would have been possible either, as what possible survival advantage does a partial backbone impart?

Venom is another example of a structure and function which seems hard to imagine having arisen from evolution. A select few animals in the world produce venom, which is a toxin secreted by the animal for the purposes of attacking and/or killing a victim. Such animals include jellyfish, vipers, spiders, scorpions, centipedes, bees, platypus and even a recently discovered primate known as the slow loris. So we can see that there is a huge diversity in the animals which can produce venom, and we can see that they are not closely related to each other. Venom producing ability is present in several different animal classes.

Evolutionary biologists will be the first to tell you that they don't really have a good idea of how the venom function has evolved independently in so many animals. Venom is a complex structure. It is composed of intricately complex molecules which can lock onto and attack certain proteins in the victim. Venoms have various mechanisms of action: some paralyze nerves, some damage muscles, and some interfere with the blood clotting mechanism. Now, not only is venom itself a very complex structure, but the equipment needed to store, transport and deliver the venom is complex too. In a cobra, the venom is delivered through its fangs. In a scorpion, the venom is delivered through its tail. The venom can be executed in various ways: through spit, through a bite, through a sting, through ingestion of the venom producing animal and so on. If we think about it, venom-

---

* The process whereby animals develop similar traits and functions independent of one another is known as "convergent evolution", as with the example of wings in bats, birds and insects.

delivering mechanisms could be likened to the perfect weapon, perhaps a gun. The venom could be considered the bullet, and the anatomical structures of the animal which produce, store, transport and execute the venom could be considered the gun.

Now, a gun relies on all of its mechanical parts in order to successfully shoot a bullet. If one part of that gun fails or is removed, there is a good chance that the bullet will not fire. The gun cannot be built in stages with each stage offering a higher level of functioning. Similar to the gun, the venom-delivering mechanism is a weapon. Either it is a successful weapon or it is not. Natural selection would not allow for the slow build-up of the weapon if there was no functional benefit of its transitional states. For example, why would an animal who could produce a very potent venom, store it, transport it around his body without self-mutilation, but had not yet evolved a system for executing it, be favoured by natural selection? There would be no functional benefit to his venom. Similarly, why would an animal who had all the infrastructure for storing, transporting, and executing venom, but lacked the ability to produce venom, be favoured by natural selection? It would be like having a gun with no bullets, except it would be an internal gun which could not even be seen by predators so as to act as a deterrent.

Also, can we expect that an effective venom poison evolves instantly through one random mutation? Because, if not, then venom seems unlikely to have evolved at all, as it would be unlikely to evolve gradually through natural selection. Natural selection would see no benefit of a venom that was ineffective (remember, it either works or it doesn't – there's no in between). There are no known examples of species with an ineffective venom. Even when we cook a meal, it takes us a while to perfect the recipe. So it seems illogical to suggest that a random mutation can suddenly give an animal an effective venom when the animal's parents had no venom at all. This would appear to be one of the fundamental flaws of evolutionary theory – it dictates that functionality evolves gradually along with the gradually evolving anatomical structures that give rise to this functionality. Sight, flight and use of venom all gradually evolved, according to evolutionary theory.

We have just shown that it seems illogical for venom to have gradually evolved, however, let's play with the idea that it did, along with sight and flight as well, for the purposes of the argument that we are about to make. For these functions to arise from 0% functionality and gradually evolve all the way up to 100% functionality, then all the infrastructure and components that enables this functionality would have had to have evolved in tandem as well. The brain would have to evolve with the eye, the body shape would have to evolve with the wings, and the storage and expelling devices would have to develop with the venom. As we said earlier, random mutations are mostly harmful, and it seems reasonable to presume that only one beneficial change happens per mutation. One structure, or one component, is altered at a time. This contradicts gradually evolving functionality, which would need several independent components and structures to develop simultaneously and evolve in tandem. A random mutation creating venom is not good enough. We need the mutation to also create the storage, transport and delivery mechanisms at the same time. You can't just add a steering function to a car by adding a steering wheel. A whole apparatus of a steering wheel connected to the wheels via a steering shaft with a rack-and-pinion mechanism is required. Without just one of these components, the whole apparatus is pointless and serves no function. So presumably you can see the problem. It just seems too far-fetched.

The peculiarity of convergent evolution

Convergent evolution is the fascinating suggestion by evolutionary theory that similar structures and functions can evolve independently. There are multiple examples of this, including eyes, ears, feathers, wings and stingers. Even complex functions like echolocation are said to have evolved independently in at least four different animal types (whales, bats, swiftlets and shrews).

Evolutionary theory has no option but to suggest that these structures developed independently, because otherwise they cannot be explained by the phylogenetic tree. If structures and functions are present in evolutionary cousins but absent in their ancestors, evolutionists have to propose independent (or convergent) evolution of these structures and functions. Otherwise, they have to redraw the tree to suggest closer relationships between animals that share these rare structures and functions. However, in such cases redrawing the tree is problematic, as other criteria that have gone into creating the relationships shown on the tree, such as DNA sequence analysis and cladistic morphological analysis, would then have to be compromised. Obviously, it is easier to promote the idea that a swiftlet is more closely related to other birds than it is to a whale.

The fact that venom-producing ability is present in most of the animal classes tells us that venom must have developed and evolved independently multiple times if evolutionary theory is true. This in itself is remarkable when you think about it – inert nature has somehow managed to create the same tool producing the same function several times, all independent of each other. Most of the greatest inventions in history, such as the mechanical clock, the steam engine, the light-bulb and the telephone, are thought to have arisen only once, with the technology then spreading across the world from the original location of invention. Even the invention of the wheel is thought to have happened only once in human history: there was no wheel in the whole of the Americas when the first European travellers arrived there a few centuries ago. Conscious intelligence can only create motion through wheels once, yet inert nature can create flight through wings thrice?! This seems illogical. Are we are expected to simply accept that inert nature can create similar structures and functions independent of one another? The tornado sweeping through and assembling an aeroplane by chance is one thing, but for it to separately and independently also assemble a helicopter through the same means would be quite something.

Even the idea that two resembling species can evolve independently through convergent evolution is interesting. For example, the triceratops is reportedly more closely related to a chicken than it is to a rhinoceros. Evolutionary theory is forced to suggest this because the triceratops is a dinosaur whereas the rhinoceros is a mammal: evolutionary theory proposes that dinosaurs and mammals branched off from a common ancestor hundreds of millions of years ago and therefore are not closely related. But there seems to be more physical similarity between the triceratops and the rhinoceros than there is between the triceratops and the chicken. In fact, the highly esteemed 19th Century American palaeontologist Othniel Charles Marsh, who was considered an expert on dinosaurs, initially thought the partial skull-fossil of a triceratops found in Western America was that of a bison. According to evolutionary theory, that mistake he made was pure coincidence. Pure coincidence that a bison skull could resemble that of a rhinoceros, as the two developed their similarity completely independently.

Also, many marsupial mammals in Australia and South America share remarkably similar anatomy with placental mammals in other continents. For example, it is very difficult to tell apart a Tasmanian marsupial wolf from a European timber wolf, or a marsupial jerboa from a placental jerboa, or a marsupial flying phalanger from a placental flying squirrel. Yet, evolutionary theory claims that these pairs evolved thousands of miles apart, independently and coincidentally, from an ancient common ancestor (a small shrew-like mammal) that was dispersed across the globe through continental separation.

As we mentioned earlier, Sir Fred Hoyle considered the probability of complex organisms arising through evolution to be extremely low. So to claim that similar, complex structures evolved through independent random mutations on multiple isolated instances is beyond imagination. The remarkable thing is that evolutionary theory proposes that this idea is much more feasible than the idea that abiogenesis occurred more than once. This is because evolutionists claim that the chances of the same four-letter code of DNA originating twice to form independent organisms is unimaginable. But logically, this does not seem that much more improbable than a single cell organism evolving into a man. Is the jump from the free-floating components of a cell to the first organism that much more improbable than the jump from that first organism to a man? If a complex function like echolocation evolved more than once, it seems reasonable to presume that the same four-letter code of DNA could evolve more than once in separate organisms. So there is a contradiction here that does not fit. Evolutionary theory states that there is no chance the same four-letter code of DNA evolved more than once, but they are happy to say that eyes, ears and wings all evolved on multiple separate occasions. Of course, if they were to acknowledge the possibility of life arising more than once, the theory of *common* descent is invalidated.

The presence of rare complex structures and functions in far-related animals should actually create severe doubt over the plausibility of evolutionary theory. As should the presence of remarkably similar species that have reportedly evolved independently. But, due to probable hindsight bias, proponents of the theory find a way to fit these extraordinary observations into their theory.

The absence of intermediate functionality

There are no species which appear to have organs, structures or functions in mid-development. Evolutionary theory states that this is because they have been selected out by nature. But evolution is a continual process which is ongoing, therefore we would expect such structures to exist.

There don't seem to be species with half a wing or half a venom-producing mechanism in place. In fact, there does not appear to be any species that has a structure or organ that would appear incomplete. So it seems that nothing is wasted. Every structure seems to offer a benefit (note that we are talking about the species as a whole rather than individual members of a species who, of course, can develop unwanted defects). Even though pro-evolutionists quote examples of the eye in transition from the shallow pits in flat-worms to the deeper pits in snails to the complex lens-equipped eye in humans, the earlier forms cannot be considered partial or incomplete. When you compare a Mini to a Rolls-Royce, you cannot deduce that the Mini is a partial Rolls-Royce because it is smaller, less complex and has less equipment. The two are independent and separate vehicles. Similarly, the eye of the snail would appear to be its own eye and not necessarily the eye that is destined to become the eye of the human. The snail's eye is perfect for its own needs and its place in its ecosystem. If we cut the Rolls-Royce in half, we would not have a functional car, even though each half may still be bigger than the full Mini car on its own. The less complex Mini is functionally better than half a Rolls-Royce, for purposes of getting from A to B at least. In fact, to create a human eye in incremental stages, with the function of adequate sight for survival being present from the beginning (and throughout), is quite remarkable. This would be like creating a watch from scratch, with the watch telling the time from the very beginning before all the parts have come together. Generally, the time-telling ability of a watch comes relatively close to the end of its production, once all the necessary springs and wheels have been put in their respective places.

To deduce that functionality perfectly increases in a linear relationship with the incremental anatomical developments of a structure seems illogical. For each change and stage of development of the eye to offer *additional* functionality for improved sight and survival, is extremely remarkable. And to propose that this is what has happened is a gross presumption which has not been based on any scientific evidence, nor on any logical thinking. This is likened to suggesting that every single change in the construction of a car results in improving function in the car. Adding just one of four wheels to a car does not mean that the car's ability to move is improved by 25%. Nor does adding just two wheels allow for 50% improvement in movement. Only having four wheels enables the car to go from 0% to 100% of its speed range. Removing one wheel means that the car goes from 100% ability to move to 0% ability to move. Everybody knows that the separate parts of a car's basic make-up all complement each other, and individually they serve no functional purpose.

We just don't see structures or organs in animals which appear to be developing parts which offer no benefit now but could potentially offer benefit in the future if the necessary additions were made. For example, we don't find ciliary muscles or the beginnings of ciliary muscles in a snail with no lens, even though technically this should be possible.* Just to mention, we are not talking about vestigial structures or atavisms here, which are deemed by evolutionary theory to be previous traits of ancestors: instead we are talking about completely new structures developing which appear to have no functional benefit and have no historical presence in the species or the species' ancestors.

Another remarkable piece of information that we can use to highlight this point is the uniqueness of certain functions displayed by many animals all over the world. Humans are the only animals to display an intellect (more on this later). Bats are the only animals to fly using flaps of skin stretched between the bones of the arm, and they are the only mammals to fly. Kangaroos are the only large animals to use hopping as a means of locomotion (and this is not primitive: they can reach speeds of 40mph and cover a mile in about two and a half minutes). Dung beetles are the only animals that can navigate using moonlight, which they use to travel in a straight line while transporting their dung balls. Hummingbirds are the only birds that can hover in the air and the only birds that can fly backwards and upside down. Bees are the only animals (other than humans) who use dancing to communicate. The list goes on and on. These are all unique functions which contradict the notion of incremental changes leading to a gradation of functionality. Evolutionary theory would predict that there should be intermediary functions of any function that is found in the world.

---

* Ciliary muscles are the internal eye muscles which hold the lens in place.

Chapter 4 – The unanswered questions

There are several aspects of evolutionary theory that seem unviable. These aspects are often brushed over and not given any attention. If they were addressed, they would seriously jeopardise the eminent position that the theory currently holds in society. We are going to expand on some of these points in this chapter.

There's nothing quite like a human

Homo sapiens are the only living species in their genus. No reasonably-minded person can say that human beings are similar to other animals. How evolutionary theory has managed to convince people that human beings are no different to other animals is remarkable. No species is as different from another species as Homo sapiens is from others. The most obvious difference is one of intellect. Indian philosophy suggests that this is the main difference between humans beings and animals. Although animals do have minds, are conscious and are able to feel and express emotions, they appear to lack an intellect. They are not able to rationalise, intellectualise or understand their own existence. Also, think about the variability in human behaviour. There is more variability in behaviour displayed in the Homo sapiens species than that of any other species. And are there any other similarly aged species so far devoid of a resembling living relative? We are told that our nearest relative is the chimpanzee, but just on observation alone, we can see that we are far different to a chimpanzee in terms of appearance, behaviour and functioning. Everyone knows that a chimpanzee shares more in common in these categories with fellow primates rather than ourselves.

Think of horses. They have plenty of close relatives. The differences between horses, donkeys and zebras are relatively small. Think of crocodiles and alligators, hares and rabbits, ravens and crows – not much to separate them on the surface is there? The anatomical layout and behaviour of these relatives seem quite similar. But now think of us. We seem to have no relatives that resemble us (in appearance, behaviour or functioning) so closely.

Evolutionists tell us that the chimpanzee is more closely related to us (and a bonobo – a variant type of chimpanzee) than it is to a gorilla or any other primate for that matter. This conclusion has been made from DNA comparisons (human beings and chimpanzees share almost 99% of their DNA), not from anatomy, behaviour or functioning. But as we have previously mentioned, DNA comparisons do not *prove* relatedness between different species. So to say that a chimpanzee has more DNA similarity to us than any other primate is fair enough. However, it is also fair to say that a chimpanzee has more anatomical, behavioural and functional similarity to any other great ape than it does to us. Neither statement proves or disproves relatedness.

However, reason dictates that the latter holds more weight. Think about it; there's not even another species on the planet that walks on two legs! There is no other living species that can make a fire or that can make a weapon to hunt. Human beings seem to be able to actively choose their behaviours rather than having to impulsively act on them like other animals. It does not take a biologist to see that there are no species that hold more unique behaviours than human beings. Just think of some of the functions and behaviours that are unique to human beings: speech, language, bipedal gait, manual dexterity, blushing, clothing, cooking, altruism, suicide, racism, prejudice, fetish, homosexuality (although this is a matter of contention), asexuality, celibacy, paedophilia, schizophrenic behaviour, manic behaviour, appreciation of art and music. This is to name just a few. We could write a whole chapter on the unique traits of human beings. With all of this, evolutionary theory still wants to proclaim that we are very similar to chimpanzees. It makes no sense. The similarity is only on an equivocal biochemical level. Just to highlight this point, we are told that we share 98% of our DNA with a gorilla, and that we have a closer relation to gorillas than chimpanzees do. Now, who in their right mind would conclude that the likeness between human beings and gorillas is greater than that between chimpanzees and gorillas?!

Okay, there are some isolated species out there, for example the platypus. And we did say that we would come back to the platypus, as it is a curious animal to say the least. The platypus is a rather strange looking animal. It is endemic to Australia. It has a duck-like bill, a beaver-like tail and otter-like feet, as shown in Figure 7.

Figure 7. The platypus.

It is covered in fur, yet is semi-aquatic, and it produces venom (delivered through sharp stingers on its feet) and lays eggs for reproduction. It is deemed to be a mammal, but due to its egg-laying function, is thought to represent a descendant of one of the animals in direct transition from a reptile to a mammal. Due to its bizarre appearance, the platypus baffled European naturalists and biologists when they first saw it, with some actually thinking it was a hoax whereby someone had sewn on the various features to its body. The platypus and the echidna (a small animal that looks a bit like a hedgehog) are the only known egg-laying mammals (monotremes), but the echidna does not resemble the platypus, and nor does any other known animal. However, despite this, its functions and behaviours are still not that unique: many other animals lay eggs, many other animals swim, many other animals produce venom, and most other large land-mammals move on land on four legs. And even though its swimming style is unusual, as it uses its front feet for propulsion and its rear feet for steering, other animals, such as fur seals, use a similar mechanism whereby they use their front flippers for propulsion and their rear flippers for steering. So it is fair to say that even though, according to evolutionary theory, the platypus has fewer close relatives than the human being does, the platypus appears to resemble other animals much more than the human being does. This would appear to contradict the essence of evolutionary theory.

People may say "I share 90% of my genes with a mouse", as if this is an intriguing and fascinating fact which supports evolutionary theory, but do they really believe that they are 90% similar to a mouse?! If not, their statement is futile. It is just a factual observation with equivocal relevance behind it. It would be like me stating, "my hair colour is 90% similar to yours," in an attempt to prove relatedness between us.

A typical human being does not appear 90% similar to a mouse. The human mind seems very different from that of a mouse. Scientists may say that they have found signs of intelligence in animals, such as dolphins and chimpanzees, but this is to a very basic level and certainly does not match the intelligence shown by human beings. And besides, "intelligent" behaviour in animals appears to be immediate-reward based, whereas human beings are able to function without this approach and conceptualise potential benefits of actions further down the line. It is also reasonable to assume that human beings can function without an aspect of reward, although this is beyond the scope of this book and is rather a philosophical and spiritual matter for debate.

Think of the intelligence that you need to be reading this right now and understanding it. It is remarkable. No animal can come close to demonstrating this level of intelligence. So the question of why human beings are so different from any other animal on the planet has not been answered by evolutionary theory, and this creates a lot of doubt over whether the theory is even plausible.

Now, the question arises, if human beings are so much more intelligent than their animal counterparts, surely evolutionary theory would have to predict intermediary species of intelligence. Where are they then?? They tell us of Neanderthals and the rest, but, unfortunately, they are not around anymore, even though, according to evolutionary theory, they were the second most intelligent species on the planet at the time of their existence. Second to us (Homo sapiens) that is. That's right, even though they were the second most intelligent species around at the time, they still went extinct. Fossils of species presumed to be close relatives of Homo sapiens have been found, including Neanderthals, Homo antecessor and Homo floresiensis, but these species have all gone extinct. It is important to remember that these are not direct ancestors of Homo sapiens but cousins who shared a common ancestor. It is hard to imagine why all these presumably intellectually-advanced species would go extinct. Multiple theories have been proposed for their extinction, including extinction from violence, extinction from disease, natural catastrophe or possibly being out-competed by the evolving Homo sapiens species. Ultimately, no-one knows for sure. However, the fact they no longer exist should raise the eyebrows of anyone investigating evolutionary theory with an open mind.

Currently there are over 30,000 species of spider, close to 5,000 species of frog, about 3,000 species of snake, over 400 species of shark, more than 60 species of eagle, over 200 species of squirrel, more than 250 species of monkey, almost 40 species of wild cat, 16 species of gibbon, and even 2 species of gorilla, 2 species of orangutan and 2 species of chimpanzee. Yet how many current species are there of the most intelligent genus ever? That's right – just one! Homo sapiens, that's it. At least one of the so-called ape-humans, with intelligence that falls somewhere between that of a chimpanzee and human, would have been expected to survive. They should have been able to outdo a gorilla, seeing as they can live on the same food sources and would have had the intelligence and necessary skills to outcompete them. Could it be argued that the human species deliberately wiped out other Homo species for competition reasons? Completely eliminating an intelligent species, which theoretically could have colonised the whole world and survived in a multitude of different environments, would not be so easy, let alone practical. So we really are at a loss in trying to explain the uniqueness of the human species through an evolutionary model.

Where are the living ancestors?

Evolutionary theory proposes that all species undergo evolution but at different rates. The term "living fossils" is used to describe species that live today but evolved millions of years ago – such species have undergone hardly any evolution since arising and have not borne new species. Examples of these are few and far between but include crocodiles (reportedly evolved 55 million years ago), coelacanths (reportedly evolved about 400 million years ago), elephant sharks (reportedly evolved 420 million years ago) and horseshoe crabs (reportedly evolved 450 million years ago). Now, these species do not have any descendants. In fact, evolutionary theory has not identified any extant species that has borne a descendant species. The theory states that this is because all species eventually evolve into new species – once the evolution begins, the old species goes out of existence. Sometimes the species may change into one new species or sometimes two or more, which can be explained by Figure 8.

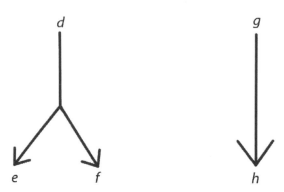

Figure 8. An example of how the phylogenetic tree depicts change from one species to either two new species or to one new species.

Essentially, as soon as the species has changed significantly, the old type dies out, presumably through a mechanism of natural selection and survival of the fittest. The term "dies out" may not be factually correct, as evolutionists will say that the species does not technically die out or go extinct as such: instead it changes or "evolves" into a new species. But for the purpose of questioning this presumption, this does not really matter; it is just semantics. The outcome is the same – the old species is no longer present. But the question arises; why does species *d* on Figure 8 have to be wiped out of existence by its descendants *e* and *f*? If we are talking about species *e* and *f* outcompeting species *d*, then surely the same logic would have to presume that species *e* and *f* would compete with each other resulting in one being victorious and wiping out the other. That is to say, if species *e* does not have to wipe out species *f*, then why does it have to wipe out species *d*? If species *e* and *f* can coexist, then why can species *e* and *d* not coexist?

So the bifurcation points on the phylogenetic tree are a curious matter. In theory the phylogenetic tree should allow for the occurrences depicted in Figure 9.

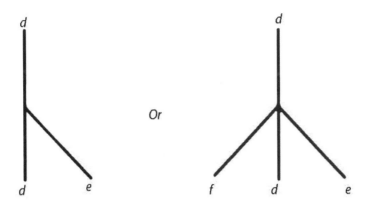

Figure 9. An example of how the phylogenetic tree *could* demonstrate coexistence of ancestors and descendants.

Referring to Figure 9, rather than a bifurcation on the tree, we have instead created new limbs on an already existing pathway to allow for coexistence of ancestor and descendant. However, this is hypothetical: we do not have examples on the phylogenetic tree, or in life today, of this phenomenon occurring. We know that species do not *have to* change in order to survive, as we have given examples of species that have not changed or adapted in hundreds of millions of years. Also, many primitive and ancient forms of life, such as single-cell organisms, bacteria, nautiloids and hagfish, still exist today, showing that they are able to coexist with their much more advanced relatives. This means that there is no reason why species *d* cannot theoretically coexist alongside its descendants species *e* and species *f*.* As we have shown, you don't *have* to change, and you don't *have* to become as advanced as your relatives in order to survive.

Figure 10a is a copy of the famous sketch made by Chares Darwin when he was formulating his theory of evolution. It demonstrates how a hypothetical section of a phylogenetic tree works and shows how species evolve into new species. Note the "I think" at the top of the sketch: quite fitting.

---

* Note that extant ancient forms of life, such as single-cell organisms, bacteria, nautiloids, and hagfish, are not living ancestors but are descendants of common ancestors. They have not borne descendant species.

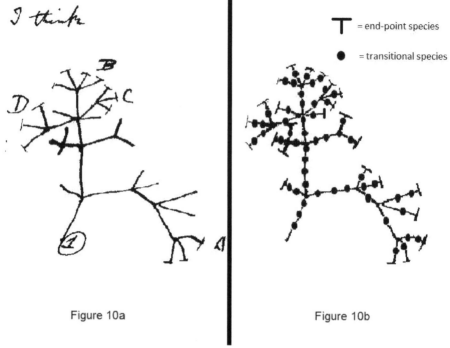

Figure 10a

Figure 10b

Figure 10a. A copy of Chares Darwin's original sketch of a hypothetical section of a phylogenetic tree.

Figure 10b. A copy of Chares Darwin's original sketch of a hypothetical section of a phylogenetic tree with modifications made to show hypothetical transitional species.

Current observations suggest that only species which are end points on a branch (the "end-point species" in Figure 10b) exist today. Of course, many of these end-point species have gone extinct (such as the woolly mammoth and the dodo bird) without providing any descendants (which is why they are the end-points of the branches). But, of course, many do exist today, like us humans. The points on the tree branches that are not at the ends of the branches represent the ancestors of species which have evolved into the species further down the branch/branches through the process of evolution. They are marked as the "transitional species" in Figure 10b. Some of these transitional/ancestor species have evolved into only one new species, whereas others have evolved into more than one. This is why these ancestor species are said not to have gone extinct as such. Instead they have evolved into a new species, as their DNA still exists, whereas a species that has gone extinct, such as the dodo bird, has not passed on its DNA to any descendants.

Why can't a species give rise to a new species and remain in existence itself? For example, why does Australopithecus africanus (a presumed direct ancestor to human beings) not exist today? In order to answer this question, we must take a look at human evolution more closely...

A section of the proposed hominid (great ape) evolution is shown in Figure 11. Bear in mind this is only one possible version of it, as there is no consensus amongst the so-called experts about the evolution of the Homo genus – there are disagreements over whether some of the species depicted in Figure 11 are ancestors of Homo sapiens or cousins who share a common ancestor. But this does not matter for the point that we are about to make, which would be relevant to any of the lineages proposed by evolutionists.

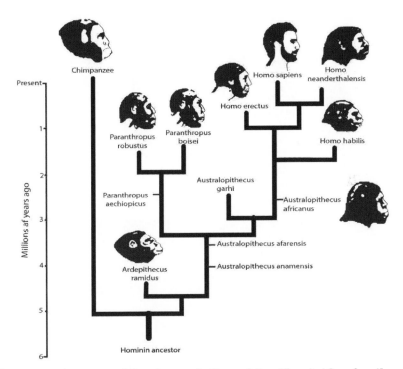

Figure 11. A proposal for the evolution of the Hominidae family.

We know with some certainty that, apart from us and the chimpanzee, none of the species depicted in Figure 11 exist today. From a logical point of view, some ancestor species could theoretically exist today and coexist with their descendants. Think about it. Homo sapiens' closest ancestor would have presumably been relatively intelligent with many attributes similar to Homo sapiens. Is it really conceivable that this species was completely wiped out (or rather completely changed) due to selection pressures or even through any other means? Even if they were outcompeted for resources by the evolving Homo sapiens species, and even if the evolving Homo sapiens were favoured in terms of disease, food or sexual reproduction, is it not at all possible that some of the ancestor species may have continued to survive and reproduce amongst themselves ensuring the survival of their characteristics and attributes?

If the evolving Homo sapiens species was a better hunter, is it not possible that the ancestor species could have sought alternative food sources and altered its diet or chosen less tasty or even less nutritious food not utilised by the evolving Homo sapiens species? Even though this food may lead to less favourable outcomes, it may not necessarily lead to the demise of the whole species. Australopithecus afarensis, which is one of our more distant ancestors (according to evolutionary theory), is thought to have foraged for fruit, nuts and seeds in a mixture of woodland and savannah, and possibly would have obtained animal protein from termites or birds' eggs. This means that they were not reliant on just one food source, and could theoretically have adapted their behaviour and continued to exist. Do we expect the ancestor species with less favourable characteristics to simply say: "well, you have better attributes, so I will just sit in this corner and wither away and die without passing on my genes?" Also, why could they not relocate to an area uninhabited by the evolving Homo sapiens species and continue to survive and procreate there? This is one of the fundamental flaws of evolutionary theory – it does not accommodate or account for any adaptability. It does not allow for coexistence of old types with new.

Also, think about how evolution is supposed to work. A random mutation occurs giving rise to a favourable characteristic, which then infiltrates the species. When this occurs in the species' timeline is unpredictable. As we have seen, some species have lived for hundreds of millions of years without this occurring. Surely then, it would be likely that in many species these changes occur at a time when the species has already advanced, progressed and diversified. So in the case of Homo sapiens' closest ancestor, in theory they could already have spread all over the world before the mutations leading to the development of the Homo sapiens species took place, and therefore certain groups of this ancestor species could have formed their own niches. Now, obviously these mutations are rare occurrences and only happen in one member of the species. Bearing this in mind, is it really plausible that this one member and its descendants are then able to infiltrate the whole of the species across the whole of the world and set in motion change in every member of the already existing species? Even if one thinks that this is likely in the vast majority of species, surely a reasonably minded person would concede that this should not have happened in at least one of the reported 5 billion species that have ever existed. Remember, time is not relevant, as we have given examples of species that have been unchanged for hundreds of millions of years. Therefore, there is no rule that all members of a species *must* change, meaning that it is plausible that not all of the members of a species do change, which would result in coexistence of ancestors and descendants.

We can use another example to make this clearer. Think of the Darwin finches of the Galapagos Islands which we mentioned before. The theory states that all the original finches on the archipelago underwent change of some sort to create new species of finches, which are distinct and have favourable characteristics for the environment in which they are in. But logic tells us that an original ancestor finch *could* have survived and not undergone change, resulting in it coexisting with its descendants albeit in different environments or islands. Remember, the coelacanth has not changed in 400 million years, so why should every ancestral finch change into a new prototype? There's no law that says it should be so. Even if this was not the case with the finches, surely there is one species out there where this *has* been the case?! But there isn't.

We can use one final example to demonstrate this point, which will be more of an analogy rather than an example of evidence. If we consider the two distinct human races of black people and white people, it is evident that they reproduce to create what is termed as a "mixed race" offspring, which is a mix between the two races. Through large-scale integration and mixing, these two original races have become three races. Now, in theory, it is possible to turn the two original races into just one race by ensuring that every black individual procreates with a white individual and no same-race procreation occurs. This would create one mixed race and eliminate the previous black race and white race. Of course, we think of this as being preposterous, as it seems unfathomable that this would ever happen.

However, this is what evolutionary theory proposes *does* happen and *has* happened. It proposes that one new feature or characteristic is passed on entirely and exclusively so that the older type goes out of existence completely, which is why we have no living ancestors. It is not difficult to see the strangeness of this assertion. It defies reason. In our race analogy there is no obvious evolutionary or survival advantage to being one race over the other, however, the analogy is useful in terms of thinking about the practicalities of what evolutionary theory proposes has happened.

The suggestion that a newer model of a species can exhaustively eliminate the older type through a mechanism of outcompeting them just seems a little hard to swallow. We know today that many different species which have similar niches and eating habits do coexist, for example red squirrels and grey squirrels. Evolutionists also suggest other mechanisms for older types going extinct, including disease, predation, changing environments plus others. But ultimately our point remains – we would still expect at least one ancestor species to have been able to adapt and survive alongside its descendants. The new group may be *better* adapted to the environment, but this does not mean that the old group are badly adapted to the environment. In fact, they existed in it at one time, so their *total* demise would not necessarily be expected. They would be expected to show some adaptability.

Evolutionary theory states that these former ancestor species do not exist today because they have all evolved into newer species (or end-point species). The theory justifies this by claiming that all species eventually evolve, and that natural selection with evolution has been operating for millions of years, meaning that ancestors are likely to go extinct. But this is nonsensical. According to evolutionary theory elephant sharks have not evolved in 420 million years. So at least *some* transitional/ancestor species which evolved after the elephant shark would be expected to exist today (to put this into context, the Homo heidelbergensis species is only 1.4 million years old). Thus, time cannot explain the lack of living ancestor species. Also, the idea that the fittest (or most adapted) species of a lineage is the only one that can exist is not consistent with evolutionary theory's assertion that a species can evolve into two or more species which can coexist. If evolutionary siblings and cousins can coexist, we would expect ancestors and descendants to also.

This is an important point because if we had living ancestors, this would be the strongest evidence for evolutionary theory – we could actually observe and study these ancestor species and formulate specific genetic pathways of how they evolved into the newer descendant species. For example, the specific morphological, functional and behavioural changes between ancestor and descendant could be identified, and then a genetic pathway could be proposed to account for these changes – an actual scientific model proposing evolution of one species to another could be postulated. This is virtually impossible to do when you have no DNA for these supposed ancestor species and only a few fossilised remains which tell you next to nothing about the functioning and behaviour of these species.* Such fossilised remains cannot even reveal accurate anatomical and physical characteristics of the species, such as the anatomy of internal organs or the presence of body hair. For example, the closest identified ancestor to Homo sapiens, according to evolutionary theory, is Homo heidelbergensis, but only a handful of fossils for this species have been found, most of which are fragmented skulls and jaw bones which yield no DNA for analysis. Considering this, it is not possible to formulate an accurate theory on how Homo heidelbergensis genetically and morphologically "evolved" into Homo sapiens.

Genetic studies today can reveal exact mechanisms for morphological changes, diseases and abnormalities in an organism. A person's DNA can be analysed to determine their geographical and racial ancestry. Similarly, *if* we had a living ancestor species, we could theoretically establish speciation through genetic studies. So it seems rather inconvenient for sceptics of evolutionary theory (or any reasonably minded person wanting to evaluate the theory) that there aren't any ancestor species alive today to examine. As we have mentioned, this inconvenience is unexpected. And there are really only two possible explanations for this: either we are desperately unlucky or evolutionary theory is false.

The chicken and egg dilemma

The famous dilemma of which came first out of the chicken and the egg has been a question in philosophical thought for many centuries. The question asks, how can the first chicken have come from an egg when that egg would have had to have been laid by a chicken, and how can

---

* Due to degradation, DNA only survives within a fossil for a limited time. The world's oldest sequenced DNA genome comes from a 700,000-year-old horse. DNA from ancient ancestor species is unavailable.

the first egg have come from a chicken when that chicken would have had to have been hatched from an egg? Evolutionary theory believes it has answered this question. It surmises that the foetuses in eggs laid by previous ancestors of the chicken would have undergone the necessary mutations in order to eventually bring about the chicken so that one day a chicken hatches from an egg, hence the egg would have preceded the chicken. Fair enough. However, evolutionary theory has not answered the deeper question raised by this philosophical dilemma: how do you get an egg from no egg? Or which came first, the first egg-laying creature or the first egg? And evolutionary theory has no answer to this question. In order to demonstrate this, we need to go back in time to look at the evolution of reproduction and egg-laying...

The last unicellular (single-celled) ancestor of animals is thought to be a flagellate eukaryote form of life, similar to the Choanoflagellate organism that exists today.* Choanoflagellates are used by scientists as a useful model for reconstructing the last unicellular ancestor of animals. The way that such an organism reproduces is asexually through binary division, whereby the organism duplicates its genetic material and then separates into two new bodies. The evolutionary theory model states that this type of organism went on to become the first animal, which is surmised to be a type of sea sponge (a multicellular organism with a body). Sea sponges reproduce both asexually and sexually. Sexual reproduction is achieved by the sponge having eggs and sperms and allowing fertilisation to occur (the sponge can do this themselves as they are hermaphroditic and have both eggs and sperms, but it also occurs between sponges). So where did these first eggs come from? Presumably, evolutionary theory would have to state that somehow a sponge derived from asexual reproduction underwent mutations in its DNA that enabled it to then create sperm and eggs and allow for sexual reproduction. Asexual reproduction to sexual reproduction from a mutation.

Now, evolutionary theory defends the concept that features can develop incrementally. It says that an eye evolves and develops from a single light-sensitive cell to the complex eye that we see in the human today, and a wing develops and evolves from a small stub that aids gliding into a fully formed wing that enables flying. This is how

---

* A Choanoflagellate is a unicellular, eukaryote organism that lives in water. It is not thought to be a direct ancestor of the animal kingdom but is presumed to share the same ancestor as the animal kingdom. This ancestor is thought to be similar in morphology to the Choanoflagellate, making it a good organism to study when evaluating the evolution of the animal kingdom.

evolutionary theory explains how complex structures come into existence. While this claim does appear extravagant, it does not seem *completely* implausible. But how on Earth can evolutionary theory justify an egg coming from no egg or sexual reproduction coming from asexual reproduction through chance random mutations? Think about it. Fair enough, theoretically you *may* be able to get a random mutation that creates a light-sensitive cell that then undergoes further mutations and natural selection, resulting in a fully functional eye, but how do you go from reproducing asexually by duplicating your DNA to reproducing sexually through fertilisation of an egg with a sperm? It is illogical to think that a single random mutation could create a sponge that suddenly has egg and sperm-making ability. To create an egg that is capable of carrying an organism's offspring is a vastly complex procedure: sexual organs have to be created that produce the egg; then the egg itself has to have various features including an ability to be penetrated by a sperm, an ability to nourish and support the unborn foetus, and an ability to be housed or expelled in the parent's body. These are all gross changes which surely cannot come about by one chance random mutation of DNA. And this cannot be justified through a gradual process of evolution either. You either reproduce asexually or sexually. There is no in between. You cannot gradually change asexual reproduction to sexual reproduction, unlike the ability to see or fly which *theoretically* can be gradually improved through stages.

While evolutionary theory may justify change of features gradually over time, it cannot justify sudden dramatic functional change, such as that from asexual reproduction to sexual reproduction, where no intermediate functionality between the two states can exist. You cannot gradually develop sexual organs or an egg through an evolving process. Of what use is half an egg? Either the egg is able to sustain life and allow for successful reproduction or it isn't. You cannot have eggs becoming gradually more complex until eventually they are able to facilitate reproduction. The egg is of no use if it is unable to facilitate reproduction, and it offers no survival advantage without reproduction ability. So there is no reason why an evolving sexual organ would be favoured and selected by nature to allow for a gradual evolution of sexual organs. Also, today we have no organisms that reproduce asexually yet have sexual organs that don't work or are half-complete. So in this example it is binary, one or the other, and the change from one to the other cannot be justified through a single random mutation. In fact, evolutionary theory has not even proposed any possible mechanism for how sexually reproducing organisms have "evolved" from asexually reproducing organisms, and it would seem that this is a very large piece of missing information if one wants to claim that their ancestor was an asexually reproducing sponge. The suggestion that asexually reproducing organisms give rise to sexually reproducing organisms appears to significantly increase the implausibility of evolutionary theory.

Where to draw the line?

Evolutionary theory states that species gradually develop changing features and characteristics over time through a natural selection process until a point arrives where they are grossly different to their ancestors and are deemed to be a new species altogether. But *when* exactly this point arrives is a matter of curiosity. If we take any one direct lineal branch of the phylogenetic tree and try to establish the points on this branch where new species arose, it will not take long before we start getting ourselves into a mess.

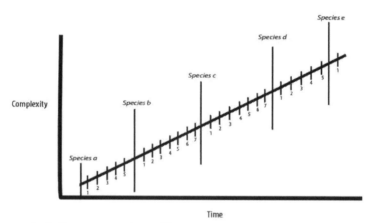

Figure 12. A demonstration of how one species evolves into another along a lineal branch of the phylogenetic tree.

Figure 12 shows how species are reported to evolve over time. The intermediate (significantly morphologically-different) creatures between species are listed as the number variants on Figure 12. For example, in the dog species we could hypothetically consider the first dog (the wolf) as creature $d1$ and the American Bulldog (one of the most recent dog breeds to come into existence) as $d5$ which is then going to go on to develop a new species e (obviously this has not happened [yet?!]).* The higher the number, the closer the creature is to becoming the next species. For example, creature $b7$ is close to becoming a new species (species c). Remember, this is only a hypothetical depiction for explanatory purposes – in evolutionary theory it is presumed that there would be many, many more intermediate creatures between the two distinct species, but for purposes of our explanation, this makes no difference. Now, species differentiation can be clearly separated by an objective and binary measurement, namely the ability to reproduce. Either you can reproduce with another creature or you cannot – there is no in between whereby you can partially reproduce with them. If you are the same species, you can reproduce. If you are different species, you cannot reproduce. Obviously, creature $b7$ is still a member of the b species and therefore technically should be able to reproduce with any member of the b species all the way down to creature $b1$. However, the morphological differences between $b1$ and $b7$ are going to be much greater than that between $b7$ and $c1$, meaning that it makes no sense why $b1$ and $b7$ can reproduce but $b7$ and $c1$ cannot. You cannot say that the theoretical ability to reproduce gradually reduces as species get more advanced and get closer to becoming the next species – this would be nonsensical. Similarly, we cannot say that creature $b7$ can reproduce with creature $c1$, as this would defy the principle that different species cannot reproduce. So there is this strange transition from when one species becomes another (marked by the large vertical lines on the graph in Figure 12) where the two creatures either side of the line are mysteriously unable to reproduce with each other yet are very similar (they must be very similar as the latter is derived from the former).

Pro-evolutionists argue that you cannot determine or demarcate when one species becomes another, as it is a gradual process, rather like a boy turning into a man where no single point can be identified for this transition. However, in the case of evolutionary theory, we do have an exact point of reference for separating one species from another, namely the ability to reproduce, and therefore we can actually determine and separate species clearly. In essence, evolutionary theory does, in fact, state that one species gives direct birth to a new species –

---

* Note that figure 12 is only showing one species' lineage, and not the whole tree for this particular section. For example, only the lineage of the American Bulldog would be included here without its cousins who have followed a different lineage.

it is a well-defined, specific moment in time. Creature $b7$ belonging to the b species gives birth to creature $c1$ belonging to the c species, and members belonging to $b7$ variant are unable to reproduce with members belonging to the $c1$ variant. Clearly, it is the not the same as the gradual transition of a boy turning in to a man.

This would appear to be the greatest conundrum that arises out of evolutionary theory. There is no plausible explanation of how one species can give *direct* birth to another. And there are no examples that we know of, either extant or extinct, of a species that can successfully reproduce with variants either side of it on the lineal branch of the phylogenetic tree whereby the two variants are unable to successfully reproduce with each other – there is no species known with dual and unique reproductive abilities. For example, if species y can reproduce with both species x and species z, it is expected that species x and z can reproduce with each other. We would not expect a white European person to be able to reproduce with a Black African person and an Asian Chinese person, yet for a Black African person to be unable to reproduce with an Asian Chinese person. Similarly too, if it was found that a white European person could successfully procreate with a chimpanzee, we would also expect this of a Black African person and an Asian Chinese person.

It is true that hybrids between species have been created, but these are very few and far between in the animal class. In most cases the offspring have severe defects and are infertile (interbreeding is only considered successful if it yields fertile offspring). Examples of these include the liger (a lion-tiger hybrid), the zebroid (a zebra-donkey hybrid), the hinny (a horse-donkey hybrid) and the cama (a camel-lama hybrid). However, these examples do not help us with the dilemma of how one species can give rise to a new species, since these are examples of unsuccessful interbreeding of species from different branches of the phylogenetic tree, and not from species belonging to the same lineage. Also, any successful hybrid derived from two very closely related species, would raise the question of whether its parents are actually different species or rather variants of the same species. That is to say, the phylogenetic tree may have made an error in presuming that two different looking creatures belong to different species *if*, in fact, they can successfully reproduce with each other.

The conundrum of human races

Explaining the human racial distribution pattern across the world appears to be a significant problem for evolutionary theory. To address this issue we need to explore aspects of human history in some detail...

Part I   The history of human races
Part II   Prehistoric migration
Part III   Explaining racial distribution

Part I – The history of human races

Evolutionary theory states that human beings (Homo sapiens) evolved in Africa about 200,000 years ago and split into two groups, with one venturing out of the African continent into Eurasia about 70,000 years ago. Human beings then colonised the various corners of the Earth and are believed to have reached the Australian continent (Oceania) about 60,000 years ago and the Americas about 30,000 years ago. The separation of the continental land masses happened hundreds of millions of years ago. So human migration into the Americas and Oceania would have had to have happened across oceans. Some suggest that a land-bridge known as the Bering Strait may have existed between North America and Northeast Asia, connecting the two land masses and making migration between them more feasible. However, this idea does not seem to have strong support, and there is little physical evidence to suggest it.

The written history of humankind dates back about 6,000 years. Prior to this we don't have much information about human civilisation and history. From this point up until only a few centuries ago, the records tell us that there was relatively little inter-continental migration of humans. Different ethnic races and groups appeared to reside in different areas of the planet.

Throughout history most anthropologists have recognised three basic racial categories of human beings – the mongoloids, the negroids, and the caucasoids.* Historically, there were multiple groups for each

---

* Mongoloid, negroid and caucasoid are the historical terms used to describe the three traditional races of the human species. These may now be considered to be offensive terms - we are only using them here in a scientific manner to illustrate a point. Historically, the mongoloid group refers to the indigenous people of the Americas and Asia (excluding the Indian subcontinent), the negroid group refers to the indigenous people of the

of these categories, for example an American mongoloid was differentiated from a Chinese mongoloid, an African negroid was differentiated from an Australian negroid, and a Hamitic caucasoid from Northern Africa was differentiated from an Aryan caucasoid of Northern Europe. Many modern-day scientists disagree with this classification system and the concept of race, as they say that there is only one human race with a gradation of features from one end of a spectrum to another. However, one cannot deny that prior to the mass inter-continental movement of people a few centuries ago, the people inhabiting Sub-Saharan Africa, Northern Africa, Europe, The Americas, South Asia, South-east Asia, Australia and the Pacific islands, could all be told apart from one another. They all looked different, and a smooth gradation or transition of features was not observed geographically. There are clear and distinct anatomical differences between the three main racial categories.* Obviously, today these distinctions are not as clear-cut as they were a few centuries ago, due to the movement of people and the mixing of different human groups in recent times. But why were they so clear-cut previously? We'll come onto this in a moment.

The Meyers Konversations-Lexikon from the 19th century illustrated the distribution of the different racial groups across the planet.† It was evident that the different racial groups existed in different parts of the planet (see Figure 13). This uniformity of racial type is the pattern that we saw across the whole world up until relatively recently – only one specific racial group being found in a given area. Until several centuries ago, you would not find a white man in Australia, nor would you find a black man in the Americas.

Human records tell us that the major empires of the world from the Akkadian Empire of 2300 BCE up to the Neo-Babylonian Empire of 626 BCE, did not know of lands and people far beyond the borders of their own empires.‡ There is no evidence that contact between

---

Australian continent and Sub-Saharan Africa, and the caucasoid group refers to the indigenous people of Europe, Northern Africa and the middle-east extending into the Indian subcontinent.

* There are various anatomical differences between the three main racial groups, such as with skin colour, hair structure, craniofacial structure, nasal shape and skin-folds of the upper eye-lid (epicanthic folds).

† The Meyers Konversations-Lexikon was a major German encyclopaedia from the 19th century.

‡ The oldest known map of the world is from the Neo-Babylonian empire from about 600 BCE. This map and all other world maps of the time were localised

different racial groups or cohabitation of different racial groups occurred before the time of the Neo-Babylonian Empire of 626 BCE. Evidence would be expected if such contact or cohabitation occurred. Thus, this absence of evidence is evidence of absence, in the same way that the absence of evidence for elephants existing in the Pacific Islands is evidence to suggest that elephants do not exist in the Pacific Islands.

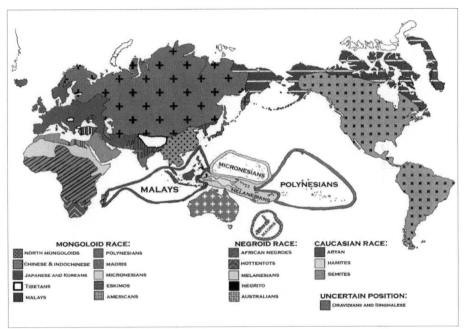

Figure 13. A modified version of the ethnographic map from the Meyers Konversations-Lexikon (c. 1885).

From a Eurocentric point of view, at the time of Alexander the Great (born 356 BCE), Greece was considered to be the pinnacle of civilisation, and the place where the greatest thinkers and academics resided. The *oecumene* was the term used by the ancient Greeks for the known world. According to maps, the ancient Greeks thought the oecumene was limited by Western Europe to the west, Northern Africa to the south and India to the east (see Figure 14). They had no knowledge of sub-Saharan Africa, China, South-East Asia, let alone Oceania or the Americas. Of course, there are great geographical

to the area in which they were created. They did not include any lands beyond the ocean, as the ocean was thought to be the end of all lands.

barriers separating these lands, which explains this. The Sahara Desert separated Northern Africa from sub-Saharan Africa, the Himalayan Mountains along with other mountains and deserts separated the Eastern borders of the then-known world with the rest of Asia, and, of course, the oceans separated Eurasia from Oceania and the Americas. Considering this, it seems reasonable to extrapolate that the ancient Greeks did not know of the racial groups from the mongoloid and negroid categories.

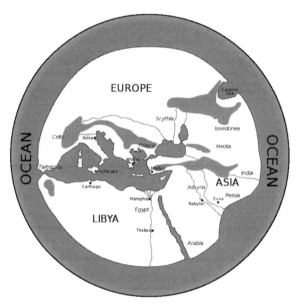

Figure 14. The oecumene by Hecataeus of Miletus (died c. 476 BCE).

Eratosthenes (276–194 BCE) drew an improved map of the world, based on new information from the campaigns of Alexander the Great and his successors (see Figure 15). The island of "Taprobane" in the Southeastern corner of the map was the name given to the island which is known today as Sri Lanka. The map shows that at the time of Eratosthenes, there was a better knowledge of the geography of Eurasia and Northern Africa, however, there was still no knowledge of China, Southeast Asia, Oceania or the Americas. European knowledge of China appears to have arisen around the time of the Roman conquest of Egypt in 30 BCE, whereby the Silk Route facilitated regular communications and trade between Europe, the Middle-East, North Africa, India, China and Southeast Asia.

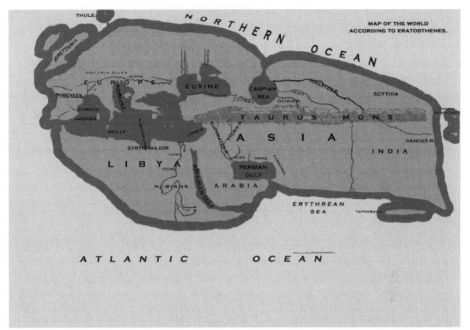

Figure 15. A reconstruction of the oecumene by Eratosthenes (died 194 BCE).

When sub-Saharan black Africans became known to European populations is somewhat unclear. Some historians claim that at the time of Jesus Christ, the Roman Empire was aware of the presence of black Africans, as there are some Roman writings and pictures referring to them. They referred to them as "Aethiopians". At latest the sub-Saharan black Africans became known to Eurasians by the 6th and 7th centuries AD. This was due to the spread of Islam into the African continent. However, exploration of the sub-Saharan African region by Europeans (starting with the Portuguese) only occurred in the 15th Century. By this time there had been small-scale migrations of people across known trade routes in Eurasia and parts of Africa, and miscegenation would have occurred amongst different racial groups in these regions. For example, in the 13th Century the Mongol Empire led by Genghis Khan extended from Beijing in the east to almost the gates of Vienna in the west. Genghis Khan himself was thought to have fathered hundreds of children across his empire, and miscegenation between invading mongoloid groups and indigenous caucasoid populations of the Middle-east and Eastern Europe would have occurred.

Thomas Huxley, who was known as Darwin's Bulldog due to his strong advocacy of Charles Darwin's theory of evolution, produced a map of racial distribution in the world and classified the human races into four main categories (australoid, negroid, mongoloid and xanthocroic) and several sub-categories or groups (see Figure 16). He split the caucasoid race into two groups – the Xanthocroi were the fair whites of Northern Europe which became known as the Nordic race, and the Melanochroi were the dark whites of Southern Europe, Northern Africa, the Middle East and India, which became known as the Mediterranean race: this group also included Hamites and Moors. More recently, in 1962 Carleton Coon (a physical anthropologist and professor at Harvard University) created his own map demonstrating racial distribution in which he identified 5 main racial categories (australoid, capoid, congoid, mongoloid and caucasoid) – see Figure 17.

The ethnographic maps of Huxley, Coon, and the Meyers Konversations-Lexikon are all remarkably similar. It seems likely that if a random sample of one hundred individuals was taken from any part of the world a few centuries ago, most modern-day anthropologists would easily identify which of the fourteen racial groups on Huxley's ethnographic map the sample belonged to. All the maps identify at least three main racial categories and locate these in very similar positions. There are minor discrepancies, such as with the Indian subcontinent and the Horn of Africa. In fact, Huxley himself identified certain areas of the world which demonstrated complex or uncertain ethnic compositions that didn't fit into his paradigm, including the Indian subcontinent and the Horn of Africa. But overall there is a general consensus amongst the three maps regarding the major patterns of distribution of the main racial categories and even, to a large extent, the specific racial groups. Coon's map is dated much later than the others, and it shows the Siberian and Central Asian regions as being occupied by the caucasoid race rather than the mongoloid race, unlike the earlier maps. The Russian conquest of Siberia took place in the 16th and 17th centuries which resulted in a rush of European-Russian settlers and raiders moving into Siberia and displacing the indigenous mongoloid populations. This could account for the differences observed in the racial type of Siberia in more recent ethnographic maps.

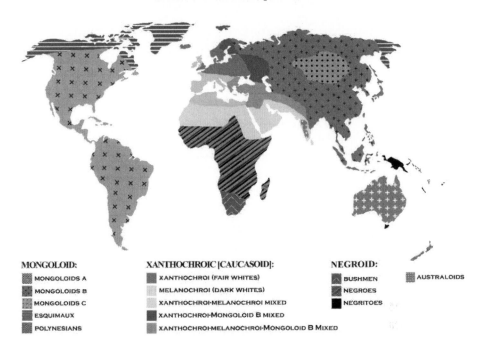

Figure 16. A reconstruction of Thomas Huxley's ethnographic map from *On the Geographical Distribution of the Chief Modifications of Mankind* (1870).

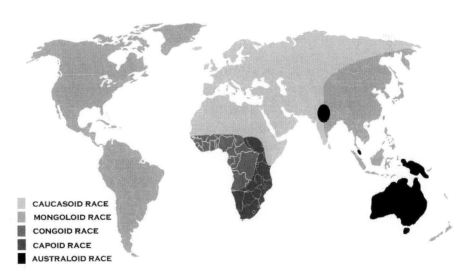

Figure 17. Carleton Coon's ethnographic map (1962).

From the ethnographic maps of Coon and the Meyers Konversations-Lexikon we can see that the caucasoid racial category was thought to extend into the Horn of Africa (modern day Somalia and Ethiopia). People occupying these areas today are dark-skinned. However, the Romans had previously referred to the "Aethiopian" people occupying these areas as "White Aethiopians", suggesting they were light-complexioned. The 1st Century Greek travelogue known as the Periplus of the Erythraean Sea extensively described the Horn of Africa but did not mention dark-skinned individuals living there. Strabo, the Greek philosopher and geographer of the 1st Century, suggested that Aethiopians were the same as Indians. In the 4th Century the Greco-Roman historian Eusebius proposed inhabitants of the Horn of Africa had emigrated there from the Indus Valley. Leo Africanus, an established and respected explorer of the 16th Century, wrote that "olive" complexioned people inhabited the Horn of Africa. This all supports the idea that the people of the Horn of Africa may have been caucasoid rather than negroid in racial type. Coon's assessment of these people suggested that their facial features were more consistent with caucasoid than negroid features.

The idea that people of the Horn of Africa and Ethiopia have a different racial origin to sub-Saharan Africans is not inconceivable given the geographical barriers of the area, with the region being cut off from the rest of Africa by the Ethiopian Highlands, large rivers (the Jubba and the Shebelle), and the Sahara Desert. The Geographer A.T. Grove stated in 1978 that rugged escarpments overlooking the Sudan and desert plains in Northeast Kenya separated the Ethiopian Highlands and the Horn of Africa from the rest of the continent. Modern day genetic studies propose that there was gene flow between Eurasia and the Horn of Africa 3,000 years ago, which further supports the idea that people of these regions belong to the same racial category.

In the ethnographic maps of Coon, Huxley and the Meyers Konversations-Lexikon, the phenomenon of two distinct races cohabiting the same land is not recognised anywhere in Oceania, the Americas or sub-Saharan Africa. Some cohabitation of different racial groups is depicted in regions like Siberia, Russia, Northern Europe and areas along the Silk Route, which is most likely due to several centuries of migration and miscegenation among these areas. However, the ethnographic maps show most racial groups to be well-demarcated and localised to specific regions throughout the world. This appears to have been the case throughout human history up until very recently. So the human records and ethnographic maps suggest that at no point in *known* human history has cohabitation of different racial groups existed in a specific region up until a few centuries ago. But is it possible that there was *pre*historic contact between different racial groups?

Part II – Prehistoric migration

If a new racial group enters a mono-racial region, there are only three possibilities for what can happen. One, the new group may live in isolation and cohabit the same region, resulting in segregated racial groups in the region. Two, mixing and interbreeding of the two groups may occur. Three, elimination of one group may occur for various reasons, such as genocide, disease or lack of resources. If there is no evidence of at least one of these occurrences, it is reasonable to presume that prehistoric cohabitation of races did not exist.

For there to have been cohabitation of different racial groups *prior* to human records beginning, we would expect cohabitation of different racial groups to have been evident *throughout* history. We would not expect ethnographic maps to show well-demarcated and localised racial groups throughout the world. This is because it is not feasible for different segregated racial groups to merge into one type. Evolutionary theory states that the specific racial features of a racial group developed gradually over thousands of years. The problem with this suggestion is that the specific features of a particular race don't clearly offer evolutionary advantages, therefore they should not be naturally selected. There is no obvious evolutionary benefit to having mongoloid features in Japan and caucasoid features in France. We would not expect a segregated Japanese community in France to change into a caucasoid racial type, even if given tens of thousands of years to do so. So the idea that various distinct racial groups may have once existed in a region yet through natural selection processes "evolved" to become one type does not seem feasible. Today, major cities of the developed world, such as New York, London, Paris and Sydney, cannot be categorised into a racial group as they could have been in the past. This is due to the variation and diversity of racial groups residing there today. It seems a peculiar idea to suggest that given time all the people belonging to one of these individual cities would merge into one racial type as an inevitable consequence of evolutionary theory.

Could interbreeding have concealed prehistoric cohabitation of racial groups? According to human records, crossing of major geographical barriers and miscegenation did not happen from 4,000 BCE up until a few centuries ago. As soon as these barriers were overcome, miscegenation occurred, and subsequently racial groups became less distinct. The mixing of racial groups in recent centuries has resulted in new mixed racial groups which bridge the gap between the original groups. This can clearly be seen in a country like Australia where white Europeans emigrated and mixed with indigenous Aborigine populations to the point where there are now more European-Aborigine mixed people in the country than there are "full-blooded" Aborigines. These European-Aborigine mixed people resemble Europeans more than the indigenous full-blooded Aborigines did, thus creating a smaller gap between the pre-existing Aborigine racial group and the emigrant European (Xanthochroi) racial group. A similar situation is seen in many South American regions. If in prehistoric times different racial groups of people entered mono-racial regions and miscegenation occurred, we would expect racial variation within that region, which would result in smaller gaps between the various racial groups than were observed up until a few centuries ago. Even if you think different racial groups can merge into one type through miscegenation, it is unreasonable to presume that this has happened in every region of the world. It seems likely that some individuals may have reproduced within their racial group only, thus we would not expect complete change in every member of the group. For example, we do not see *only* a mixed-race European-Aborigine group existing in Australia today: instead we have the original Aborigine group and the original European (Xanthochroi) group *in addition* to the new mixed-race European-Aborigine group. Also, the idea that a poly-racial region may "evolve" into one type due to artificial selection seems unrealistic. For this to happen, populations would have to have a unique fancy for certain features and then *artificially* select these for reproduction. For every single society to intentionally come to look homogenous in this manner seems a peculiar idea.

But could one group eliminate another group, thus removing evidence of previous cohabitation? Australia is a relevant example. The white European emigrants pursued deliberate policies of extermination and genocide against the native Aborigines through various methods, including direct killing, withdrawal of resources and government policies. Through an "assimilation programme" there was a deliberate effort to remove the indigenous full-blooded Aborigines

126

from the land, as only mixed-race Aborigines were given the opportunity to integrate in society while full-blooded Aborigines were neglected in the hope they would "die out" through a process of natural elimination. The European immigrants did cause extinction of full-blooded Tasmanian Aborigines in the relatively tiny island of Tasmania to the south of mainland Australia.* However, this was a much harder task to achieve on the mainland of Australia due to its size (over seven million square kilometres) and much larger indigenous population. Consequently, a significant number of full-blooded Aborigines still exist in Australia today, which demonstrates the difficulty of eradicating or changing an existing indigenous population in its entirety. North America has a similar history, but we still have indigenous native American-Indians cohabiting with non-indigenous settlers today.

As demonstrated by these examples, attempts to homogenise a group are extremely difficult. If we look at Australia in the 1950's (before the "White Australia Policy" for migration was removed), we see the presence of white Europeans and indigenous Aborigines cohabiting the same land – two distinct races cohabiting the same land (in addition to a mixed-race European-Aborigine group). This suggests that the total elimination of a racial group by another through genocide or miscegenation is extremely unlikely, especially with a large population spread over a large distance. So prior to 6,000 years ago, it seems very unlikely that different racial groups cohabited the same land and then, due to total elimination, only one group was left standing.

We have shown that prehistoric segregation, miscegenation or extermination of different racial groups in a given area seems highly improbable. So we can presume that different racial groups never cohabited in the same lands prior to human records beginning (if such a time existed), and all the world regions were *always* mono-racial up until relatively recently. Following on from this, it is logical to presume that the reason for this is because different racial groups never visited each other until relatively (from an evolutionary theory point of view) recently in human history.

---

* The Tasmanian Aborigines were the indigenous people of the island state of Tasmania in Australia. They are now generally considered to be an extinct race with no "full-blooded" members of the race left today.

Part III – Explaining racial distribution

The historic pattern of racial distribution across the world is not consistent with evolutionary theory. The differences between all the racial groups identified may be subtle, but they are significant, as they allow for the correct identification of populations across the world. As we have shown, up until relatively recently, different racial groups were well localised and demarcated across the world, and people living in a specific area all belonged to the same racial group. Evolutionary theory cannot explain this phenomenon. This pattern of distribution is more indicative of polygenism (the theory that different races have different origins) than it is with monogenism (the theory that all races originated from one original source). To claim that all non-African racial groups originated from migrating African cliques seems extremely infeasible.

We identify the current geographical barriers as being the cause of the previous segregation of racial groups. The suggestion that cliques of humans had the ability to cross great geographical barriers tens of thousands of years ago with limited technology and equipment is questionable. Presumably these cliques were relatively primitive, yet from Africa they somehow discovered the Americas and Australia, a feat not achieved by European explorers until the 15th and 17th Centuries respectively. As we established, the ancient Greeks, with their advanced mathematics and astronomy and large warships requiring 170 men to row them, were unaware of the Americas and Australia, yet evolutionary theory claims that primitive nomads migrating out of Africa tens of thousands of years ago stumbled into the Americas and Australia with limited resources. Granted, evolutionary theory proposes that this migration happened over a few thousand years between 60,000 to 70,000 years ago. But considering knowledge of Australia to non-indigenous Australians was absent for the first 5,600 years of the 6,000 years of recorded human history, this is still a remarkable and unexpected achievement.

In known human history, whenever new land is discovered, knowledge of the new land quickly gets back to the homeland. A new communication channel emerges with the new route between home and the new land. People move back and forth, and knowledge is passed on to the descendants. When those first supposed pioneering groups landed in distant lands like the Americas and Australia, they had knowledge of the land where they came from and an idea of how to get back there. It would be expected that some would return with knowledge of the new-found land, or at least some descendants would hear of tales of their motherland and venture out in search of it. Granted, the initial journeys were made by primitive nomads over generations, but we are not suggesting complete return to the starting-point in Africa. We would expect new-found segmental migration routes to be active and to show fluidity with groups moving back and forth. For example, the first Australians are thought to have got there in one journey from islands in Melanesia, such as Papua New Guinea. So it is reasonable to expect subsequent migrations back and forth between these lands. However, throughout human history the indigenous people occupying Australia and the indigenous people occupying the Melanesian islands have belonged to different and distinct racial groups, suggesting that they have been living in separation and segregation since time began. A similar story is seen in other segmental migration routes, for example the Sahara Desert crossing whereby, up until recently, we had different and distinct racial groups living north and south of this route. No group outside of sub-Saharan Africa knew about the land that they supposedly originated from until tens of thousands of years later: when the first European explorers arrived in America, the native American-Indians were shocked that there was a world outside the Americas, and when the first European explorers arrived in Australia, the indigenous Australians were shocked that there was a world outside Australia. The idea that these pioneering groups were too primitive to return, communicate or pass on knowledge of navigation is not in keeping with the skill and ability that they would have needed to make those journeys in the first place.

Reportedly, indigenous people first arrived in Australia 60,000 years ago, traversing large distances across the oceans, presumably on rafts of some kind. So it would be expected that somewhere in the subsequent 59,600 years a different racial group might have also been able to make that journey and cohabit the largest island in the world. If humans were able to migrate to the distant lands of Australia and the Americas 60,000 and 30,000 years ago respectively, logic would dictate that different racial groups would also have made that trip (as they have done in the last few centuries). When Captain James Cook discovered Australia for the Europeans in 1770, the population of the indigenous Aborigine people was estimated to be around 1 million. The population of England and Wales at this time was around 9 million. So it's clear that Australia was heavily underpopulated, and there would have been plenty of room for different racial groups to cohabit the island.

For monogenism to be true, one would have to propose that individual groups from Africa crossed great geographical barriers tens of thousands of years ago and colonised different regions of the world and then "evolved" into specific and distinct races. This suggests that each group was uncontacted by other distinct racial groups during this "evolution" process. Monogenism supposes that these first "colonisers" of mono-racial regions lived in these regions in isolation and never returned to the lands where they came from. If different racial groups cohabited the same regions, there should not have been the clear and distinct patterns of geographical distribution of racial types that were evident prior to the last few centuries. But there was no cohabitation or difference in the racial type in world regions prior to the Neo-Babylonian Empire of 626 BCE. So the distribution of the human race cannot be explained by evolutionary theory. Now, creationism may have an equally hard time explaining this phenomenon, but remember, we are not establishing what caused this phenomenon, but rather whether it is compatible with evolutionary theory. And it doesn't seem to be. It would appear to be one of those mysteries that cannot be solved.

The same explanatory problems arise from a Biblical-Genesis version of creation with a single Adam and single Eve being the original ancestors of all humans, because how would they too have gone on to create distinct and clear races across the planet? Who knows!? Perhaps there was an instantaneous creation of all racial groups by a supernatural intelligence, or perhaps the different groups were created in stages. But remember, not knowing the answer does not mean that evolutionary theory gets it by default!

Chapter 5 – The reliability of the evidence

There are several levels on which evolutionary theory can be attacked. So far, we have attacked it on the grounds that it is not scientific, it lacks evidence, it seems highly illogical, and it has significant flaws in its methodology. But there are also some who dismiss the theory on the premise that the evidence is wrong, is misinterpreted, or, in some cases, is fraudulent. Some also claim that evidence that contradicts the theory is suppressed or ignored. There are even some who give a detailed argument to support the idea that evolutionary theory is a huge hoax.

In Chapters 1 and 2, we established that the evidence proposed for evolutionary theory does not provide a strong case for it. However, we will now look at the authenticity, validity and interpretation of this evidence in order to establish whether it is reliable in the first place. Even though some or many or all of the arguments about to be made in this chapter may not be shared by you (or by me), they are shared by a significant proportion of people in the world, including various eminent scientists. For that reason, they should be given the appropriate consideration. A fair and thorough evaluation of a theory can only be made once *all* the major arguments for and against it have been heard.

Interpreting the evidence

Some scientists disagree with the theory that the earth is billions of years old and believe it to actually be only a few thousand years old, consistent with historical, religious teachings: this is known as "young Earth creationism". They say that there is no actual evidence for the Earth being more than a few thousand years old. In order to date the world, you have to use scientific dating methods. There is no other way of knowing, as there are no records or documents that show that the world is over a few thousand years old. Now, the problem with these dating methods is that they rely on various assumptions, as we briefly touched on earlier.

Radiometric dating is the main process used for determining the age of rocks and fossils. Many older fossils don't contain elements that are susceptible to radiometric dating, so their age is determined by dating the rocks in which they have been found in or next to. The process which makes this possible is the radioactive decay of various element isotopes. We don't need to go through this in great detail, but essentially, by knowing the rates at which certain element isotopes decay and change, scientists are able to deduce how old a rock is: consequently they can establish how old a fossil within the rock is. Now, it is well known that dating through radioactive decay relies on some assumptions. For example, one has to *assume* that radioactive elements in the past have always behaved and decayed in the same way as they do today. But it cannot be known for sure that the rate of change in the past was the same as it is in the present. Many scientists claim that this nullifies the dating methods used and means that the Earth cannot be *proved* to be more than a few thousand years old using such methods. Also, if the dating of the rock is inaccurate, the dating of the fossil is inaccurate. While evolutionists have dated many prehistoric animals to be hundreds of millions of years old, certain scientists dispute this, stating that there is no actual proof for this and that no species, extinct or extant, is over a few thousand years old. Of course, if the age of fossils is questionable, the whole of evolutionary theory comes into disrepute.

Many other arguments are put forward to suggest that the Earth is not as old as suggested by evolutionary theory: for example, some coal deposits which are meant to be 300 million years old based on their location, have been shown to still contain radioactive carbon-14, which would make them under 100,000 years old according to the currently accepted scientific dating methods. Also, some scientists claim that the electromagnetic field around the Earth has been shown to have a 7% reduction rate every 100 years. If you apply this same rate of decline retrospectively for the Earth, it shows that 20,000 years ago the electromagnetic field would have been so strong that it would have dissolved the core of the Earth.

Despite this confusing debate, the age of the Earth is actually irrelevant to proving evolutionary theory. If the earth is proved to be billions of years old, even though "young Earth creationism" is disproved, evolutionary theory has still not been proved. This would only make evolutionary theory *possible* but not probable. By contrast, if the Earth were proved to be only a few thousand years old, evolutionary theory would be automatically disproved.

On another note, many of the reconstructions of transitional or extinct species are hypothetical reconstructions based on gross presumptions. Many individual specimens of presumed extinct species have only a very small proportion of the skeleton present when they are found. Often the fossil is a single isolated piece like a partial skull, a jaw bone, a pelvis bone, a limb bone or even just a single tooth. Experts then reconstruct the whole skeleton based on what they *think* it would have looked like. All the complete images that you see of extinct and transitional species are theoretical, as, of course, even an expert cannot tell what the species' external appearance would have been from an incomplete skeleton. Many critics state that gross errors are made when extinct species are reconstructed, with the reconstructors creating the species in a way which deliberately and intentionally fits in with the evolution hypothesis.

Also, some scientists say that the fossils representing the so-called transition of apes to humans are very questionable indeed. These are the "hominid fossils". Most of these fossils are found as only a few fragmented pieces of bone, and then presumptuous reconstructions of the whole skeleton are made from these. One of the few examples of an almost complete skeleton being found for one of these fossils is the specimen of "Turkana Boy". This fossil was found in Kenya in 1984, and pro-evolutionists think it to be an example of Homo erectus (a possible ancestor of human beings). What is interesting about this fossil skeleton is that it looks like a typical human skeleton apart from the skull which is much smaller. Some experts argue that this actually *is* a human skeleton with a deformity resulting in a small skull – such skull shapes are found in humans in existence today (representing disease and deformity). Because this skeleton was found in isolation, pro-evolutionists can presume that it represents a different species to humans. However, had the skeleton been found amongst multiple other human skeletons, for instance at a burial site, then it most likely would have been concluded to be a human skeleton.

Another example of confusion over a hominid fossil involves the specimen "Lucy", a famous fossil of a hominid ancestor named Australopithecus afarensis. This is thought to be one of the links between ape and modern man. The fossil was found in Ethiopia in 1974. Pro-evolutionists saw this as a great discovery to further support evolutionary theory. However, only about 40% of the skeleton has been found and there is much debate over it. Some scientists disagree that this is a close ancestor of humans, and suggest that the skeleton is much more ape-like than human-like. There is also discrepancy over Lucy's gait, with some saying that it was bipedal like a modern man, and others saying that it was more like the typical gait of an ape. So there is a gross problem with interpreting fossils, with different experts saying different things. As the evolutionary writer J. Shreeve says: *"Everybody knows fossils are fickle; bones will sing any song you want to hear."*

The variability of anatomical make-up *within* a species can be so huge that if you were to examine two skeletons on either side of a species distribution curve, then there is a good chance that you would conclude that they were different species. This can clearly be seen by examining the skulls of various dogs, as shown in Figure 18. It is clear that there is huge variation between dog skulls, yet all skulls shown in Figure 18 belong to creatures of the same species.

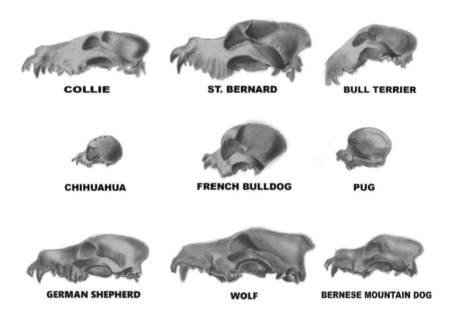

Figure 18. A picture of various skulls of the canis lupus species.

The difference between the Chihuahua's skeleton and the German Shepherd's skeleton is huge, yet they are the same species. Opponents of the so-called hominid evolution theory would say that the difference between some of the above-described hominid fossils and humans is not even as great as the difference between the Chihuahua and the German Shepherd, and therefore to automatically conclude that these hominid fossils are different species to humans is illogical. In fact, to conclude so could be considered a form of hindsight bias whereby the pro-evolutionists are seeing what they *want* to see based on their assumption that evolutionary theory is correct. So to make presumptions of speciation based on skeletal morphology is fundamentally flawed.

Erroneous evidence

Some evidence that is used to support evolutionary theory is claimed to be erroneous. The structural essence of the evidence may be genuine, however, it is presented in a misleading and incorrect manner which falsely promotes the theory. Whether this is done intentionally or unintentionally is unclear. It is, of course, possible that promoters of this erroneous evidence are blinded by psychological bias, and are not acting maliciously, but are just seeing what they want to see based on their underlying bias. (How this happens will be explored in more detail in Chapter 8).

One of the classic examples for this is "Nebraska man". This was the discovery of an unidentifiable tooth in Nebraska in 1917. This tooth was thought to be derived from a higher primate which led to the scientific world believing that they had unearthed the first ape-man of North America. A famous scientific journal of the time announced this discovery to the world. From this tooth, glamorous illustrations of the appearance of this ape-man were made. A few years later, further field work on the site of the initial discovery revealed that the tooth had been incorrectly identified. The tooth did not belong to a man or an ape but to an extinct species of pig. The journal retracted their previously announced discovery, acknowledging that a mistake had been made. There was no suspicion of foul play, and the misidentification was thought to be a genuine error.

Another example is the horse series of transitional fossils that we discussed in Chapter 2. While this shows a *relatively* good series of transitional fossils for establishing horse evolution, it is considered by even some evolutionists to be misleading. The series was founded on certain fossilised specimens, and following the proposal of the series in the late 1800's, it has been a regular cited example in school text-books for promoting evolutionary theory. However, critics of this series state that fossils of the evolving species (the transitional species) were found in the same sites, suggesting similar dates of existence, which contradicts the idea that one evolved into the other. In addition, the geographical distribution of fossilised members of this series is spread throughout the world on different continents in a way that does not support a progressive evolution of one species to another. Also, at least one of the intermediate species is claimed by the critics to have more ribs and more lumbar vertebrae than the species above and below it on the proposed evolutionary lineage – of course, this does not make sense from a genetic-evolution point of view. And finally, the variation in size in the modern horse is greater than the variation between the average modern horse and some of its supposed ancestors, suggesting that size is irrelevant in determining evolutionary lineage.* However, size appears to have played a part in proposing the series, as the intermediate species could not be dated on other methods due to being found in the same sites. The fact that one of the most decorated pieces of evidence supporting evolutionary theory has so many discrepancies associated with it should certainly be worrying for proponents of the theory. But pro-evolutionists do not acknowledge these discrepancies, and instead continue to cite this series as evidence for evolutionary theory – these discrepancies, which may actually contradict evolutionary theory rather than support it, are ignored. Whether this is intentional or accidental is certainly difficult to establish.

Ignoring evidence

A common criticism from anti-evolutionists is that evidence or information that contradicts evolutionary theory is largely ignored by pro-evolutionists. A blind eye is turned to anything that seriously challenges their assertion that evolution is the cause of all biodiversity. Such examples include the horse series mentioned above and the earlier mentioned embryological studies that contradict developmental homology of certain similar structures and organs in different species. There are numerous other examples where evidence is brushed over and ignored in a similar manner...

Anti-evolutionists cite the Cambrian explosion as providing evidence that contradicts evolutionary theory. The Cambrian is the last descending layer of stratum that has any complex-organism fossils in it. None of the layers of strata below the Cambrian have any fossils other than simple, single-celled organisms, such as bacteria and algae. The Cambrian layer is full of fossils representing a vast array of complex organisms, accounting for most major animal phyla. So there is a sudden jump from very primitive species in the Pre-Cambrian

---

* There are breeds of horses known as "miniature horses" which are typically about 3 feet tall. Clearly this breed of horse is substantially smaller than some of its supposed ancestors.

strata to complex species in the Cambrian strata, with no intermediate species in between. This Pre-Cambrian strata should, according to evolutionary theory, be filled with more primitive forms of these Cambrian fossils which are in the process of evolving upward. The sudden appearance in the fossil record of complex organisms without precedents goes against evolutionary theory's proposal of a slow accumulation of changes accounting for all species.

We mentioned 300 million-year-old coal deposits with radioactive carbon-14 in them, but other evidence has also been provided which discredits current scientific dating methods. For example, scientists have used current dating methods to date certain rocks and lavas as over a hundred million years old even though they are known from recorded observations and history to be only a few hundred years old.

Another observation made by critics of evolutionary theory is that there are currently no fossiliferous rocks forming anywhere on Earth. The millions of shells and bones of deceased creatures are simply eroded by weather and predators – the skeletons of animals just don't seem to get slowly buried and preserved in sediments. For example, millions of buffalo were slaughtered in a short space of time on the great plains of America, yet today there is no physical evidence of this in the ground. Consequently, it is claimed that fossils, especially those of larger creatures, represent creatures that are buried rapidly in some type of cataclysmic event. Proponents of this view provide evidence which they believe supports cataclysmic events, such as the Old Red Sandstone of Northern Scotland where a 100-mile area reveals billions of fish fossils appearing to have died suddenly and catastrophically. Similar observations have been made in numerous parts of the world. Also, whale skeletons have been found on the top of glacial deposits in Michigan, as well as several hundred feet above sea level in parts of Canada. The Siwalik Hills of North India, which are 2,000 to 3,000 feet high, contain remarkable extinct species, including multiple elephant species, a giant tortoise, rhinoceroses, pigs, apes and oxen. Other graveyards of terrestrial animals are provided, including a dinosaur graveyard in New Mexico where dozens of dinosaur skeletons were found interlocked and on top of each other, and a hillside in Wyoming which was covered with large dinosaur bone fragments. Such observations point to cataclysmic events resulting in rapid deposition and fossilisation. Anti-evolutionists claim that this evidence is ignored by pro-evolutionists, as it points to events that contradict current scientific thought on geology and dating of the Earth.

Analysis of common protein sequences in species shows that all species can be classified into isolated groups on these grounds: however, these groups are very distinct with no transitional groups bridging the gaps, which contradicts the notion of evolution with a gradation of morphology. Also, DNA similarity does not necessarily correlate to anatomical and functional similarity. For example, a bat and blue whale share more genetic similarity than do certain different frog species. Pro-evolutionists appear to overlook such conundrums and instead continue to use biochemical similarity in support of evolutionary theory.

And here's one final example of pro-evolutionists ignoring evidence: some anti-evolutionists claim that dinosaurs are not millions of years old, as evolutionists believe, but that they are only a few thousand years old and walked alongside humans. They provide evidence of dinosaur accounts in folklore and history, adjacent fossilised human and dinosaur footprints, and artefacts and cave paintings of dinosaurs from all over the world. This evidence is not given any credence by pro-evolutionists, and it would seem that it is dismissed *ad lapidem* rather than with any intelligible rebuttal. But we have to remember that there are educated people who promote this evidence. Most educated people in the Western world would find the proposition of dinosaurs and man coexisting preposterous, but this supposition is a result of the conditioned education that they have received, one which is written by the pro-evolutionists. Of course, no-one can *scientifically* disprove that man and dinosaurs coexisted.

Proven forgeries

In the history of discoveries of fossils supporting evolutionary theory, many proven forgeries have been demonstrated. One of the most infamous is the case of the "Piltdown Man" wherein a human skull, found in Southern England in 1912, was deliberately distorted to make out it belonged to a new species of ape-man. In 1953, the fossil was exposed as a forged composition: the skull belonged to a human, the jaw to an orangutan, and the teeth had been filed down to make them appear human.

In 2004 a previously significant Neanderthal fossil was found to be a hoax: a skull fragment, found in a peat bog in Northern Germany, was dated as 36,000 years old but was later found to be a 7,500-year-old skull fragment of a human being. The professor involved was a distinguished anthropologist and was considered an expert in carbon dating. His "discovery" had been considered a major development, as emphasised by the archaeologist who discovered the hoax, Thomas Terberger:

> *"Anthropology is going to have to completely revise its picture of modern man between 40,000 and 10,000 years ago... [His] work appeared to prove that anatomically modern humans and Neanderthals had co-existed, and perhaps even had children together. This now appears to be rubbish."*

The consequences that such a forgery can have were highlighted by Chris Stringer, the head of human origins at London's Natural History Museum, who said: *"What was considered a major piece of evidence showing that the Neanderthals once lived in northern Europe has fallen by the wayside. We are having to rewrite prehistory."* Reportedly, the scandal only came to light when the professor in question was investigated for fraud after being caught trying to sell his department's entire chimpanzee skull collection to a dealer in the United States of America. Further investigation then revealed he had forged multiple other fossils: "Binshof-Speyer Woman" was dated as over 20,000 years old but was later found to be less than 3,500 years old, and "Paderborn-Sande Man" was dated as over 29,000 years old but was later found to be under 300 years old. The anthropological museum that owns the fossil skull of Paderborn-Sande Man was so disturbed by the finding that they tested the skull themselves: Barbara Ruschoff-Thale, the museum's director, said: *"We had the skull cut open and it still smelt... We are naturally very disappointed."* It is extraordinary to think how such a gross forgery can escape detection and be used to support a "scientific" theory.

A Japanese archaeologist, who became known as "God's hands" due to his prolific archaeological discoveries, unearthed multiple human artefacts dating between 30,000 years ago to almost 600,000 years ago. His findings rewrote history and text-books, and had huge implications for human evolution. However, in 2000 he was proven to be a fraudster, when he was videotaped digging holes and burying objects which he later dug up and announced as major discoveries. Investigations revealed that almost all the artefact discoveries that had been made by him were fraudulent.

Other examples of inauthentic fossils include Archaeoraptor, which was acclaimed as the missing link between dinosaur and birds (more on this in a moment), and Acinonyx kurteni, a discredited extinct cheetah fossil. This fossil was found to have segments of the skull glued together from disparate bone pieces so that it resembled the skull of a modern cheetah. There have been forgeries with other evidence too. One example is the infamous Errnst Haeckel's embryo fraud, in which the German zoologist forged drawings of embryos of various mammals, including a human, in order to establish relatedness. For years, these diagrams were reproduced in biology text-books and taught as fact, forming a significant part of the evolutionary theory doctrine.

In evolutionary theory's defence, these deliberate forgeries are rare. However, they do exist and have been used by scientists and evolutionists to support evolutionary theory. The motives behind these forgeries are unclear, and it is possible, if not probable, that they were instigated by a few individuals acting deceptively for personal gain rather than to falsely promote evolutionary theory. The problem is that once it is apparent that forgeries can easily be introduced and used as evidence in support of the theory, then the credibility of all evidence, and consequently the theory itself, comes into question.

Is evolution a hoax?

Theodore Tahmisian, a former physiologist for the United States Atomic Energy Commission, said: *"Scientists who go about teaching that Evolution is a fact of life are great con men, and the story they are telling may be the greatest hoax ever. In explaining Evolution we do not have one iota of fact."* This idea is shared by some, who claim that evolutionary theory is just simply one big hoax...

Evolutionary theory is a very powerful weapon for challenging orthodox Christianity. When the theory was first proposed by Charles Darwin, it directly challenged Christian notions of an intelligent designer creating nature and the Earth being only a few thousand years old. As put by the famed writer Robert Ingersoll (nicknamed "The Great Agnostic") in 1884, *"Charles Darwin destroyed the foundation of orthodox Christianity."*

After the proposal of evolutionary theory around 160 years ago, it soon gained huge popularity and shot into science classrooms across the world. Some people think that this was a deliberate ploy from governments and the science community to deliberately indoctrinate people with this false theory on the basis that it reduced the power and hold of the Christian Church, while promoting secularism. Such people argue that that the establishment responsible for this has continued to facilitate this process hitherto in order to maintain the status quo. Such a view is not about individual cases of fraud, which are seemingly done for reasons of personal gain, but fraud on an institutional scale.

If this is true, it seems likely that only a few select people will probably "know" that evolutionary theory is a hoax, while the majority of scientists, and even evolutionary biologists, will not, because they are simply provided with the necessary information to believe in, support and promote the theory. For example, the fossils could be provided and deliberately placed in locations which fit in with evolutionary theory. Fossils could be artificially manufactured. Dating methods could be intentionally manipulated to provide an age of the Earth and age of fossils which fit in with evolutionary theory. If any evidence is found which contradicts the theory, it could be suppressed and not brought to the attention of the public. Eminent speakers and supporters of the theory could be heavily promoted, while sceptics would get little air-time and be branded as foolish. This does all sound far-fetched: however, it needs to be considered as a possible alternative explanation.

Human evolution

Human evolution has been a contentious issue since the inception of evolutionary theory. Experts agree that there is little fossil evidence for the divergence of the gorilla, chimpanzee and hominin lineages.

The fossil record for human evolution is scanty to say the least, and it is very difficult to interpret. Scientists often disagree on what the fossil findings (and subsequent DNA findings) represent. New findings often contradict previous models of evolution, forcing the theory to change its standpoint, which it frequently does. A case in point is Australopithecus africanus. This species was originally claimed to be a direct ancestor to human beings but has now been relegated to a side branch of the supposed family tree due to subsequent discoveries.

Evolutionary theory states that the Australopithecus genus, which is believed to be a cross between apes and humans, evolved into the Homo (human) genus. The Homo genus encompasses human beings (Homo sapiens), as well as the extinct human species, which are either ancestral to or closely related to human beings. The genus is believed to be between 2-3 million years old. It includes species such as Homo habilis, Homo naledi, Homo erectus, Homo ergaster, Homo antecessor, Homo heidelbergensis, Homo rhodesiensis, Homo floresiensis, Homo neanderthalensis, and, of course, Homo sapiens. There is much debate amongst evolutionists about the exact evolution of the Homo genus: however, there are general agreements regarding certain elements of it. One such proposed evolutionary model is shown in Figure 19.

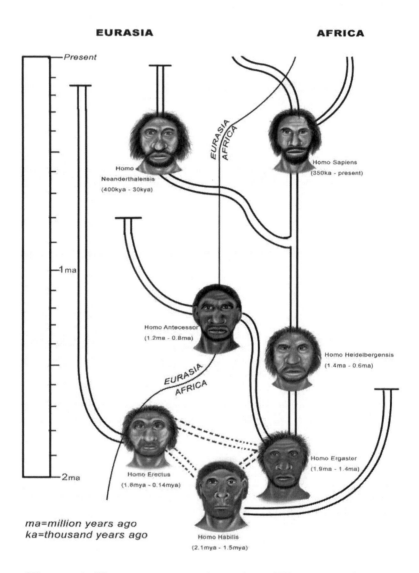

Figure 19. The most accepted version of Human evolution.

In order to critique the theory of human evolution, we need to describe what it states. Most evolutionists agree that the Homo genus originated in Africa and migrated out of Africa to colonise the rest of the world. The most popular theory about how the Homo genus evolved goes something like this:

> Homo habilis is the oldest identified human (Homo) species, living between roughly 2.1 and 1.5 million years ago. This species evolved into Homo erectus in Africa. Homo erectus was the first human species to leave the African continent, which they did about 2 million years ago. They managed to colonise much of Europe and Asia, however, they did not evolve into other human species outside of Africa and subsequently went extinct around 140,000 years ago. While this migrating Homo erectus group were travelling the world, the non-migrating Homo group which stayed in Africa (thought by some evolutionists to also be Homo erectus [African Homo erectus] but by others to be a different species known as Homo ergaster) evolved into Homo antecessor, which existed in Europe around 800,000 years ago, suggesting that either Homo antecessor had evolved in Africa and migrated out to Europe, or Homo ergaster (or African Homo erectus) had migrated to Europe and evolved into Homo antecessor in Europe. As with the migrating (non-African) Homo erectus group, Homo antecessor did not evolve into other human species outside of Africa and subsequently went extinct. The African group of Homo ergaster (or African Homo erectus) that did not end up in Europe stayed in Africa and evolved into Homo heidelbergensis. A group of this ancestor species of Homo heidelbergensis then migrated out of Africa and into Europe around 600,000 years ago. Around 300,000 years ago, the group that resided in Europe evolved to become Homo neanderthalensis (Neanderthals), and the group that had stayed behind in Africa evolved to become Homo sapiens (human beings), making Homo sapiens and Homo neanderthalensis evolutionary cousins. A group of Homo sapiens then ventured out of Africa and colonised the rest of the world, while the Homo neanderthalensis species, for reasons unknown, became extinct about 40,000 years ago.

Many of the fossil discoveries of the extinct species of the Homo genus have been made within the last few decades. Only about 3000 fossilised bones of these humans have ever been found. This might sound like a lot, but many of these fossils are isolated teeth: it is obviously very difficult to prove anything from a few teeth. Of the remainder, most are single, fragmented pieces of bone. Where bones are found at the same site, they are sometimes presumed to belong to the same individual although they may be found metres apart and even, in some cases, as with "Java Man", months apart (the femur of Java Man was found 1 year after and 15 metres away from where the skull-cap was found).

Of the ancient Homo species, Homo erectus is probably the most famous and most revered by evolutionists. The discovery of "Java Man" between 1891-1893 and "Peking Man" between 1927-1937 gave evolutionary theory a much-needed boost. These fossils represented, according to evolutionary theory, a new species of "ape-man" which became known as Homo erectus. Up until the Java man discovery, the only evidence to support human evolution was a few Neanderthal specimens. When it comes to the so-called Homo erectus fossil specimens, as well as all the other specimens of ancient humans, anti-evolutionists claim that they do not represent an ancient ape-man species but can be explained through other means.

It is often suggested that these specimens are fraudulent and have been tampered with or manipulated, as was the case with Piltdown Man. Other arguments against these specimens include the idea that, rather than representing an ape-man (or creature in transition from ape to human), these specimens actually represent either an ape or a variant type of human being, perhaps a diseased human being or an extinct race of human being. Consequently, anti-evolutionists claim that there is no solid evidence for the existence of direct ancestor species to Homo sapiens.

Up until relatively recently, Neanderthals were the only known close evolutionary cousin of Homo sapiens. However, over the last couple of decades, two new species have been identified. These are Homo floresiensis and Denisovans (yet to be classified), and they are also believed to be close relatives of our species. Homo floresiensis, Homo neanderthalensis, Denisovans, and Homo sapiens are the most recent species of the Homo genus, and all of them co-existed about 50,000 years ago according to evolutionists.

The first Neanderthal was found in 1856 and was initially classified as 100% human. Since then, more than 300 Neanderthals have been discovered, and due to certain differences, they are now considered to be a distinct species from human beings. Neanderthal fossils have been predominantly found in Northern Europe and Northern Asia, suggesting that their habitat ranged there. While it is agreed that there are identifiable anatomical differences between Neanderthals and human beings, their anatomies are essentially similar in scope. They have the same number of bones, which have the same functionality. There are minor differences in the thickness and strength of the bones, but these differences are claimed by anti-evolutionists to be trivial and can be seen as normal variations within a population. However, there are traits which do appear characteristic of Neanderthals, and these include larger teeth, a sloping forehead, a lack of chin and a slightly larger cranial capacity. However, such variations are seen *within* a species as well. As previously mentioned, the anatomical and morphological differences between the Great Dane and Chihuahua could be considered greater than those between Neanderthals and human beings, thus suggesting that one cannot definitively conclude that Neanderthals and human beings are distinct species based on anatomy and morphology alone. There are, of course, observable differences between different races of humans, yet they all belong to the same species. Some anti-evolutionists believe that Neanderthals and human beings belong to the same species, and Neanderthals were simply a racial group of human beings that went extinct, like the Tasmanian Aborigine.

Homo floresiensis was identified in 2003 following the discovery of relatively recent human fossils that did not appear like any other Homo species. These were found on the island of Flores in Indonesia. The fossils revealed a skeleton that would have stood at about 1.1 metres (3 foot and seven inches) tall. Since then, one complete skull and the bones and teeth of several other similar individuals have been recovered at the same site. This is the only site in the world where such individuals have been found. In total about twelve individuals belonging to this presumed species are thought to have been identified. The findings suggest a human species that would have been hobbit-like in stature with large teeth, relatively large feet and a small cranial capacity compared to human beings. Dating of the fossils and tools made by these individuals reveals that Homo floresiensis existed between 190,000 and 50,000 years ago at least. No Homo floresiensis DNA has been found from the fossils so nothing is known about their genetics. The marked anatomical differences between Homo floresiensis and other Homo species led scientists to conclude that they were a distinct species. Some evolutionists think that they evolved directly from the migrating non-African Homo erectus which could have reached these locations. But the problem with such an assumption is that there is no evidence for it whatsoever.

As we mentioned earlier, presumptions of speciation based on skeletal morphology are fundamentally flawed. The anatomical difference between Homo floresiensis and Homo sapiens is no larger than that between a Chihuahua and a Great Dane. In the nineteenth century, Jean Louis Armand de Quatrefages de Bréau, a French biologist, extensively studied and described the negrito race of the Philippines. He referred to them as "Les Pygmees" owing to their physical similarity with Pygmies of Central Africa (although most anthropologists recognise the Philippine negritos as a distinct race from the African Pygmies). Along with African Pygmies, they were distinct from other human races known at the time. They were described as dwarf-like in stature (mostly under 5 feet tall) with large clumsy feet and short, flat skulls. The negritos demonstrate the anatomical variation *within* the Homo sapiens species. The differences between negritos and Homo floresiensis may not be significantly greater than that between negritos and other human races. Thus, it is not possible to conclude with any degree of certainty that Homo floresiensis is a distinct species as supposed to being another variant of the human being race.

Furthermore, it is the premise that evolutionary theory is true that leads one to justify the existence of Homo floresiensis in evolutionary terms. So it is a form of circular reasoning. The fact is, there is nothing to say that these individuals evolved from anywhere. From a logical point of view, these individuals could represent a unique species or a unique racial group, or they could even represent a group of diseased Homo sapiens, possibly with a genetic disorder which rendered them short in stature. Such genetic disorders exist in populations today. Perhaps they were deliberately isolated from the mainstream Homo sapiens community because of their disorder. Such an idea is not inconceivable given what we know about historical human behaviour. Either way, we lack the evidence to conclude one way or the other. So these hobbits don't seem to add much to our knowledge of human evolution.

The discovery of Denisovans occurred in 2010 when a finger phalanx bone of a juvenile female, who lived about 41,000 years ago, was found in the remote Denisova Cave in the Altai Mountains in Siberia.* Two teeth belonging to different members of the same population were also found. DNA from these specimens was found and

---

* A phalanx bone is one of the segment bones that makes up the fingers, thumbs and toes of a human.

studied. Analysis of the DNA showed it to be genetically distinct from that of Neanderthals and human beings, thus leading scientists to conclude that they had identified a new species, which they named Denisovans.

It is really DNA analysis that has led to the identification and relationships of the various recent species of the Homo genus. Fossils demonstrated the existence of Neanderthals, but DNA confirmed their relationship to human beings. Denisovans have been identified purely from DNA analysis of a fragmented finger bone and two teeth, which showed the DNA was neither that of a human being nor a Neanderthal but belonged to a separate species altogether. With only DNA and no significant skeletal evidence, a skeletal reconstruction of Denisovans cannot be postulated, and no-one has any idea what they looked like.

DNA analysis of Neanderthal fossils suggest that 99.7% of the nucleotide sequences of the human being and Neanderthal genomes are identical, compared to humans sharing around 98.8% of sequences with the chimpanzee. Some scientists state that every human being is 99.9% genetically similar, while other scientists state that on average, in terms of DNA sequence, each human being is only 99.5% similar. If the latter is true, the DNA variation *within* the human being species is greater than the variation than that *between* the Neanderthal and human being, meaning that one cannot conclude that Neanderthals and human beings are separate species based on genetics alone. If the former is true, then relatively speaking, it is difficult to determine whether the 99.7% difference between Neanderthal and human being DNA is statistically significant enough to consider them distinct species.

The cave in Siberia where the Denisovans fossils were found had also reportedly been inhabited by Neanderthals and human beings. DNA studies in the last few years have suggested that Denisovans shared a common origin with Neanderthals and human beings, and that they ranged from Siberia to Southeast Asia. These studies have also shown that approximately 4–6% of DNA that is specific to Denisovans is also found in modern Melanesians (inhabitants of the islands off the northeast coast of Australia) and Aboriginal Australians. Neanderthal DNA is comparably similar to DNA in human beings. Approximately 2–4% of DNA specific to Neanderthals can also be found in modern European and Asian people. African populations generally do not have any of this specific Neanderthal DNA. This suggested to evolutionists that Africans evolved separately to non-Africans. These findings led evolutionists to conclude that there was interbreeding between Homo neanderthalensis and Homo sapiens in Europe and Asia, and that Denisovans also lived among and interbred with Homo sapiens at least in Southeast Asia.

Now, where do we begin with this one? Firstly, DNA analysis cannot definitively identify whether two organisms belong to the same species or not. This determination is made through the observable knowledge of successful interbreeding between the different types. As we previously established, different species do not interbreed and reproduce. In fact, this is the defining criteria for a species. Therefore, it seems hugely bizarre for evolutionists to now claim that Neanderthals and human beings interbred but were still different species. It makes no sense. The obvious question that arises is: don't these recent DNA findings suggest that Neanderthals and human beings belonged to the same species? Of course, there are huge anatomical and morphological differences within a species, for example with the dog species, so it is not inconceivable that Neanderthals were just a different-looking type of human being.

Secondly, DNA analysis is a disputed and debatable art, with different scientists concluding different outcomes. For example, some scientists say that, based on DNA analysis, our closest relative is the chimpanzee, while others say that it is the orangutan. Some say that we are genetically 99% similar to a chimpanzee, whereas others say that the similarity is only 94%. As already mentioned, there is even disagreement on the genetic variation within the human being species, with ranges varying from 99.5% to 99.9%. Considering this, it seems completely redundant to make presumptions of relatedness on DNA analysis alone.

Species are defined as a group of organisms which can successfully interbreed with each other. Different species should theoretically not be able to interbreed. As we mentioned in chapter 4, successful interbreeding between species is not observed in the world (although granted, there is some circularity in this statement). The question that should be dawning in your mind is: why have evolutionists suggested interbreeding between these various Homo species when it contradicts the very essence of what defines a species? The reason for this claim by evolutionists is because... it is necessary.

Neanderthals were previously considered to be a distinct species from human beings, but this recent DNA evidence, which reveals specific Neanderthal DNA being present in Europeans and Asians but not Africans, has to be explained. If human beings evolved separately in Africa to Neanderthals in Europe, then specific Neanderthal DNA should not be restricted to European/Asian human beings and excluded from African human beings. It is evolutionarily incompatible. So evolutionists have two options. They can either propose a bizarre and paradoxical theory of interbreeding amongst Neanderthals and human beings, or they can accept Neanderthals as a type of human being that has gone extinct rather than a distinct species to human beings. The problem with the latter option is that it brings the whole of evolutionary theory into disrepute. The evolutionists are pot-committed.* They have invested so much time and support into the Neanderthal theory, they simply cannot retract it now. Neanderthals are the only convincing Homo species that could have co-existed with Homo sapiens, with evidence of 300 specimens compared to one phalanx and two teeth of Denisovans and 12 isolated hobbits. To not have any other Homo species that existed at the same time as human beings would render evolutionary theory significantly more dubious than it already is. For evolutionists to concede now that Neanderthals are actually the same species as human being would be a huge blow for the theory, and one which they would seemingly struggle to bounce back from. So evolutionary theory has decided to stick with the idea that Neanderthals are a different species to human beings and convince society that somehow these separate species were able to transcend the known laws of nature and interbreed. It is, once again, a form of circular reasoning, whereby the premise that evolution is true is put first, and then evidence is interpreted in a way which fits in with the premise.

This same conundrum exists for the newly found Denisovan "species". As Denisovan-specific DNA is found only in some human populations, and as it has some specific Neanderthal DNA in it as well, evolutionists are forced to propose a theory of interbreeding between all three groups. Otherwise they would have to contend that they all belong to the same species. It is extraordinary how society seems to be accepting the evolutionists' version of events: we will explore why this might be in chapter 8.

---

* Pot-committed is the term used in the game of Poker where a player has committed so much of his stake to one hand that it becomes unwise (or emotionally difficult) to fold from that hand, and the player is obliged to see the hand through. The term can be used as an analogy for when one commits to something so much that they, figuratively speaking, reach a point of no-return.

Dinosaur denial

We could not go through the book without mentioning dinosaurs. Many of you know dinosaurs as the massive reptile-like creatures that roamed the world but went extinct before humans came into existence.

The vast majority of dinosaurs are only known due to fossils of them being found in the last 150 years or so. It may interest you to know that there are people out there who deny dinosaurs ever existed. They are fittingly called "dinosaur deniers". There is a hugely detailed conspiracy about exactly how this was achieved. We won't dwell on this for too long, as it seems that this should not be a decisive factor in your judgment, but it may be of some interest to you. If it is not of interest to you, please feel free to jump to the next section, as it is not directly relevant to the case at hand anyway.

In 1676 a large thigh bone fossil was discovered in Southern England. Scientists at the time could not identify the fossil but were amazed by its size. An illustration of the fossil was made by Robert Plot, a curator of a British Museum, who thought the fossil was a thighbone of a Roman war elephant. The fossil then disappeared without a trace. Almost 150 years later, the illustration was examined by William Buckland, an English geologist and palaeontologist, who reportedly came under pressure to classify the creature. He then collected several other fossil fragments (a piece of a right lower jaw with a single erupted tooth, a cervical rib, another rib, two vertebra, a sacrum, an ilium of a pelvis, a piece of pubic bone, a part of an ischium, a thighbone and the lower part of a second metatarsal) belonging to different members of what he believed to be the same species. in 1824 he eventually fully classified the fossils and assigned them to a species which became known as *Megalosaurus*. In 1822 large teeth that had never been seen before were discovered in Southern England. In 1834, a more complete specimen, presumed to belong to the same species, was found in Southern England: however, it was still significantly   incomplete   (and   later   discoveries   revealed misinterpretations of this original specimen were made). The teeth and specimen were assigned to a species named *Iguanadon*, as it resembled a large iguana. In 1832 Gideon Mantell, an English geologist and palaeontologist, discovered, again in Southern England, a more complete fossil skeleton of a large reptile-like previously unidentified creature. The skeleton was missing most of the head and forelimbs, and consisted of only the rear of the skull, possibly the lower jaws, ten vertebrae, both scapulae, both coracoids and several spikes and armour plates. A species named *Hylaeosaurus* was established from this creature.

Sir Richard Owen, a renowned British anatomist, is credited with "inventing" dinosaurs. In the early 1840's, he came across a spine-fragment fossil of *Iguanadon* in a collection, which reportedly got him thinking. He thought that the three large prehistoric animals of *Megalosaurus*, *Iguanadon*, and *Hylaeosaurus* were in many ways similar to each other but different from all other animals. Thus, he concluded that these three large prehistoric animals belonged to a unique group of animals which he termed *dinosauria*. So essentially, he made his hypothesis of dinosaurs based on the scarce fossil evidence and grossly incomplete skeletons of *Megalosaurus*, *Iguanadon* and *Hylaeosaurus*. Following Owen's proposal, dinosaurs became of great interest to people and the media alike. Subsequently, within a few years, more complete dinosaur fossils started emerging. Dinosaur deniers find this all too convenient. They claim that it is extraordinary how for all the centuries before, no extensive dinosaur fossils had ever been discovered. Then, as soon as a hypothesis of dinosaurs emerged, and there was an enchanted audience awaiting their arrival, the first extensive fossils started appearing. Why did the Native American-Indians (living in areas where many of these fossils have been found), or any other ancient civilisation, not discover such fossils and mention them?

Before the 1800's no-one knew that dinosaurs existed. Then, after the first dinosaur fossils were found, "The Great Dinosaur Rush" ensued whereby dinosaur hunting became a fad, as there was much fame and fortune associated with successful discoveries. Due to this, many forgeries emerged. The dinosaur deniers find it suspicious that almost all of the discoveries of dinosaur fossils have been made by people with vested interests, such as palaeontologists and museums rather than accidental discoveries from people such as farmers, ranchers or diggers. More accidental discoveries would be expected.

You may question what the possible motive for creating a dinosaur lie would be. The motive proposed is two-fold. Firstly, dinosaurs help explain certain puzzles of evolutionary theory, such as the evolution of reptiles to birds. Secondly, the dinosaur business is huge: dinosaur merchandise is financially lucrative, while museums and the movie business have both benefited financially from the presence of dinosaurs. Dinosaurs capture the imagination of the youth and become a main part of children's fun and fantasy. You may then ask: if dinosaurs are made-up, how have dinosaur fossils emerged? Well, dinosaur deniers claim that hardly any complete dinosaur skeletons have ever been found. In most cases only a few isolated bones are found, and then a presumptuous reconstruction of the whole animal is made. Some animals have been constructed on just a few teeth alone. Dinosaur deniers also claim that these fossils could be forgeries and not real fossilised bones. In museums, the real specimens are not on display, and what you see are reconstructed models from the original specimens that are kept hidden away in locked vaults. Only a few select palaeontologists reportedly have access to these original fossils: no independent researcher has ever handled or examined these specimens.

Dinosaur deniers propose that many of the dinosaur fossils are actually forgeries of a mix-and-match of various animals like crocodiles, whales, giraffes, elephants, rhinoceroses, ostriches and so on. They also claim that dinosaur bones can be, and actually are, directly made as forgeries and then planted to look like genuine fossils. Proven fake fossils have been in circulation. One such example was of a fossil representing a transition from dinosaurs to birds (known as "archaeoraptor") which was presented by one of the largest scientific institutions in the world. Later it transpired that this fossil was a complete hoax and had been artificially made of other animal bones, which caused much embarrassment for the scientific institution concerned. The dinosaur deniers also claim that there are structural incompatibilities with many of the dinosaurs, for example with the famous "tyrannosaurus rex": its heavy head and forward-leaning torso means that it would not have the right centre of balance to be able to move. In summary, the following arguments have led to the phenomenon of dinosaur denial:

1. There have only been dinosaur discoveries in the last two centuries.
2. Dinosaur discoveries are not made by laypersons, whereas this would be expected.
3. The actual fossils are not handled or examined by independent researchers.
4. The reconstructions of dinosaurs are gross presumptions and in many cases are not viable.
5. Established forgeries have been produced bringing the credibility of any fossil into question.

Chapter 6 – The alternative view

In order for evolutionary theory to be disregarded, there would have to be a viable alternative theory to explain biodiversity. There are several alternative theories in circulation. We won't attempt to establish any of these or make the case for them, only to assess whether they can offer a plausible explanation for biodiversity and give an alternative explanation for the evidence used to support evolutionary theory.

It is important to remember that evolutionary theory does not attempt to answer the question of the initial cause of life; it only attempts to explain the great biodiversity that we have and how all organisms came to be from an original life source. On a side note, the question of the initial creation of life is in itself of great interest, and may indirectly play a role in the promotion and acceptance of evolutionary theory. We will look at this in more detail in Chapter 8. For now, we will just concentrate on the process of evolution following the occurrence of the first life form.

What other theories can explain biodiversity?

The main alternative to evolutionary theory is creationism. Creationism is the hypothesis that the universe and life were created through supernatural processes by a cosmic or supernatural intelligence, known as God. Obviously, for this theory to be true, God would have to be able to defy the known laws of nature, meaning that theoretically anything would be possible for God.

Other theories are possible as well, such as an alien species invading Earth and creating all life, or perhaps Rene Descartes' "Evil Demon", or even the "brain in a vat" theory proposed by Gilbert Harman (we will explore this later).* There is also the theory of non-creation, as proposed in the Hindu scripture of the Mandukya Upanishad.† These theories are considered philosophical, and none of

---

* Rene Descartes' Evil Demon concept proposes that an evil demon has presented to you a complete illusion of an external world in a deliberate effort to mislead you. The "brain in a vat" theory is a follow-on from this.
† The theory of non-creation, as proposed in the Mandukya Upanishad and explained by Swami Yogeshwarananda, states that there actually is no creation or material world - the whole thing is a construct of your own

them have a big level of support or promotion, so we will not spend too much time discussing them, and we will focus primarily on creationism.

Evolutionary theory attacks creationism in several ways, arguing that certain observations about the natural world are incompatible with creationism. For creationism to remain viable, it would need to be able to defend itself against such attacks. There are, of course, various versions of creationism. Some people argue that God created all species instantaneously in one go, while others say that the different groups of life forms were created separately, as stated in the book of Genesis in the Bible: the plants first, then the birds of the air and the animals of the sea, and then the land animals, and lastly the humans. Some people may create their own versions of creationism, such as a supernatural intelligence creating initial organisms within a class, order or family of animals for evolution to then take over and produce all the biodiversity within these groups. Or perhaps a supernatural intelligence creating an initial life form and thereafter creating new species or groups of species periodically. This variability in creationism is inconsequential for the purpose of establishing whether there are adequate counter-arguments to the case put forward by evolutionary theory. Essentially, creationism is about a supernatural intelligence being the intentional cause of any life forms (apart from an initial, solitary common ancestor), thus negating evolutionary theory's claim that *it* is the explanation of all species and organisms following the presence of the first life form. Some people even adhere to a model whereby a creator or God set in motion the process of evolution and retains control and responsibility for it, so that God and evolution coexist. For the sake of our case, this is also inconsequential, as we are not trying to establish whether such coexistence might be true, but whether evolutionary theory is a solid theory that has been proven to a reasonable degree. Whether it is driven by an underlying intelligence or not is irrelevant to the question we are trying to answer. However, we will look at the concept of the coexistence of God and evolution in the next chapter, as it is a point of interest.

Remember, we aren't trying to substantiate creationism or the other alternative theories. All we need to establish here is whether the evidence for evolutionary theory is good enough in view of the possible alternative theories. In order to establish this, the alternative theories

---

mind, in much the same way that a dream is a product of your own mind and does not exist without you (the dreamer).

would have to have counter-arguments to all the proposed evidence brought forward to support evolutionary theory. If there is a piece of evidence which cannot be explained through alternative means, then not only are the alternative theories significantly weakened, but evolutionary theory's position would be strengthened. And, of course, the alternative theories must be viable to a reasonable degree (but not necessarily proven).

A creationist interpretation of the evidence

In order to explain biodiversity and offer alternate explanations for the evidence and observations, we have to *assume* the existence of God. This should not be mistaken for affirming God's existence. We are only establishing how the evidence, observations and biodiversity *could* be explained by creationism *if* God exists. So we need to examine what creationism could say about the main observations and pieces of evidence that were brought out in chapter 2...

All life shares similar characteristics and is made of the same core materials (DNA and RNA). To a pro-evolutionist, this suggests relatedness and common ancestry. However, a creationist could easily challenge this assertion by stating that God would simply choose to use the same material to create all life, the same way that a potter chooses to make all his pots from clay. Similarly, all life shares the basic characteristics of life such as metabolism, catalysis, replication and hereditability because that is the way God chose to make life. It is not illogical. Think about it. If you've got a tried and tested formula for making something, why would you change it?

The phylogenetic tree is a hypothetical construct, derived mostly from circular reasoning. It is not proof of evolutionary theory. It may be true, it may not be. There is no way we can empirically prove it. However, even *if* the proposed phylogenetic tree is correct, this still does not disprove creationism: the nested hierarchies could have been created this way through a series of separate creation and extinction processes guided by God. Perhaps God changed his mind. Perhaps God did not like his creations. Perhaps God deliberately changed animals for reasons that we do not understand. The phylogenetic tree itself does not prove *evolution* of one species to another. It just shows different species existing at different times. So one cannot rule out creationism based on the phylogenetic tree. Also, remember, as we have just mentioned, the phylogenetic tree is not a fact. It has been created within evolutionary theory using circular reasoning, and it may be completely fictitious. If this is the case, of course, a creationist could pitch almost any model of creationism against evolutionary theory and come out on top.

The fossils of extinct species do not disprove the possibility of God. Even if the fossils were to decisively show that there has been gradually increasing complexity of species over time, this does not prove speciation. The reasons why the species represented by the fossils became extinct have not been established. It is no less reasonable to say that God, for whatever reason, decided to cause extinction of a species with recreation of a more complex type, than it is to say that evolution did it and the one species evolved into the other. There is no actual evidence for either, and both are as logical as each other. You may question, why would God do that? Surely if God is intelligent enough to create life from nothing, God would be intelligent enough to create it perfectly without needing to amend it. We will address this question shortly.

Vestigial structures, atavisms, and imperfect designs (like the left recurrent laryngeal nerve described previously) appear to be the favourite pieces of evidence used by pro-evolutionists to dismiss the possibility of God. Jerry Coyne, a well-known American biologist and pro-evolutionist, in his book *Why Evolution is True*, says:

> *"...if organisms were built from scratch by a designer—one who used the biological building blocks or nerves, muscles, bone, and so on—they would not have such imperfections. Perfect design would truly be the sign of a skilled and intelligent designer. Imperfect design is the mark of evolution; in fact, it's precisely what we expect from evolution."*

Pro-evolutionists argue that if God is intelligent enough to make species, why would God make such careless mistakes? But this line of argument presumes that these features *are* accidental mistakes. Each species, and even each member of a species, *could* have been created by God in a very deliberate manner. With your limited understanding, you may question, "why did God create abnormalities, why did God create disease, and why did God allow for suffering?" But these are all questions posed from a human understanding of life, and what you as a human think life should be. Of course, if you want all life forms to have perfection and immortality, life as we know it does not work. Every creature has to die eventually otherwise populations would grow exponentially which would be unsustainable. It appears that imperfection would have to be created on all levels in the system for it to work. Death and destruction would always need to be incorporated into the design of any environment with life in it. God is faced with the task of creating a world which reportedly allows for the coexistence of 10 million species. In order for all these species to coexist, there has to be a harmony of the ecosystems in which they abide in. If the balance is not right, the ecosystem fails. Too much or too little of one species can lead to the demise of others. A species in the middle of a food chain has to be good enough to escape from its predators but not so good so that its predators never catch it. Otherwise, the demise of the predators ensues, which is likely to result in an increase in the aforementioned species, which in turn is going to lead to a demise of their prey. With our limited intelligence and foresight, it seems unreasonable for us to question the methods in which God uses to achieve this perfect balance. Vestigial structures, atavisms, abnormalities and diseases may all appear futile or even callous to us, but that may be because we judge them with a limited intelligence. We don't know how to run a planet! We don't want to digress too much into a philosophical or theological debate here about the role of suffering and the plausibility of God allowing for this, but it suffices to say that one cannot dismiss the possibility of God just because one disagrees with the designs or doesn't like them.

The geographical distribution of species is also thought by pro-evolutionists to represent evolution. However, we have dismissed this argument on the grounds that it is unscientific and does not prove *evolution* of one species to another. It is only an observation of the here and now. It is not unreasonable for a creationist to argue that God puts animals in the best environment to suit their needs. Anti-creationists claim that the fact that some species do not exist in environments suitable to their needs, such as elephants not existing in the Pacific Islands, is evidence against creationism. However, this is not a strong argument against creationism. As, these environments only *appear* suitable to us from our narrow perspective. We may be wrong. Species hold ecosystems in a delicate balance, and ecosystems have been devastatingly changed by the artificial introduction of a new alien species. The effects that this new species has on the ecosystem are often unpredictable. We may *think* that elephants would do well on the Pacific Islands, but there is a possibility that the whole ecosystem could fail if they were introduced there. And even if it was true that elephants would survive well in the Pacific Islands and keep the ecosystem running appropriately, this still does not disprove creationism. God could simply choose only certain locations for species for reasons unknown to us.

The information and observations from the finches, both past and present, show no actual evidence of evolution. Modern day studies of finches only show oscillating patterns of populations and finch types rather than any actual change in species. Over the last few decades, it has been observed that finch populations vary with the natural conditions. For example, in drought conditions, there is a shortage of soft seeds available, meaning that the main diet of a finch has to be tough nuts. Subsequently, there is an increase in the population of finches with beaks that can crack these tough nuts. Then, when conditions change to provide lots of rainfall with a subsequent increase in soft seeds, the finches with the more suitable beaks for eating these soft seeds increase in population. Modern day studies have only shown finch type populations oscillating back and forth like this with no actual net evolution of the finches. So creationists would have no problem refuting a claim that finch beak observations suggest evolution rather than creationism.

In terms of the experimental and observational evidence showing evidence of natural selection, this does not negate the presence of God either. Remember, this evidence only suggests evidence for natural selection, not for evolution or common descent – a gross inference would have to be made to get from the former to the latter. A species evolving into another has never been observed or reproduced. Natural selection is just the species adapting to its environment. It's no big deal, and no real shock either. For example, before the industrial revolution in Great Britain, most peppered moths had a pale colouring which meant that they were camouflaged against the pale birch trees that they would rest on. Moths with a "mutant" black colouring were easily spotted and eaten by birds. This gave the pale variety a survival advantage over the "mutant" black moths. However, with the industrial revolution, airborne pollution in industrial areas resulted in soot blackening the tree barks which the moths would rest on. The survival advantage of camouflage was now changed from the pale colour to the black colour. Subsequently, the black peppered moths became far more numerous than the pale moths in the urban areas. Most creationism advocates would not deny that these events happened, but they would argue that they have nothing to do with evolution. They would also argue that such examples of natural selection are not incompatible with God. Why couldn't God accommodate this? There's no reason why God couldn't have pre-empted environmental changes and created variant types of a species to allow for the continual existence of that species.

It seems that creationism is a viable alternative theory for explaining evolutionary theory's observations and evidence. It is a theory which is supported by eminent thinkers, academics, scientists, mathematicians and philosophers. So to dismiss it *ad lapidem* would be considered unreasonable.

Naturalism versus supernaturalism

Naturalism is the philosophical belief that all known phenomena arise through naturalistic or materialistic processes. It excludes the possibility of supernatural processes that cannot be explained through the known laws of nature. Evolutionary theory is a naturalistic explanation for biodiversity whereas creationism clearly incorporates supernatural processes.

Evolutionary theory is considered the best naturalistic explanation for biodiversity, which is why it is taught in science classrooms across the Western world. This in itself is questionable, as one could argue that there is as much evidence for other naturalistic theories to explain biodiversity. For example, there appears to be as much evidence for multiple descent as there is for common descent (as there is no direct evidence for either). So evolutionary theory is *a* naturalistic explanation for biodiversity, but not necessarily the *best* explanation. But, leaving this aside, it is difficult to compare the strength of a naturalistic explanation to a supernaturalistic explanation, as this will come down to an individual's belief and acceptance in supernatural processes. An atheist is unlikely to find creationism a *viable* theory for explaining biodiversity. However, this should not lower the bar of the burden of proof for a naturalistic explanation. Any naturalistic explanation would still need to be proven to a reasonable degree. A naturalist clearly wants to explain all phenomena through naturalistic means, and will therefore always consider the best naturalistic explanation as the *best* explanation. But the best naturalistic explanation does not necessarily equate to being a *good* explanation.

To impose naturalism on life is a peculiar activity. Life appears very different to non-life. These two phenomena in the universe can be referred to as the animate and the inanimate respectively. The animate refers to life. The inanimate refers to non-living phenomena. These are distinguished from one another based on certain characteristics. Intelligence is found in the animate but not in the inanimate. The animate is very different from the inanimate and has characteristics which are not susceptible to being explained through naturalistic causes. That is not to say that they cannot be explained through naturalistic means alone, but a strong case would have to be made. It seems paradoxical to exclude the *possibility* of supernaturalistic causes for the animate – if intelligence is present in the animate, how can intelligence be excluded as a possible cause of the animate?

To insist that all organisms bar one could only have arisen through naturalistic means seems bizarre. Why would supernatural processes be discounted? And if they are not discounted, one would have to consider them a viable alternative theory. A genuinely open-minded person should be able to see that the observations and evidence used to formulate evolutionary theory do not negate the possibility of the presence of a supernatural intelligence or God.

Belief in supernatural phenomena does not necessarily equate to belief in God. Supernatural phenomena includes ghosts, miracles, astrology, prophecy, reincarnation and extrasensory perception (psychic abilities) such as clairvoyance, telepathy and mediumship. These phenomena cannot be explained through naturalistic means. Contrastingly, the presence of aliens or extra-terrestrials in the universe could *theoretically* be explained naturalistically, in the same way that life on Earth is. So believing that aliens visited Earth and created life on Earth is not *necessarily* a supernatural belief: interestingly, a 2005 poll from Gallup revealed that 24% of people in the United States of America do believe that extra-terrestrials visited Earth in the past. This poll also revealed that 41% believe in psychic abilities, 32% believe in ghosts, 20% believe in reincarnation, and, most notably, 73% believe in at least one of the poll's listed supernatural phenomena. Now, the acceptance or belief in supernatural phenomena invalidates a *necessity* to explain phenomena naturalistically: there is no obligation to explain biodiversity naturalistically. And, as we have shown so far, there is no compelling naturalistic explanation for biodiversity, so it is illogical for people who believe in supernatural phenomena to accept evolutionary theory: for such people, a bad explanation is not better than no explanation.

Of note, naturalism can be linked to atheism; in fact, they appear dependent on each other. On the other hand, supernaturalism and atheism appear incompatible, as God is considered a supernatural entity and therefore supernatural processes affirm God's existence. Naturalism may not include an overt objection to God or theism per se, but it supposes that all natural phenomena can be explained by the laws of nature. Thus, it indirectly removes God and theism from any explanation of natural phenomena: we will explore the importance of this in Chapter 8.

The illusion of evolution

Attempting to establish the motives and reasons for the possible actions of God would appear to be a pointless excursion. Based on the *ability* to create various life forms, God theoretically exhibits a high degree of intelligence. Our intelligence cannot match this. This means that we are unlikely to be able to comprehend God's actions, as God functions on a level which is unfamiliar to us. When a scientist performs intelligence tests on animals, the animals would not be expected to comprehend the reasons for the tests or the motives of the scientist, even though the animals may be able to successfully complete the tests.

Even if you refute the possibility of God doing everything specifically in a way which is beyond our comprehension but has some unknown purpose, there are still other explanations for the *appearance* of evolutionary theory. Perhaps God is testing our faith. Perhaps God is testing our intelligence. Perhaps God is trying to trick us into thinking evolutionary theory is true. Perhaps God is trying to hide. Perhaps God is creating an industry for evolutionary biology with occupations for the proponents and opponents of it. Think about it; I wouldn't have written this, and you wouldn't be reading this, if it wasn't for the controversy circling evolutionary theory.

The suppositions mentioned above are all based on God intentionally creating an *illusion* of evolution. (Of course, if God actually uses evolutionary theory to create, the theory of creationism is redundant.) But why would God intentionally create such an illusion which seemingly diminishes recognition and appreciation of creationism and even seemingly diminishes the idea that God exists? Now we are in the realms of trying to establish the motives and intentions of God, which, as we previously stated, appears a futile task. Ultimately though, it does not matter, as the actual motive is not what is relevant here. Instead it is the *possibility* of there being a motive that is of importance.

The claim that God is intentionally creating an illusion of evolution may seem absurd to you, but it is certainly not inconceivable. And when you think about it, is it really less likely than the idea of a single-cell organism evolving into all of the life forms in existence today through a series of chance random mutations?

The dilemma of causality

Natural selection, as suggested by Darwin's observations of the finches, could be challenged by a philosophical argument on causality. You could think of it as a chicken and egg scenario; have the finches adapted to their environment, or is the necessary environment provided for the finches (by God)? That is to say, perhaps the finches changed first, and subsequently God assisted them by changing their environment to suit them better. Or perhaps God changed them simultaneously.

This demonstrates the dilemma of causality whereby one cannot prove the cause of an observation or correlation. This idea is present in Indian Philosophy and was descriptively brought out in the Yoga Vasistha, an ancient Hindu scripture. In this, the analogy is given of a crow landing on a palm tree just as a coconut from that tree falls to the ground. An inference is then made by the observer that the crow landing on the tree directly caused the coconut to fall from the tree. However, these two events may not be causally related and may just be coincidence, or related in a subtler manner. To conclude that one event has led to the other is an assumption.

Similarly, Darwin observed different finch beaks on different islands of the Galapagos, and assumed causality. He assumed that one observation had led to the other (the islands' environments had led to the specificity of the finch beaks). But this was an unnatural conclusion to draw, and one led by a bias of how *he* thought nature functions. This would seem to be a naturalistic or materialistic bias, whereby every natural, observable phenomenon has to be explained through the known laws of nature. It may *seem* natural to draw the conclusion of a species adapting to its environment, but this conclusion can only be drawn from a naturalistic-biased perspective. Just the same way that one cannot decisively conclude that the crow landing on the branch was the cause of the coconut falling to the ground, one cannot assume the islands' differing environments led to the evolution of different beak shapes and sizes. The mere appearance (or illusion) of causality is not evidence of causality.

The brain in the vat theory

If you reject God as a viable alternative to evolutionary theory, then you could use the brain in the vat option. This suggests that your existence as you experience it is an illusion: your brain has been removed from your body and placed in a vat where it is connected to a supercomputer which transmits electrical impulses identical to those that a brain normally receives. Thus, the computer is able to simulate reality, making you believe that certain things are happening which aren't actually happening, not outside your own realm of consciousness anyway. The process requires a producer, and this is attributed to a mad scientist who is carrying out the experiment for unknown reasons.

Now, if this is true, then technically speaking, the mad scientist is the creator of all life. Or actually, he has made *you* the creator of all life, as all life originates from your brain only. However, we have to accept that even if this is true, there are certainties in life that we accept, such as undisputed scientific laws, as the mad scientist has ensured that they have met the necessary threshold to be considered as such. But certainly evolutionary theory is not such a case.

Also, with a mad scientist at the helm, we could not put it past him to deliberately try to deceive us into believing evolutionary theory is true – leaving little clues to make it look like evolution could be true but not giving enough to conclude with certainty that it is. Perhaps he does this for his own amusement. Or perhaps he does this to distinguish the intelligent from the less intelligent! Now, is this suggestion really less plausible than the suggestion that your ancestor was 5,000 times smaller than the size of a garden pea? An unbiased mind would have to conclude that it is not. The difference between the two is that no evidence will be found to support the former, whereas we might be able to obtain small amounts of evidence to fit in with the latter (but not prove it). Considering this, people opt to go for the latter, possibly because they assume (wrongly) that a small amount of evidence is better than none. But in reality it seems that their preference towards evolutionary theory is more likely to be due to other factors, which we will discuss soon.

Chapter 7 – Evolution and God

There are many religious people who accept evolutionary theory as true, and many who say that there is no contradiction with evolutionary theory and a belief in God or religious affiliation. In fact, polls of the Western world suggest that many people believe in both evolution and a supernatural being, and believe that evolution has been influenced by that being. These people are known as theistic evolutionists.

Pope Francis, who is the current Pope of the Catholic Church, declared in 2014 that evolution is true, and that God is "not a magician with a magic wand". He went on to say that evolution and creationism were both correct, and that God created the Earth and all living forms through the "Big Bang" and evolution respectively. He also declared evolution as an "effectively proven fact". Many religious leaders have come out supporting a similar position. Now, the question arises as to whether this is a logical position to take or not. Several prominent atheists declare it is not, and that God and evolution cannot coexist. In order to explore this further, we need to consider *how* God could coexist with evolution. For this, we need to assume God exists and take into account the following three separate processes (as evolutionary theory requires all three processes to have taken place):

1. The origin of the physical universe (considered by many to have arisen through the "Big Bang");
2. The origin of the first organism (known as abiogenesis), and;
3. Common descent and evolution of species through (random) mutations in DNA.

We need to relate these separate processes to God through hypothetical models. It seems reasonable to presume that if God is responsible for some or all of the above processes, then God should precede or coincide with the first process (creation of the physical universe). We would not expect the creation of the physical universe to have come about through accidental physical causes and for God *then* to somehow come into existence and create life. So this kind of model will not be included in our following hypotheses. Similarly, the above processes are sequential, and we would not expect God to be responsible for a later process without being responsible for the former processes. This leaves us with four potential models of how God and evolution could coexist:

The four possible models of evolution and God coexisting

a) God could have created the universe, including Planet Earth, and then left it there with no plan or intention of life ever coming about (responsible for process 1 only).

b) God could have created the universe, including Planet Earth, and then activated abiogenesis and stopped there with no plan or intention of this first organism evolving into other species (responsible for processes 1 and 2 only).

c) God could have created the universe, including Planet Earth, and then activated abiogenesis, and then partially assisted inert nature with bringing about all species on Planet Earth through the process of evolution (responsible for processes 1 and 2, and partially responsible for process 3).

d) God could have created the universe, including Planet Earth, and then activated abiogenesis, and then, with a complete plan and full intention, brought about all species on Planet Earth through the process of evolution (responsible for processes 1, 2 and 3).

We have to attribute at least one of these models to God, otherwise God is completely redundant and serves no purpose. There would be no point in God's existence, as God would have had no impact on the world or life. Such a belief system is more fitting with an atheistic outlook.

In all of these models, the full process of evolution from start to finish has to be present, in other words the assumptions all have to be compatible with evolutionary theory in its entirety. You may wonder why we have not included a model whereby a mix of evolution and supernatural processes (creation) are responsible for life on Earth. For example, some of the transitions may have required supernatural processes rather than evolution. Or maybe *some* of the groups of animals were supernaturally created (and not evolved), like the insects (for which we have very little fossil evidence). The reason that this is not considered as one of our possible models is because it defies evolutionary theory. Evolutionary theory is about *all* life descending from an original common ancestor, so we cannot allow some life forms to be excluded from this process and be explained through other means, such as supernatural processes. This would nullify evolutionary theory. The theory would have to be changed to say that only partial evolution is true, which is a completely different theory. We are examining common descent, not partial descent. Let us now look at the possibilities above one by one....

a) *God could have created the universe, including Planet Earth, and then left it there with no plan or intention of life ever coming about.*

This would be a very peculiar belief structure to have. It implies that God had no intention of life ever coming about. Despite God having the intelligence and ability to create an entire universe, God did not have the intelligence to foresee the possibility of life arising by chance out of the composition of elements that God himself had brought about. The "fine-tune universe" model proposes that dimensionless physical constants must lie within a very specific range in order to accommodate matter, astronomical structures, chemical elements and subsequently life. If any of these fundamental constants were even just slightly different, the universe would not be functional. It follows that the universe, if created, required a high degree of skill and knowledge from its creator. For this creator to not foresee life arising in the universe would be paradoxical. So there is a contradiction here which makes this position untenable. It seems irrational to conclude that God exists but never intended for life to arise.

This model leaves us with a conundrum as to how the first organism came into existence. Many atheists argue that it is possible for life to come from non-life through random chance processes, and this view can be accepted. But a mixture of this with the presence of God just seems illogical. Life has never been reproduced from non-life since, so we can say that it was a hugely unlikely event that happened by chance and is unlikely to ever happen again. Fair enough. But to say that this very unlikely event was overseen by God who played no part in it, seems illogical. Why would God be an inactive bystander in this process? It seems that either God was directly involved or God does not exist and the process happened by random chance. So the problem of how it would be possible to get life from non-life with an inactive God being present but uninvolved, is created by this position, which makes it unreasonable.

This position also leaves us with the aforementioned dilemma of the extremely unlikely probability of random mutations leading to the development of all life forms from the original single-cell common ancestor. Without God guiding or directing evolution, the process would be random and left purely to chance. Inert nature would thus be responsible for abiogenesis and the existence of all life forms on the planet.

b) *God could have created the universe, including Planet Earth, and then activated abiogenesis and stopped there with no plan or intention of this first organism evolving into other species.*

This model has the same shortcomings as the previous one. Although, this creator demonstrates more intelligence and skill than the one in the previous model, as they have not only created matter from non-matter but have also created life from non-life.

The distinction between matter and life (inanimate and animate) is not always clearly understood, and the definition of life is somewhat controversial. Life forms (organisms) maintain homeostasis, are composed of cells, undergo metabolism, grow, adapt to their environment, respond to stimuli and reproduce. They are constituted of living cells which contain DNA, and they share certain characteristics such as metabolism, catalysis and replication. Inert matter does not have such biological processes. Life forms are considered to have a unique level of functioning, and they can have sentience: the ability to feel, perceive and experience subjectively. Inert nature does not have this. A rock cannot think or feel and has no subjective sense of reality.

Atheists generally adopt the view that Planet Earth came into existence about 4.5 billion years ago, and abiogenesis occurred about 3.8 billion years ago. So for approximately 700 million years, according to them, there was only inert nature on Planet Earth, and there was no life present. They then attribute abiogenesis to inert nature through a series of random and accidental processes whereby physical elements turned into the first living organism. This first organism had an intrinsic drive to survive and replicate, and subsequently it brought about all the life forms we see on the planet today.

In biology, there is a well-established idea known as the "minimal gene-set concept", which we will look at in more detail later. This suggests that a minimum of around 380 genes is required to create a living life form, such as a single-cell organism. This is because a life form requires multiple characteristics, such as metabolism, catalysis and replication. In theory, as atheists argue, inert nature can achieve this through random chance just as, in theory, a monkey can create great literature through random typing of a keyboard. However, if we are to attribute this feat of abiogenesis to God, one would have to say that this God has demonstrated an incredible level of skill and ability in accomplishing this feat. Even though a monkey could theoretically create Shakespeare's *Macbeth* without any intention, this does not take away from the skill and ability Shakespeare demonstrated in *intentionally* creating *Macbeth*.

It could even be argued that the intentional creation of abiogenesis is more impressive than the creation of the physical universe without life. So we have reached a similar point to the one from which we refuted the previous model: it seems irrational to conclude that this God could not foresee the evolution of new species from this first life form. Also, why would this God want to create a very primitive life form and leave it at that? There is a contradiction here which makes this model untenable as well. For God to be responsible for abiogenesis, which is a deeply complex process, and then inert nature and random chance be responsible for the origin of all other life forms on Planet Earth, seems paradoxical. It seems implausible that evolution could proceed without God's intention *if* God exists.

c) *God could have created the universe, including Planet Earth, and then activated abiogenesis, and then partially assisted inert nature with bringing about all species on Planet Earth through the process of evolution (responsible for process 1 and 2, and partially responsible for process 3).*

We have presumed that the act of creation of the physical universe is a single act. Abiogenesis can also be considered a single act. Evolution, on the other hand, is a gradual process occurring over billions of years through a multitude of different stages. So in theory, it is possible that it could be partly due to God and partly due to randomness brought about by inert nature. For example, perhaps God is responsible for the mutations that lead to changes in the characteristics of a species, but then inert nature is responsible for the selection of these characteristics resulting in their prominence. Or perhaps God is responsible for the gross changes and changing one species into another, but inert nature is responsible for everything else in between, such as the micro-evolution of a species.

The problem with this model is similar to the previous ones. A God adept enough to create the universe, create life, and now also contribute to evolution, should have the ability to complete the processes of evolution without the need to rely on inert nature. In addition, the process of evolution does not lend itself to being shared, as it is the very gradual accumulation of small changes leading to big change. For God to induce a mutation in a land mammal that creates a tiny wing-stub seems a pointless activity unless God directs the whole process of converting this wing-stub into a fully functional wing so that the mammal can fly. There would have to be a full plan and intention from the start, meaning that none of the acts resulting in the evolution of the wing can be random. It seems irrational to conclude that a Shakespearean play could be part written by Shakespeare and part written by a monkey randomly typing. If you accept that Shakespeare is responsible for part of the play, it seems logical to conclude that randomness cannot be responsible for the other part. It follows that evolution is a phenomenon which is all or nothing: all inert nature or all supernatural intelligence. So this model of coexistence is not a viable option.

d) *God could have created the universe, including Planet Earth, and then activated abiogenesis, and then, with a complete plan and full intention, brought about all species on Planet Earth through the process of evolution.*

This would appear to be the most popular model adopted by religious evolutionists. It supposes that God is directly responsible for creation of the universe, abiogenesis and evolution. *How* God achieves this is irrelevant to the issue of whether God and evolution can coexist. You may hear terms like "activating evolution" or "setting evolution in motion" or "directing evolution" branded about by theistic evolutionists, but such statements are devoid of any meaning. Whether God activated evolution or was directing it as it went along is insignificant. Either way, there is an intention behind the process, which is the paramount issue.

If the mutations leading to evolution are the result of an intelligence, they are not random. They may appear random to us, but this is only because we cannot identify any mechanism for how they came about. In the same way, a clean lottery draw is random, but a fixed lottery draw is not random. Even though a fixed lottery draw may *appear* random to us, this is only because we do not have knowledge of the corruption. With such a corruption, there is an intelligence who has fixed the draw with intention so that the numbers produced by the draw are predetermined and not random. Similarly, if God has fixed these mutations with the intention of inducing evolution, they are predetermined and not random, even though we do not understand the mechanisms by which they occur.

Of note, it is argued by some that there is no such phenomenon as randomness, as everything is predictable through the laws of nature and it is only a lack of information or intelligence that renders certain events unpredictable. Even a coin toss is *theoretically* predictable and thus non-random. This is because the laws of nature determine what side the coin lands on: the power of the flick, the air resistance, the weight of the coin and the distance to land are all factors which mean that the side that the coin lands on is based on various physical factors, and consequently it is predictable with the right knowledge. However, an atheistic proponent of this view is still obliged to accept that the laws of nature that create predictability have arisen out of random chance – even though the laws of nature may produce orderly outcomes with predictability, they themselves are the result of unintentional and accidental processes. Anything which is derived without the intent of an intelligence has no meaning or purpose: its origin is accidental. So even if you assert that the mutations leading to evolution are non-random due to theoretical predictability, they are still the result of chance and accidental processes and therefore should be considered as random. This can be better understood using the analogy of the monkey typing *Macbeth*: Shakespeare's creation of *Macbeth* is non-random, as Shakespeare intentionally wrote it: however, the monkey's creation of *Macbeth* (even though exactly the same as Shakespeare's version) is the product of chance and randomness, as it has come about through unintentional and accidental processes. Considering this, it seems reasonable to define randomness by whether or not there is intent behind the event. Consequently, we can say that if there is evolution without an intelligence behind it, the mutations are random. But if there is evolution with an intelligence behind it, the mutations are non-random: this is known as the deterministic approach to evolution.

Back to the issue at hand. This model states that God is behind every stage of evolution, causing every mutation intentionally, and causing the extinction of species after species and replacing them with newer, more advanced versions. Remember, evolution is a grossly inefficient and cumbersome process that creates a huge amount of waste. It takes, according to evolutionary theory, 250,000 generations to make an eye from a flat retina. Evolutionary theory predicts that it generally takes about one million years to convert one species into another. It has reportedly taken about 4.4 million years to get from the first bipedal hominid to the first man. So the question that should arise in a logical mind is: "why would God bother with this arduous and tiresome process?" A God capable of creating the universe and creating life from non-life would surely be capable of creating and extincting species without the need for such a process – inefficiency cannot be part of God's nature.

Theistic evolution versus atheistic evolution

Evolutionary theory is considered the best naturalistic explanation for the presence of all species on Earth – it is a phenomenon which can be explained through the known laws of nature without the need for supernatural processes. Theistic evolution is the idea that God plans and guides evolution. Atheistic evolution assumes that God does not exist and therefore cannot be responsible for evolution – evolution occurs without any supernatural guidance. Both, however, explain evolution *naturalistically*.

It appears that the attraction of theistic evolution is that it negates the dilemma of the improbability of evolution. This improbability has been likened by Sir Fred Hoyle to a tornado sweeping through a junkyard and assembling a fully functional aeroplane by chance. As we've established, if an intelligence is behind evolution, the processes involved in evolution are not random. However, this theistic evolution would still not be considered supernatural, as the processes involved in evolution are still explainable through the known laws of nature. Similarly, a deterministic belief system assumes that *all* phenomena are due to an underlying supernatural intelligence, yet phenomena relating to the material world should still be explained through the known laws of nature where possible.

This brings us on to the distinction between the natural and the supernatural. This is not a clear distinction to make. For all intents and purposes, we consider the supernatural to be that which theoretically can never be explained through naturalistic means. Christian doctrine proposes that Jesus Christ was born of virgin through a miraculous conception. If one is to accept the occurrence of such a miraculous conception, one would have to accept this as a supernatural phenomenon. This is because the known laws of nature suggest that the only way a woman can conceive is through the physical introduction of a sperm. Most religions in the world claim that God and God's incarnations on Earth have demonstrated miraculous powers. Jesus Christ reportedly performed various miracles, such as healing the blind, walking on water and turning water into wine: such acts would also need to be considered as supernatural phenomena, as we cannot explain them through the known laws of nature. So creationism is a supernatural (unexplainable) phenomenon, whereas evolution is a non-supernatural phenomenon whether it is guided by God or not.

If God exists, this is clearly a supernatural phenomenon. This is by definition, as God's existence is not defined by the known laws of nature. God would have to have supernatural abilities. Therefore, as opposed to what Pope Francis said, it is only logical that God *would* be a magician, in fact, much more than that. If God can create life from non-life, or if God can create a planet from no planet, then God is much greater than a magician already. To claim that God is not a magician (if God exists) is a paradox. Therefore, creating the various forms of life that we see in existence today through supernatural means seems unlikely to be out of God's capabilities. There would be no need for God to rely on the process of evolution, which is a tedious and cumbersome process, to bring about all species (if that is what God intended from the beginning). So if you accept the presence of God, you should accept that evolution is not *necessary* for the creation of species – the origin of a species can, in theory, be brought about by supernatural processes. The question then arises: why *might* God rely on evolution to produce the various species?

The only obvious reason why God would use evolution as a means to create species, would appear to be deliberate misdirection rather than necessity or limitation. Perhaps God is trying to deliberately mislead people into atheism. Perhaps God is hiding. As it is not possible for us to know the motives and intentions of such an intelligence, this idea should not be considered inconceivable. However, it does seem a little extreme. And God could just give the *illusion* of evolution without *actually* using evolution if the primary motive is to hide. So really, there is no reason to believe in evolution over the illusion of evolution.

Some theistic evolutionists claim that God is confined and restricted by the laws of nature, and can only operate within this framework. Consequently, they do not believe in supernatural phenomena in the material world. They argue that there are no supernatural phenomena, and all phenomena are explainable through the known laws of nature. Miraculous conception and resurrection simply didn't happen. Now, the problem with this position is that the existence of God automatically suggests the presence of supernatural forces that defy the known laws of nature. So it is paradoxical for a theistic evolutionist to insist that all phenomena, apart from God, must be explained through naturalistic means.

The question does arise: if there are supernatural events occurring in the world, why are they not evident? Many atheists argue that they would accept the presence of God *if* God could present them with a supernatural phenomenon. It is further argued that the lack of supernatural phenomena in the material world suggests that there are no such occurrences. This is a reasonable argument for atheism, but, for reasons mentioned above, it is not an argument for theistic evolution.

Atheistic evolutionists deny any supernatural processes being present and therefore have a consistent position of accepting inert nature as the cause of all phenomena. Theistic anti-evolutionists also adopt a consistent position of accepting that if God exists, supernatural processes are going to be part of the phenomena that occur on Planet Earth. But theistic evolutionists adopt a somewhat inconsistent position, because, on the one hand, supernatural processes are accepted for the creation and presence of God, yet, on the other hand, they are excluded for explaining the biodiversity of life. Of course, however, theistic evolution is an acceptable position if the evidence strongly supports evolutionary theory. If not, as our case so far suggests, then there is no reason why a theist should accept evolutionary theory as the mechanism for biodiversity on Earth.

The rise in popularity of theistic evolution could in part be due to the belief that this ideology incorporates the best of both worlds. Acceptance of evolutionary theory is generally considered the intelligent position and is on the side of science. So by adopting a position of theistic evolution, people are able to hedge their bets and adopt a form of Pascal's Wager at the same time.* However, as we have shown, theistic evolution is not an intelligible or rational position to hold.

---

* Pascal's wager is the position of accepting a particular religion for fear of punishment if it is true, as one stands to lose more by rejecting the religion and it turning out to be true than by accepting the religion and it turning out to be untrue. The argument is named after Blaise Pascal (a 17th century French philosopher and mathematician) who first proposed it.

If God caused evolution, what caused God?

Another conundrum that arises from supposing a coexistence of God and evolution is how to explain the cause of God. We briefly alluded to this point in Chapter 3. A paradox arises because evolution is all about complexity arising from simplicity through a gradual evolutionary process. So to suppose that God, which is more complex than anything else in the universe, existed before this process of evolution started, is somewhat contradictory. To say that life forms can only come about through a gradual evolution of increasing complexity but have the most complex life-entity at the start, is illogical.

By definition, this God or supernatural intelligence is an entity of life and consciousness, and must be the most complex presence in the universe. God may or may not have a cause. We do not have the ability to establish this. The only thing that we do know with a degree of certainty is that evolution is *not* the cause of God. Evolution cannot explain God's existence. Therefore, a theistic evolutionist, who explains the origin of all species on Earth through evolutionary theory, is required to accept that the most complex life-entity in the universe arose through means other than evolution.

If God can be brought about through means other than evolution, it suffices to say that any life form could theoretically be brought about through means other than evolution. God, or the cause of God, should be able to bring about life in any manner. God or that cause does not have to fiddle around with DNA mutations and take 250,000 generations to make an eye from a flat retina! If this cause can create God, or if God has arisen without a cause, surely an eye could be made in an instant. Granted, this reasoning does not disprove evolutionary theory. But considering evolutionary theory can explain all life on Earth bar God and the original common ancestor, God does appear to be a significant problem for the theory. (Note that the original common ancestor does not pose the same problem: we will expound on this in Chapter 8).

Remember however, these dilemmas arise due to the supposition of a *coexistence* of God and evolution. If you take God out of the equation, these problems don't arise. Atheistic evolution doesn't have such problems. So why people accept both God and evolution is turning out to be as much a mystery as the mystery of life itself!

Contradictions between evolution and religion

If we take the Christian God, it suffices to say that this God has extraordinary abilities and powers. This God reportedly incarnated a man, Jesus Christ, into the world through a miraculous conception in a virgin, thus escaping the whole process of evolution. Of course, this defies evolutionary theory – the 23 chromosomes and genetic material that should have come from a sperm were created out of nothing.* If the Pope is to accept miraculous conception, it suffices to say that he would have to accept that God can create an organism outside of evolution. Following on from this, logic would dictate that such a God *could* create any animal out of nothing and would not have to rely on fiddling around with DNA in order to turn one animal into another. So the Christian God does not *need* to rely on evolution for creation of life.

Remember, evolutionary theory is based on the naturalistic philosophy that all life is biologically related. If even just one member of a species arose outside reproduction and through other means, the whole theory collapses – if one member of a species escaped the process of reproduction, it suffices to say that the origin of a species could have as well. If non-naturalistic means are used to explain one organism, they could also be used to explain past organisms and species, thus nullifying evolutionary theory and rendering biological similarity equivocal to the evolutionary theory hypothesis.

Another curious dilemma for theistic evolution has to do with purpose. Religion generally dictates that there is a purpose to human existence. Atheism suggests that there is no purpose. It is clear that in all religious ideology, a clear distinction is made between animals and human beings (Homo sapiens). Religious doctrine is intended for human beings and not for animals. The reason is that animals do not possess the intellectual ability to understand their own existence. In spiritual philosophy, the difference between animals and human beings is the intellect. Animals are thought to possess a body and mind, but lack the additional intellect that human beings possess. This intellect predisposes a human being to religious evaluation and judgement. Evolutionary theory does not make a clear distinction between human beings and animals. Human beings evolved from ape-humans which in turn evolved from more primitive animals. On the

---

* A chromosome is the structure that contains the DNA for any living organism. A human being has 23 pairs of chromosomes making a total of 46 chromosomes. 23 come from its mother's egg and 23 from its father's sperm with the union of these chromosomes occurring at fertilisation.

evolution timeline, there is no clear point at which a human being arises. So it is a strange idea to believe in evolution *and* a religion, as the religion is only accessible to one species (out of millions of species) which developed nonchalantly with no clear origin. Also, life on Earth, according to evolutionary theory, has been developing for 3.8 billion years, yet human beings have only been around for a couple of hundred thousand years. If God exists, why would God take so long to create the one species that can appreciate God? More than that, why wait up until only a few thousand years ago before releasing any religious theology? If God exists, the whole purpose of existence is to do with God, yet God only brings this purpose into play after a few billion years from the creation of the first life form?! A theistic evolutionist, such as Pope Francis, believes that God created the world 4.5 billion years ago, created life 3.8 billion years ago, developed human beings 200,000 years ago, and then only introduced God and the doctrine of salvation and enlightenment a few thousand years ago. Clearly, there is a strange paradox here which makes theistic evolution hard to swallow.

The crucial problem with the hypothetical models of coexistence between God and evolution is that they do not account for the difference between man and animals, and they do not account for the soul and the afterlife. What the human soul actually is, is a matter of contention. For now, let us consider it to be your human individuality which is made up of your mind and driven by consciousness. Now of course, this is not relevant if you take an atheistic view and dismiss God. But any inclusion of God would have to incorporate these ideas, as every religious tradition that has a God at its centre does. For example, the Christian traditions talk about an afterlife of Heaven and Hell. Man is given a code to live by, which determines the afterlife he takes. As far as we can tell, there is no religion that advocates and implements such a code for any other species. The problem then arises; why would this code apply only to human beings? Remember, evolutionary theory dictates that there is a smooth transition of all organisms. It implies that there is no significant difference between man and other animals. Man has simply gradually evolved from his primate ancestors. The transition is so smooth that evolutionary theory dictates that you would not actually be able to identify a single point in time when the change happened, rather like a boy changing into a man. So it would not be logical or compatible with evolutionary theory to state that suddenly when Homo heidelbergensis (supposedly the closest ancestor of human beings) turned into Homo sapiens, a soul emerged, and it is this soul which is subject to religious and spiritual matters.

As evolutionary theory has suggested, it is not possible for a structure or function to just emerge – it has to gradually develop. Many religious people do actually believe that all animals have a soul too, but then another problem arises; why are their souls not subject to the same religious judgment as the human soul? Also, it seems illogical to argue that the soul is developed through a different system (one controlled by God), while the physical body is controlled through the process of evolution. This appears incompatible. There cannot be two separate systems functioning independently of one another, the former directed by God through non-naturalistic means and the latter by either God through inefficient naturalistic means or inert nature through randomness. It is logical to assume that the soul and body are dependent on one another. Through some mechanism the soul is able to express itself through the body. Also, it gets all its experiences through the body. So how can God efficiently control the soul system without control over the body system as well? Many pro-evolutionists accept that explaining consciousness is a big problem for evolutionary theory, and as yet it has no answer to this problem. So the problem of humans having a unique religious code to live by is a problem which theistic evolutionists are unable to give an answer to.

We have shown that it is illogical to accept evolutionary theory *and* maintain a belief in God. That is why evolutionary theory is so powerful. It really isn't compatible with the presence of God. The only plausible explanation for the two coexisting would be for God to be behind every stage of evolution and to have done this in a deliberate effort to conceal himself. Ironically, this possibility seems more likely than the possibility that evolution is driven purely by inert nature. Evolutionary theory actually works better with God behind it. This is because to get these random mutations that cause so much diversity can be likened to the tornado sweeping through a junkyard and accidentally assembling a fully functional aeroplane from the parts therein. It is hard to accept that the tornado has done this by pure chance, whereas, if you are told that God, who is not subject to the known laws of nature, was the cause of this and willed it to happen, then suddenly it becomes a more plausible event. So actually, even though evolution *with* God is an illogical view to adopt, it seems more probable than evolution *without* God. But, as we will see in the next chapter, there is an understandable attraction to atheistic evolution; there is no understandable attraction to theistic evolution.

Chapter 8 – Explaining its success

We have briefly touched on the question of how evolutionary theory has gained such a high level of support from experts as well as non-experts, but let's try and understand why this might be. When the theory was first proposed by Charles Darwin, it caused a huge uproar due to it demoting the role of God in creation. Most people seemed to understand that evolution and God were just not compatible. Even Charles Darwin apologised for his so-called discovery, as he knew it would have huge negative implications for religion. It is quite extraordinary how many people have managed to adopt a compromised position between the two, as we established in the previous chapter. The effect that evolutionary theory has had on religion appears to be the greatest impact that it has had in the world. There is probably no scientific theory that has caused more controversy since time began. And it would seem that evolutionary theory does not directly offer any benefits to society: it is not used to produce new species, it is not used in the conservation of species, modern medicine doesn't rely on it, and it doesn't give us a better understanding of how animals function and behave. So its anti-religion function appears to be its greatest use. Otherwise, its only use appears to be academia. As stated by Louise Bounoure, the former Director of Research at the French National Centre for Scientific Research: *"Evolution is a fairy tale for grown-ups. This theory has helped nothing in the progress of science. It is useless."*

Up to now, we have established the following about evolutionary theory: there is no scientific case for it, there appears to be only a weak non-scientific case for it, it seems highly illogical, there are many inconsistencies with it, there are questions over the validity of the evidence used to promote it, and it would appear to contradict the existence of God. That being said, the question then arises: why do so many people accept it and believe in it? Ludwig von Bertalanffy, who was an Austrian biologist known as one of the founders of General Systems Theory, said, regarding evolutionary theory: *"The fact that a theory so vague, so insufficiently verifiable, and so far from the criteria otherwise applied in 'hard' science has become a dogma can only be explained on sociological grounds."* It seems that these sociological causes are multi-faceted: in order to understand these, we need to firstly establish and categorise the different positions that one can hold regarding both evolution and God, as they appear to be significantly related – see Figure 20.

Belief in evolution

	Evolution (*a*)	No Evolution (*b*)	Unsure (*x*)
God (1)	1*a*	1*b*	1*x*
Atheist (2)	2*a*	2*b*	2*x*
Agnostic (9)	9*a*	9*b*	9*x*

Belief in God

Figure 20. The various positions that one can hold regarding belief in evolution and/or God.

Technically speaking, any one of the derivatives shown in Figure 20 is possible, all the way from the 1*a* to the 9*x* position. It is a point of curiosity as to why almost every atheist you encounter has a strong belief in evolutionary theory, resulting in hardly any people belonging to the 2*b* or 2*x* categories which are highlighted in Figure 21. It seems that every other category of person is easily found in the world. We will attempt to explain this phenomenon in addition to examining the causes that lead people to accept evolutionary theory.

Belief in evolution

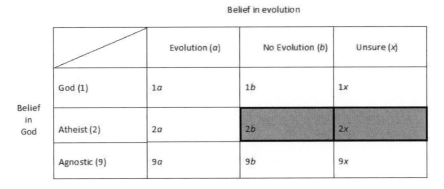

	Evolution (*a*)	No Evolution (*b*)	Unsure (*x*)
God (1)	1*a*	1*b*	1*x*
Atheist (2)	2*a*	2*b*	2*x*
Agnostic (9)	9*a*	9*b*	9*x*

Belief in God

Figure 21. The rarely seen positions (highlighted) that one *could* theoretically hold regarding belief in evolution and/or God.

It should be noted that we are referring to people who have given these issues some thought, and consequently have made active decisions to either accept, reject or remain agnostic/unsure on them. Those who are unaware of evolutionary theory, and those who have not considered the presence of God, are not categorised or considered for the arguments that are about to be made.

A weapon for atheism

Before the advent of evolutionary theory, atheism was unable to answer one of the most important questions in life: how did we get here? This would always create doubt in the minds of agnostics when considering atheism. Suddenly, with the appearance of evolutionary theory, atheism could finally answer this question. But, as we mentioned in the last chapter, theistic evolution actually seems a more plausible proposition than atheistic evolution (even though both seem highly illogical for the reasons mentioned so far). This is because to get DNA mutations, which result in perfect structural and functional improvements, by pure chance just seems unfathomable. If you add an intelligence behind them, it makes the whole thing a bit more plausible. But either way the theory is still not significantly plausible, in the same way that the difference between a probability of 2% and 4% is significant, but 4% is still a very low probability. Just because one option is *more* likely, it does not make it *actually* likely. So it could be said that evolutionary theory cannot live with God, and it cannot live without God either!

So if evolutionary theory with God is more likely than evolutionary theory without God, why is evolutionary theory a powerful tool for contradicting God? Why does it promote atheism if it actually requires God more than it doesn't? This can be explained logically...

Prior to evolutionary theory, God was the most logical explanation for biodiversity, thus biodiversity affirmed God's existence. Then along comes evolutionary theory. The theory seems unscientific and illogical, so people who already believe in God refuse to accept it. There is no reason for them to adopt a position of accepting both evolutionary theory and God to explain biodiversity, as they already have an explanation for this – creationism. So the position of evolution and God coexisting is not going to be supported by people with a bias towards God. Neither will it be supported by people with a bias or predisposition towards atheism (obviously, as it supposes God's existence). But these people with a bias or predisposition towards atheism will be drawn to the even lower chance that evolution driven by inert nature is the cause of biodiversity, thus nullifying the need for God. For atheism, this weak weapon of evolutionary theory without God is better than no weapon at all. So atheism takes this position under its wing and uses it to promote itself. The new theory of evolution-driven-by-inert-nature becomes an effective weapon for atheism. It is evolutionary theory sponsored by atheism. The evidence and logic for the theory is secondary.

The strong drive to promote atheism has resulted in evolutionary theory being pushed into the limelight against all the odds and against reason too it would seem. Many atheists have seen evolutionary theory as the ideal opportunity to promote their true underlying cause of atheism, and they have used it as such. In fact, almost all atheists seem to do this, which is why you struggle to find atheists who reject evolution (the positions 2*b* and 2*x* in Figure 21). This is a point of interest, as it is grossly unexpected for this to be the case when we have pointed out that evolutionary theory with God seems more likely than evolutionary theory without God (from a logical point of view). This suggests that there are underlying processes involved that lead atheists into the acceptance and belief of evolutionary theory.

Atheists appear to be drawn to evolutionary theory for reasons of self-affirmation. They feel that evolutionary theory supports their atheism and justifies their outlook. But what they don't realise is that anti-evolutionism and atheism can coexist. Remember, evolutionary theory is an advent of the last 160 years or so, whereas atheism has been present for many centuries, dating back at least to Socrates around 400 BCE. Many great thinkers and philosophers through the ages have adopted an atheistic position without knowledge of evolutionary theory. Like we have said, evolutionary theory does not actually disprove the existence of God; it only makes belief in God seem illogical. So evolutionary theory is not essential for an atheistic outlook on life. There are other models whereby atheism and no-evolution can coexist. The position of atheism can actually be logically deduced to some extent, which is why historically it has been a position held by various intellectuals. However, as we have seen, evolutionary theory is not a position which can be logically deduced, and it is not an intelligible doctrine to adopt. Essentially, atheists are fighting with an ineffective weapon.

But evolutionary theory does appear to have given atheism a real push at a time when the Church was ruling like a dictator in the Western world. It is not inconceivable that there would have been many people wanting evolutionary theory to be true for purposes of redistributing the balance between state and Church as well as promoting atheism. You could even theorise that many of the initial promoters of evolutionary theory were not necessarily pro-atheism but instead anti-Church.

It is fair to say that atheists cannot be blamed for their bias against religion. When we think of all the atrocities that have been committed in the world in the name of religion, and also directly by religion, it not surprising that there is a huge bias against it. Many people are disgusted by the behaviour of the Church, so they develop a bias against it. They associate the current Church with the actions of the Church of the past: the burning of witches, the condemnation of free thinkers, the financial exploitation of people and the wars fought in the name of religion are all examples of this behaviour. Naturally, an animosity develops towards the Church and everything it represents. This anger has the power to blind a person and delude them. Subsequently, they start believing things which go against good reasoning and intellect.

Atheism explains why evolutionary theory was accepted and promoted so strongly. However, it is important to note that we are not necessarily saying that the initial promoters of evolutionary theory did not believe in it. They may have or may not have. We don't know whether they were biased towards it or brainwashed into believing it or actually promoted the theory with *mens rea*, knowing full well that the case for it was very weak. Here we are just giving a probable cause for why, against all the odds, the theory has blown up into the huge success it is today.

The biased mind

We have touched on the concept of a biased mind in previous chapters, but now we will expand on this, as this seems to be the main cause of the growing popularity in evolutionary theory. Separating out brainwashing from conditioning due to an underlying bias is difficult. The brainwashing process refers more to how a person is convinced (most likely from a young age) that a doctrine is true. They may or may not have an underlying bias. But what they do have is psychological vulnerability to new teachings. The same way a child can be groomed from a young age into believing a religious dogma, so too a young mind can be convinced of any scientific theory. If the theory is taught as fact by science teachers in school, and then promoted heavily by the scientific community, and then supported by the wider society, then it is natural for one to get drawn into the doctrine as well. And this is what is happening in the Western world. Evolutionary theory utilises strong promotion and hard-selling. This is also the method that most religions adopt. It is a form of brainwashing leading to indoctrination. Religions make many irrational claims, yet many people believe them because of the hard-sell that they have been victim to.

For many people, the acceptance and promotion of evolutionary theory may not be due to an intentional ploy to promote other causes, nor due to brainwashing, but instead due to an underlying bias. Bias refers to a person's preconceived ideas and beliefs about the world. Most intellectually curious people have asked themselves the fundamental questions of life and considered the presence of God. Many people have a strong inclination one way or the other on the presence of God in the universe, and it seems that this is likely to play a crucial role in determining their position on evolutionary theory. This is because people have a tendency to see things the way they want to see them, in a way which fits in with their already existing views and beliefs.

A person with an unshakable belief in the six-day creation story, as told in Genesis, is unlikely to be able to evaluate the case for evolution with an open and rational mind. In much the same way, a staunch atheist is unlikely to be able to evaluate the case against evolution with an open and rational mind. This is because the staunch atheist so badly wants evolution to be true to substantiate and affirm his already existing values, beliefs and ideals in life, so he fails to acknowledge anything which would contradict these. He only sees what he wants to see. It is wishful thinking. It is not a case of intentionally supporting a fallacious theory. It is due to him being subconsciously drawn to this position based on an underlying atheistic bias.

This is the power that bias has. It can blind a person and cause them to make decisions which aren't fitting of their own intellect. This is why a jury member is always advised to remove himself of any bias which may impact on his ability to make a fair decision in a trial. If a jury member has a strong belief in a particular cause, his decisions are likely to be biased towards that cause which, if relevant to the trial at hand, will impact on his verdict. In fact, many trial lawyers will try and capitalise on this fact by ensuring jury members *are* biased towards their cause: the classic example of this is race bias, whereby it is thought that a jury member of the same race is likely to be more sympathetic (or biased) to a suspect of the same race in a relevant crime. Even though this is a matter of race and not of ideology, it is the psychological process of identifying with a particular position, and then making decisions based on that position, which makes this a form of bias in the same way as the atheistic bias leading one to favour evolutionary theory.

So people with a strong inclination towards atheism will accept the theory of evolution with a lower threshold of evidence than they would usually require for other theories where they have no bias or incentive. They accept the theory and *then* look for the evidence to support their acceptance rather than analysing the evidence and drawing a conclusion from it. This is known as putting the cart before the horse. This can be understood with the previously used hypothetical scenario of being told a monkey had written some great literature by accident. Presumably, if an intelligent person was told this, they would not just blindly accept it – they would ask further questions about how this was achieved in order to validate the authenticity of the claim, even if it had come from a trusted source. This is because most people would not have a motive or incentive to put the cart before the horse in this case. They derive no benefit from the statement being true or not, unlike with evolutionary theory where individual bias seems likely to play a huge part. The fact that no-one had proposed evolutionary theory before Charles Darwin, which was relatively recently when you consider all of the major scientific accomplishments prior to this, is not a surprise, and it is not remarkable either. There was no way evolutionary theory could be considered logical from examining a few finch beaks and the other observations that he made. This is quite beautifully demonstrated in the following quote from the Russian scholar Immanuel Velikovsky (1895 – 1979):

> *Most controversial is the evolutionary question. I have done a great deal of work on Darwin and can say with some assurance that Darwin did not derive his theory from nature but rather superimposed a certain philosophical viewpoint on nature and then spent twenty years trying to gather the facts to make it stick.*

A friend of mine once, when discussing evolutionary theory, said he knew it was true because he could see it all around him. He said he looked at all the life forms around him and could see the physical connection between them and the theory just made sense. He was a staunch atheist. Despite being a very intelligent man, this was a classic example of bias, and how bias can overpower one's reason. It is simply not possible to just look at nature and deduce evolutionary theory, because the evidence for it is just not there. Sure, lots of species look alike, but there would be no reason to conclude that they all came from an original common ancestor. For one to conclude so would suggest that they are seeing what they want to based on their underlying bias. In the case of a staunch atheist, it is most likely to be an underlying bias against God and religion, meaning that they are psychologically drawn to any position that negates these. However, even though there is a scarcity of atheists who reject evolution, there are many theists and agnostics who accept evolution (theistic evolutionists). Now, this position contradicts the idea of an underlying atheistic bias driving belief in evolutionary theory. We have established a possible explanation for this being non-atheistic indoctrination through brainwashing and education, although it is apparent that other forces are in play too, which we need to consider...

The underlying bias influencing one's opinion on evolutionary theory is not limited to religious affiliation or atheism. There are many types of *cognitive* bias. There is a subtle difference here, in that these biases may not be as overtly motivated as the atheistic bias we have just touched on. A naturalistic (or materialistic) bias is a bias towards explaining all phenomena through naturalistic means, and therefore eliminating the possibility of supernatural causes. Its tendency is to suggest that the best naturalistic explanation for a phenomenon is the best explanation for a phenomenon, regardless of the evidence.

Many scientists have a bias towards science and the scientific process – they have a tendency to see things that appeal to their scientific perspective. It is not that they are deliberately choosing to avoid the case *against* evolution; instead it is that they are drawn to the case *for* evolution, as this is promoted as the side of science. Also, an evolutionary biologist, who bases his career on evolution, needs it to be true, so he is more likely to see the evidence for evolution better than he sees the evidence against evolution. It is a simple case of self-preservation, not necessarily intentional. He *needs* evolution to be true in order to sustain his position in society, and this dictates *how* he interprets the evidence for evolutionary theory.

The scientific consensus

There is overwhelming support from the scientific community for evolutionary theory. The majority of scientists agree with it. The majority of biologists agree with it. The majority of evolutionary biologists agree with it, and these are considered to be the people who have the expertise to make an informed decision on the subject. So the majority of the "experts" in the field of evolutionary theory have confirmed it to be true. Now, we have already highlighted that one of the problems with this is the bias that these people will have towards evolutionary theory based on their position as an evolutionary biologist. It would be like saying that the vast majority of religious people believe in God. It is a meaningless statement – that is what we expect. But if we take the larger scientific community as a whole, they will argue that they have no underlying bias towards evolutionary theory. Let's presume that they are correct: does this make the scientific consensus of evolutionary theory significant? The answer is no. Why?

Because, in the history of science, the majority consensus has often been wrong. In fact, many of the great scientific discoveries have been made by one or a few individuals going against the consensus to great disapproval. This is known as the Galileo Effect. It is aptly named after the Italian academic Galileo Galilei who disagreed with the mainstream scientific view that the Earth was the centre of the universe. He formulated his own theory that the Earth circled the sun. Initially his theory was dismissed by the mainstream scientific community, and it took a while before it became accepted as correct. You could even apply this phenomenon to Charles Darwin with evolutionary theory, whereby the theory was heavily rejected initially and took some time before becoming widely accepted. The point is that the majority do not determine what is right and what is wrong. Majority is not synonymous with truth. For people to simply accept evolutionary theory because the majority of scientists say it is right, is a form of naivety and intellectual laziness. This can be appreciated by understanding the processes by which these scientific majorities are established.

The majority of scientists have not directly investigated evolution any more than the average person. They have not gone out and dug fossils, attempted to induce mutations in the DNA of organisms, or examined biochemical and anatomical similarities between the various species. This is because, for the majority of scientists, evolutionary biology is not their speciality. Based on this, their opinion on evolutionary theory is no more valid than a layperson's. It is a second-hand opinion, formulated from hearsay, just like a layperson's. They don't hold an intellectual superiority which makes their opinion more valid than anyone else's.

What about those scientists who have directly studied it? Fair enough, they *might* be in a better position to make an informed decision regarding evolutionary theory. However, as we have shown, they have simply not made a strong case for it. It can only be bias which prevents them from acknowledging this. Also, we established in Chapter 1 that evolutionary theory is not a scientific question: it is not a scientific theory, as it is not subject to the normal scientific processes and study that would make it such. So in actual fact, these so-called scientific experts are probably in no better a position to conclude on evolutionary theory than you are.

Another thing worth looking at is how these scientific majorities are formed. When a scientific theory is proposed, it is put to the scientific community. This community is like a quiet audience that sits and listens to the speaker proposing his new ideology. As you can imagine, it's not just the actual scientific validity of the theory that counts, but multiple factors will go into the process of the theory being accepted or not: promotion, marketing, selling, bias, secondary gain, to name a few. The theory may then be accepted by the scientific community, regardless of its viability. Then a process of indoctrination can begin. As mentioned previously, these are very similar processes to how any new ideology is brought into the mainstream, including religious and political ideologies. Once the theory is set in the scientific community, then the "bandwagon effect" can take place. This is the phenomenon whereby people accept an ideology based on its popularity and "jump on the bandwagon" (hence the expression). The ideology then grows, as people opt to side with the consensus rather than analyse the case themselves. So this is how an overwhelming acceptance of an unproven but popular idea can develop.

For most people, fitting in is much more attractive than being different. If you're a scientist, you want to be part of the scientific community. In order to do this, you have to accept what science tells you. Once again, it is not necessarily a case of deliberately accepting a fallacious theory for the purpose of self-preservation. It seems more likely to be another case of bias, whereby the desire to fit in and be part of this prestigious scientific community overrides one's own intelligence and reason so that one is unable to see the truth. This is known as "herd mentality", whereby the scientific herd just blindly accepts the irrational theory and then goes with the flow. Then a "groupthink" situation arises, whereby the mainstream of science has adopted this irrational view and they have to see it through. Anyone who tries to challenge it is cast outside the group. People outside the group are considered outcasts and heretics and their opinions are demonised and considered unworthy. If you don't go with the party line, you can't be a member of the party. You are demoted to the backbenches.* People inside the group are encouraged to continue with the ideology and not question it or bring it into disrepute, which results in a loss of creativity and a loss of independent thinking. This process was described by George Kocan, a biologist and science writer, in his article *Evolution Isn't Faith But Theory*:

> "*Unfortunately many scientists and non-scientists have made Evolution into a religion, something to be defended against infidels. In my experience, many students of biology – professors and textbook writers included – have been so carried away with the arguments for Evolution that they neglect to question it. They preach it … College students, having gone through such a closed system of education, themselves become teachers, entering high schools to continue the process, using textbooks written by former classmates or professors. High standards of scholarship and teaching break down. Propaganda and the pursuit of power replace the pursuit of knowledge. Education becomes a fraud.*"

These processes might sound familiar to you. And that is because these are the same mechanisms that religious institutions in the world have adopted to maintain the status quo. The medieval Church would declare any free-thinker who went against the Church ideology as a heretic, and they would burn them at the stake. This is actually the reason why the first European settlers of the United States of America migrated there – it was to gain religious freedom. They wanted to be able to practise their religion and spirituality in a way which they saw fit.

---

* In UK politics a backbencher is a member of parliament who is not given a role in the cabinet or shadow cabinet, and they have to sit quietly on the back–benches without having an influential role in the government/shadow government.

Many scientists say that they have no bias and are willing to change their opinions with the evidence. But if this was the case, they would not subscribe to evolutionary theory, as we have shown that the case for it is grossly lacking. The way scientists and the public accept evolutionary theory so readily is no different to the way in which the masses so readily believed whatever they were told by the Church a few centuries ago – they would accept religious doctrine as fact because the Church told them to. It was only a few who used intelligence to question, analyse and evaluate the authenticity of the Church's claims and consequently conclude that they were false. Scientists will claim that the difference between what they do and what the Church did is that the Church did not use evidence to draw their conclusions from. However, this is incorrect. The New Testament is founded on testimonial accounts and this would be considered as evidence in a court of law. In fact, the testimonial evidence for some of the events of the New Testament seems to be stronger than any of the evidence that we have for evolutionary theory. Think of it like this: imagine there were creatures who were millions of years old and could communicate with us; if they told us that they had witnessed evolution in action, this would actually be stronger evidence for evolutionary theory than anything we have at present!

The power of bias

Earlier, we touched on the power that bias can have. It has the ability to prevent people from seeing the truth, even when that truth is right in front of them and glaringly obvious. There really is no better example than evolutionary theory for demonstrating this. The theory is *grossly* lacking in evidence, it seems *so* illogical, and it has *many* inconsistencies. Yet it is believed by so many intelligent people. It is like they have a mental block which prevents them from seeing what is right in front of them.

Bias is obviously present in all walks of life. An NBC News poll of the infamous O.J. Simpson murder trial of 1995 revealed that 77% of white people thought O.J. Simpson was guilty, whereas 72% of black people thought he was innocent!* These two groups had access to the same evidence. If we presume that they had a similar overall level of

---

* O.J. Simpson was a famous black African-American sportsman who was accused of murdering his white-American wife Nicole Brown Simpson and her friend Ron Goldman in 1994.

intelligence, the only logical conclusion to draw is that the vast difference in judgement was due to underlying bias.

Politics, religion and sport are classic examples of bias. Take opposing coaches watching their sides during a football match. During the match, an incident will often be interpreted in opposing ways by the two coaches. What appears to one coach to be a foul *on* a player is seen by the opposing coach as simulation (feigning injury) *by* the player. But, of course, they are witnessing the same event. It's all a matter of interpretation. The coaches are more likely to see the event in a way which they are expected to see the event by their peers and in a way which favours their own outlook and desired outcome. Most people in the world are born into one of the major religions. And most people in the world adopt the religion that they are born into as the religion they choose to follow and believe in. It forms part of their self-identity. This results in different people of equal intelligence living, believing and following completely different religious doctrines. Equally intelligent people of different religions argue the case for their own religion because of a bias towards it. They genuinely believe their way is correct. It is not that they are trying to deliberately mislead or deceive. They are just blind to arguments that go against their religious ideology. This is the same way political and sociological ideologies work. Contentious and hotly-debated issues in the world, such as euthanasia, capital punishment and socialism-versus-capitalism, can be argued well from either side of the debate. Strong proponents of such views interpret new observations and statistics in a way which supports their already existing ideologies. The same thing appears to happen with evolutionary theory. New pieces of information or "evidence" emerge in the field of evolution which don't really offer any meaningful insight or support towards the theory, yet supporters of the theory jump on them and start interpreting them in a way which suits their outlook and desired outcome.

Evolutionists may claim that they follow the science and evidence, and are willing to change their minds should a compelling case be brought forward to suggest that evolution is untrue. But for many strong advocates of evolutionary theory, the theory is an ideology or a doctrine which they hold firmly, the same as any other ideology. So they interpret observations and arguments in a way which fits in with their ideology, and they are resistive to arguments against their ideology.

The best example of this bias in pro-evolutionists is the circular reasoning demonstrated in estimates of previous species numbers. We mentioned in Chapter 2 how evolutionary theory claims that there have been 5 billion species in existence. Then the theory is obliged to follow this up with the claim that 99.9% of all species have gone extinct, as otherwise the bulk of these 5 billion species cannot be accounted for. But remember, these claims are founded on the principle that evolutionary theory is correct, and there is no *actual* evidence to suggest that 5 billion species have ever existed. It is not hard to see the circularity in this reasoning. It is not nearly as complex or intellectually challenging as trying to understand advanced mathematic theorems or nuclear physics. Yet many advanced mathematicians and nuclear physicists just can't seem to grasp it! Many pro-evolutionists have exceptional academic qualifications and can understand concepts and theories that most people find too hard to comprehend. But they cannot see this simple error with evolutionary theory. The only reason for this can be bias. It just goes to show how powerful this bias can be, and how it has the ability to completely delude a person and subjugate their intelligence.

Typically, an author will read his book several times in an attempt to eradicate all mistakes contained within it. Eventually, he will be satisfied that the book reads fine and there are no typos or errors in punctuation or grammar. However, errors undoubtedly would have made their way into his book. And many of these would ordinarily be picked up by the author if he was reading them with a fresh mind for the first time, or if he was reading them in someone else's work. The reason that he misses his own errors is because after a while, the mind starts interpreting its perceptual experiences in a way which fits in with the desired and expected outcome. He reads what he is *expecting* to read rather than what he is *actually* reading. His mind automatically corrects errors and fills in gaps. This is the inevitable process of mental conditioning. A point comes where the mind is no longer able to see errors nor evaluate accurately. An example of this is known as the McGurk Effect, which is a phenomenon whereby the mind interprets perceptions incorrectly based on previous conditioning. Psychological experiments have shown that people cannot identify the correct substance of a drink when the colour of that drink is changed. If strawberry juice is changed in colour to gold (resembling apple juice), people report tasting apple juice when drinking the golden strawberry juice. They *think* that they are drinking apple juice, but the reality is that they are not. There is a misinterpretation of the perceptual experience due to an underlying bias caused by mental conditioning. So the more conditioned you become, the more incapable you are of fairly and indiscriminately evaluating evidence which contradicts what you want and expect to be correct. This is what happens with evolutionary theory. Pro-evolutionists see evolution when it is not there. Like tasting apples when there are only strawberries. Because they have so strongly convinced themselves that evolution is true, they are likely to be completely blind and resistant to all the arguments that have been made in this book.

It is one thing accepting bias in sport, politics or even in religion, but it should not exist in science. In fact, it is not even compatible with science. To say that a scientific theory is biased is an oxymoron. Science is science. It cannot be biased. A scientist should not *want* a theory to be true. They should only be concerned with what *is* true. But evolutionary theory clearly has been founded on a high degree of bias. Although, it's not too late for the theory to be retrospectively re-evaluated from a neutral, unbiased position, which is what we are attempting here. This is much in the same way that a football match can be fairly evaluated from a position of neutrality after the match is over: a neutral spectator is much more likely to give a fair evaluation of a match than a biased fan is.

Even a book is more likely to get a good review if the author is already a "best-selling author". Even though independent reviewers are supposed to be impartial, they cannot help but be influenced by who has written the material, and therefore preconceived ideas emerge before they have even opened the book. It is natural, and cannot be helped. But these preconceived ideas are likely to influence the review to some degree. Similarly, previous reviews are likely to influence future reviews. This book is more likely to receive a bad review from a pro-evolutionist than it is from an anti-evolutionist. That's just the way bias works.

Generally speaking, people who read books based on *who* has written them are reading what they want to read, what they already agree with, and what fits in with their already established outlook on life. Where an individual has a bias towards a particular person, such as an eminent scientist, that bias, rather than reason or intellection, dictates what the person believes. Whatever this eminent scientist declares is welcomed and adopted by the person with no resistance. This is the process of blindly accepting rather than inquisitively determining. And it is this process that would seem to have played a huge role in the global epidemic of evolutionary theory.

Has evolutionary theory become more believable with age?

It is worth noting that Charles Darwin had no knowledge of DNA similarities between species when he first proposed evolutionary theory. This evidence has emerged since, and proponents of evolutionary theory claim that this is resounding evidence to support Darwin's initial hypothesis. However, is it actually? If you imagine that the theory had never been proposed, is it actually likely that people would look at all the information today and draw a conclusion of evolutionary theory? We would argue that this is not the case.

What appears to have happened is that a vague hypothesis of evolutionary theory gets proposed, and then with this in mind, patterns supporting the theory are observed. But in reality such patterns would not on their own lead one to the conclusion of evolutionary theory. The reason is that it's simply not logical to make this deduction. This is another example of putting the cart before the horse. For example, DNA similarity between species is only that. Is it really that surprising that there is a positive correlation between DNA similarity (to a large extent) and similarity in appearance, behaviour and functioning? The DNA similarity between a chimpanzee and a gorilla is closer than that between a chimpanzee and a woodpecker. One would logically expect this without evolutionary theory, as the chimpanzee does look more like a gorilla than it does a woodpecker. This does not prove, or even suggest, relatedness. To conclude that it does is actually a form of bias called hindsight bias. This is because the outcome of evolution is known, so one looks to reconstruct the processes of how this outcome was achieved with the outcome in mind and set as the target. The evidence is then interpreted in a way which fits in with the outcome, and is then used as support for the theory. And it appears that this is what has happened with all the evidence used to support evolutionary theory.

It is like someone who believes in aliens stating that the case for aliens has been made much stronger by the presence of crop circles. Without a concept of aliens, it would be unnatural to conclude that aliens exist on viewing the circles. A previous concept of aliens is required in order to link crop circles *to* aliens. Similarly, a previous concept of evolutionary theory is required in order to conclude that DNA similarity represents evolution. Without evolutionary theory, DNA similarity could be explained through other means.

Faith in evolution

The majority of people have not directly studied evolution themselves. They are told that it is true by teachers in school. Then the teaching is reinforced by eminent scientists who promote the theory themselves. Of course, an element of trust is required with any form of teaching – you have to trust that what you are being taught is true. It suffices to say that the majority of people adopt this trust and accept what they are told without much resistance. That is human nature. This also holds true for many who teach and promote the theory themselves. It is only a few who may question authority (in this case the scientific authority) and start to pick out flaws with the teaching which is being imposed upon them.

Henry Lipson, a British physicist, said: "*In fact, evolution became in a sense a scientific religion; almost all scientists accepted it and many are prepared to 'bend' their observations to fit in with it.*" This highlights the problem with evolutionary theory: it is not a science; it is a religion. And this religion is promoted by the church of science. The layperson has no choice but to accept it, otherwise he risks being branded a fool. But, like many religious people, it is not a case of him *choosing* to accept it as such. He has put his faith in the church of science and blindly accepts whatever they tell him is true. And, unlike most other scientific theories, even if he wanted to, he could not make his own determination because there is no way of testing, reproducing or observing the theory in action. There is no way for him to falsify it either – he can't suddenly go digging around looking for that rabbit in the Pre-Cambrian! So he blindly accepts what he is being told by the church of science. This is what is known as faith. In fact, all scientists who accept the theory demonstrate a faith in it. It is a faith, no different to religious faith, because it is a belief based on a strong conviction rather than actual proof. Faith relies on assumptions rather than evidence. Just because they dress the theory up in fancy scientific terminology, it is still a faith. As the expression goes; a hog in a silk waistcoat is still a hog.

We can demonstrate this using an idea mentioned earlier. A hypothesis of devolution whereby a man has devolved into a bacterium seems a hard one to sell. But it would account for the biochemical-evidence argument used to support evolutionary theory. It seems, however, that most people would reject this idea on intuition. This is due to indoctrination. The only reason one would reject a theory of devolution but not a theory of evolution, is because of a scientific, naturalistic or atheistic bias. The evidence for devolution and evolution is equal, which is virtually zero for both. The difference is that one is promoted by the institution of science and the other isn't. But to accept something on these grounds alone, is no different to accepting a religious doctrine on the grounds that it is promoted by the religious institution which you have a favour towards (most likely because it is the one you were born into). Evolution may also be favoured over devolution due to an urge to explain all phenomena through naturalistic means, as evolution can be more easily linked to abiogenesis than devolution can (we will explore this idea shortly). This is an example of a faith in naturalism or atheism.

Many people reject evolutionary theory on intuition. It seems reasonable to presume that an adult who has not been exposed to or brought up on evolutionary theory, would find the theory unfathomable. The same way that a pro-evolutionist may scoff at someone who believes in devolution, a person unfamiliar with evolutionary theory may scoff at a pro-evolutionist and find their belief system preposterous. Many knowledgeable atheists, like Richard Dawkins, are astounded by the indoctrination of people with religious ideology based on no solid evidence. But people unfamiliar with evolutionary theory may be equally astounded by the indoctrination of people with evolutionary ideology based on no solid evidence. The only difference is that pro-evolutionists hide behind a shield of "science" which they believe justifies their outlook. But the psychological mechanisms of accepting evolutionary theory or religious doctrine are one and the same.

It is an irony when you think about it. These were the same psychological mechanisms in place which resulted in the religious brainwashing of many people by religious institutions throughout the middle ages. People were told that certain historical events happened, representing certain truths about life. This ends up being the basis for the religious doctrine promoted by that particular religious institution. People put their faith in what they were taught and then blindly accepted it. Now however, the switch has been from religious indoctrination to non-religious indoctrination through the medium of evolutionary theory. Science is the new church. And the funny thing is that some of these pro-evolutionists are as fundamental as the most fundamentally religious people through the ages. This is because their faith in evolution is so important to them. They protect it vehemently. They are insulted when someone disagrees with it or disrespects it. They feel that they are irrefutably right. They feel a compulsion to spread their message believing that they are saving people from ignorance. So as you can see, they are the new religious fanatics of the modern era.

I can demonstrate this with a fitting anecdote. In school, I recall a biology teacher asking the class whether anyone disagreed with evolutionary theory. One boy answered saying that he disagreed with the theory. This was met by the teacher with huge anger, shouting and complete distain. The reason that I recall the incident is because it was such a surprise to me to see how a teacher could be so passionate about a subject matter. It is only now that I understand why this was so. I don't recall a teacher ever responding in a similar manner to any other subject. If a student was to disagree with a maths teacher on a mathematical proof, or a history student disagree with a history teacher on the reasons for certain historical events, or an art student disagree with an art teacher on the quality of the work of a particular artist, you would not expect such a hostile response from the teacher. The difference is that with the biology teacher, evolutionary theory was clearly his faith. So when his faith was challenged, he became irate. Faith tends to be fragile like this. And faith tends to be defended with such passion. The reasons for this are beyond the scope of this book, so we won't go there. But hopefully you can see how the acceptance of evolutionary theory is actually a faith rather than an intellectual determination.

Evolutionary theory as a cause of atheism

You may also hear some atheists say that they are only atheists because of evolutionary theory, which shows that God is unlikely to exist. They claim that they have made a rational decision to become an atheist based on scientific reasoning. This is an important consideration which we need to explore. Now, this may be true, but so far from what we have shown, there is no rational reason for firmly accepting evolutionary theory, as there isn't a strong case for it. This would therefore suggest that for atheists it is their atheism, or predisposition towards atheism, that has resulted in their firm acceptance of evolutionary theory. It could, of course, be seen as a chicken and egg scenario; which came first – the atheism or the evolutionism? In some cases, it may be the case that a misplaced trust in evolutionary theory has resulted in atheism, as other biases mentioned above may have come into play. But it seems unlikely that this would be the case for the majority of atheists: this is supported once again by the fact that we have very few examples of atheists who disagree with evolutionary theory or are unsure about it. If we remove the agnostics and unsure categories from Figures 20 & 21 so that we only include the people who have made up their minds on both issues, we can represent the table as shown in Figure 22.

Belief in Evolution

		Evolution (*a*)	No Evolution (*b*)
	God (1)	1*a* (the theistic evolutionist)	1*b* (the theistic anti-evolutionist)
	Atheist (2)	2*a* (the atheistic evolutionist)	2*b* (the atheistic anti-evolutionist)

Belief In God

Figure 22. The various positions that one can hold regarding belief in evolution and/or God without subjective uncertainty.

Regarding the categories shown in Figure 22, we have a good representation of people belonging to the 1*a*, 1*b* and 2*a* categories. But we don't have a good sample of people belonging to the 2*b* category. According to the 2017 poll numbers from Gallup, 19% of people in the United States of America believe in atheistic evolution; 38% of them believe in theistic evolution; 38% of them believe in God creating man without evolution; and 5% selected the "Other/No opinion" option. Interestingly, the possibility of believing in atheism without evolution was not given as an option: however, it seems reasonable to presume that people holding such a view would have selected the "Other/No opinion" option. The fact that only 5% of people chose this option is suggestive that atheists who reject evolutionary theory, termed as the atheistic anti-evolutionists on Figure 22, are few and far between. (It seems likely that a significant proportion of this 5% group would not actively identify as atheistic anti-evolutionists and instead have no opinion or are agnostic). This obviously implies that there is a strong correlation between atheism and acceptance of evolutionary theory. The atheistic evolutionist is likely to argue that this is because once a theistic bias is removed, one can see that evolutionary theory is correct, and the natural conclusion to draw from evolutionary theory is that there is no God. However, we have established that there is no solid case for evolutionary theory. We have also established that theistic evolutionary theory is more probable than atheistic evolutionary theory, and there are many theistic evolutionists out there. So we would expect to find atheistic anti-evolutionists out there. The fact that they aren't can only lead one to the conclusion that an atheistic bias strongly leads onto the acceptance of evolutionary theory and not vice versa.

The degree of extrapolation

Even if you were concede that certain parts of evolutionary theory are true, such as dinosaurs turning into birds, and land-mammals into whales (which is extremely generous), this still does not get anywhere near the burden of proof for establishing common descent with complete relatedness of *all* organisms. Remember, we have actual proof of only about 0.005% of the reportedly extinct species. To get from that to certainty over common descent requires an extreme degree of extrapolation. Also, studying DNA to show similarity and studying geography to show distribution cannot scientifically, logically or rationally lead anyone to the conclusion that they descended from a single-cell organism. It seems that many pro-evolutionists are interpreting the evidence to show these (questionable) evolutions within some animal groups and then concluding the following:

>   *a.*   Some species have evolved into new species.
>   *b.*   If some species evolved, God is not responsible for all species.
>   *c.*   If God is not responsible for all species, God cannot be responsible for any species.
>   *d.*   If God is not responsible for any species, common descent must be true.

This is a philosophical line of reasoning and certainly not a scientific one. But it would appear to be driven by bias or underlying motives towards evolutionary theory, as one can clearly see that the reasoning is flawed. Firstly, the Intelligent Design position would argue that statement *a* is incorrect, as no species can evolve into another. But, for the sake of argument, let's entertain the idea that they can: still, to get from *b* to *c* requires a huge degree of extrapolation (to get from evolution of *some* animals to evolution of *all* animals). Even to get from *c* to *d* requires a huge degree of extrapolation, as we have shown that common descent is not the *only* possible explanation other than God for explaining the biodiversity of life.

In fact, the mechanism of deduction illustrated above in the sequential example from *b* to *d* is a classic example of atheistic bias: "this animal has a redundant structure, therefore God cannot be responsible for it, therefore common descent is true" or "this part of the animal could have been designed better, therefore God cannot be responsible for it, therefore common descent is true." This is because there is a hidden caveat in the final statement of "common descent must be true": God does not exist. This is the hidden doctrine of anyone who concludes that common descent to be true on the grounds that God cannot be responsible for an aspect of nature. It is an atheistic bias because God's existence cannot be disproved by observations of nature.

Interestingly, the same mechanism of illogical deduction is used for many of the non-evolution arguments for atheism and evolutionary theory. For example, "there is suffering in the world, therefore God does not exist, therefore common descent is true". Or "God does not appear in front of me and perform miracles, therefore God does not exist, therefore common descent is true". Or "my ten-year old daughter died from fever, therefore God does not exist, therefore common descent is true".* This is the false dichotomy problem. People think that it's either God or evolution. But you simply cannot scientifically or logically extrapolate common descent from any of the evidence or arguments that have been put forward. And disagreeing with (or even disproving) the theory of God or creationism does not make common descent true. That extrapolation can only be made with an evolutionary theory bias. Even if you took God out of the above sequences, the extrapolations would still be severely excessive. This can be demonstrated as follows:

    a.   Some species have evolved into new species.
    b.   If some species have evolved, every species has evolved.
    c.   If every species has evolved, common descent is true.

---

* Charles Darwin is reported to have gradually lost his Christian faith prior to releasing his theory of evolution and common descent. It has been proposed that his loss of faith was due to various tragedies that he experienced, most notably the death of his 10-year old daughter Annie.

The above sequence is still unscientific and illogical. Statement *b* is a complete presumption and to get from statements *a* to *b* requires a huge degree of extrapolation.

We have touched on why it seems that the atheistic bias drives people towards evolutionary theory rather than any of the other alternative theories. There are many factors at work, but the fact that it is promoted as "science" and promoted as the intellectual position to hold would appear to make it more alluring than the other atheistic options. As mentioned, there are various different biases that can lead someone to the conclusion of evolutionary theory and not just atheistic bias. But what we have shown is that generally *a* bias is needed, as it is very difficult to get there without one.

So the actual arguments and evidence used to support evolutionary theory are not that relevant. They are just the means to an end, which is promoting the doctrine that God does not exist. The extrapolations that are made obviously create huge gaps, uncertainties and unanswered questions. Pro-evolutionists admit this but defend the extrapolations by claiming that just because evolutionary theory cannot answer all the questions, it does not make the theory untrue. This sounds very much like a religious argument: we don't know how this came to be, but we know evolution did it!

The initial creation of life

In order to appreciate the relationship between evolutionary theory and atheism, it helps to consider the origin of the first life form. This is known as the process of abiogenesis, the development of life from non-life. Now, as we have already said, evolutionary theory is not concerned with how the first life form came to be. It is only concerned with how all species came to be from this one original life form, and the theory does not offer any explanation for abiogenesis. Therefore, the question of how life arose should not impact on one's verdict on whether evolutionary theory is true or not. However, it is clear that almost all pro-evolutionists seem to have formulated a theory about abiogenesis, and there is overwhelming support for this...

This theory states that about 3.8 billion years ago life arose in a "primordial soup": a pond or pool of water where conditions were ideal for the formation of organic compounds. Energy for this process to take place was probably provided by naturally occurring events, such as lightning. These compounds then accumulated in a "soup" and by further transformation, more complex organic molecules developed, eventually resulting in the development of the first life form. Even though the idea of the primordial soup is credited to Alexander Oparin (a Soviet biologist) in 1924, Charles Darwin had suggested a similar idea at the time of proposing his theory of evolution. He described a warm pond with all sorts of compounds like ammonia, phosphoric salts, plus light, heat and electricity – all the necessary components that you would theoretically need to make life. This is where the terms "hydrogen to human" and "molecules to man" come from, as essentially the theory dictates that hydrogen and molecules turned into a man by these accidental processes (and the subsequent evolution).

Now, it is a fascinating point of curiosity as to why pro-evolutionists are so keen to attach this unrelated theory of abiogenesis to their theory of evolution with common descent. The two seem to go hand-in-hand wherever they go. It is very hard to find someone who believes in one but not the other. This also ties in with a point we raised earlier about why evolutionary theory has gone all out and claimed common descent of all species from one original single-cell organism. It could have stuck with a scaled down version of the theory stating direct relatedness of certain species, like the finch species, or even gone as far as direct relatedness within the various animal classes only. But why go all out and suggest that every species is directly related when there is simply no evidence for this? And why fiddle around with the creation of the first life form when it doesn't concern evolutionary theory? The answer is obvious. It can only be due to a naturalistic or atheistic bias.

If evolutionary theory proposed evolution of one animal to another only within an order, family or genus, it wouldn't interest anyone. It wouldn't even serve any purpose, other than meaningless academia. But if evolutionary theory can expand itself to relate *all* species, then suddenly it has a real purpose: it serves as an effective weapon for atheism. But in order to complete the attack on theism and remove God from the equation altogether, atheism needs to somehow come up with a mechanism for how the first life form arose too. Hence, the theory of the primordial soup and the origin of life. Now atheism has an effective dual weapon: it can attack theism with full force in a two-pronged attack (if you add the "Big Bang" theory, it becomes a three-pronged attack). This is the obvious motive for the development and promotion of both theories side by side. The fact that Charles Darwin concerned himself with the origin of life shows that he had an atheistic bias. He was a naturalist and therefore had no reason to be concerned with abiogenesis. Nor did he have any expertise in this area. The only logical reason that one could conclude for why he proposed such an idea with no evidence to support it, would be for the purpose of promoting atheism and completing an attack on theism. The fact that pro-evolutionists overwhelmingly support the primordial soup theory is itself evidence that pro-evolutionists are heavily driven by an underlying atheistic, or at least naturalistic, bias. There is no other reason why they would support such a theory. There is no evidence for it. It is all conjecture. It has never been shown to be true and it has never been reproduced or observed.

The primordial soup theory is grossly speculative. There's no two ways about it. The theory states that elements and molecules combined with each other to suddenly and accidentally give rise to the first organism. One moment there was no life, and then the next moment there was life, brought about by a few elements and molecules colliding with each other and possibly aided by some lightning in there to give it a good mix. This really does sound far-fetched, but due to an underlying naturalistic or atheistic bias, people believe it to be true. It seems that an atheist would be much better off going with the alien theory or the brain in a vat theory!

To put this into context, we can use the "minimal gene-set concept". As we have seen, this is the principle that you need a minimum amount of DNA and genes to create any living organism, however primitive. For example, the smallest genetic organism known to exist is the Mycoplasma genitalium which has 525 genes.* Scientists have attempted to remove the genes from this organism to see at what point it could no longer function, in other words at what point it ceases to be and dies. This would give them an idea of the minimum amount of genetic material required for life. They concluded that they couldn't actually go below about 380 genes without the organism dying. It's like removing parts of a car one-by-one and seeing at what point the car is unable to drive anymore. Sure, removing parts like the bumper, the seats and the turbo will not stop the car driving. But remove the engine and it will stop driving. The car has to have a certain minimum amount of parts in order to work. Similarly, a living cell needs various components in order to be functional. It needs genes to code for various functions, such as cell wall synthesis, glucose metabolism and DNA replication, just to name a few.

---

* Mycoplasma genitalium is a bacterium that lives in the urinary and genital tracts of human beings.

What the primordial soup theory states is that this all happened in one go by the random collision of various molecules and elements, possibly triggered by some lightning. This means that the living organism went from 0 to around 380 genes all in one go. I'm sure you don't require me to touch on the improbability of this. It is, of course, worth mentioning that DNA, RNA and lipids, which are the building blocks of life, have never been found to exist anywhere outside of a living organism. So we would not expect DNA strands to just be floating around and then by some chance come together to form a fully functional organism. Also, for decades scientists have been trying to reproduce the conditions of the primordial soup and have been trying to create life from non-life in much the same way the primordial soup theory dictates. They have never had any success in doing this. Think about some of the biological advances that have been made in recent times: genetic engineering, mapping of the human genome and cloning of an adult sheep. Considering these, it seems that it would not be too hard to reconstruct the conditions of the primordial soup and create a functional living cell from molecules in the soup. If they can't do this, suspicions should be raised. And they can't. Yet science wants us to believe that this is the process that occurred to bring about the first life form, and what's more, it happened by pure chance!

In Chapter 2 we said we would explore why Charles and Erasmus Darwin favoured progression of life forms rather than regression of life forms, and why they presumed that complexity starts with simplicity. If one has a naturalistic or atheistic bias, one will attempt to explain all phenomena through naturalistic means. It is much easier to propose a naturalistic origin of an original common ancestor that is a simple single-cell organism than one which is a complex organism, such as a man. A man has around 20,000 genes. It is obviously *easier*, but not necessarily feasible, to propose an accidental physical process resulting in an organism with 380 genes than an organism with 20,000 genes. Going from 0 to 380 genes in one go is much more *naturalistically* explainable than going from 0 to 20,000 genes in one go. The Darwins would only have presumed the former over the latter if they wanted to not only explain biodiversity, but also establish a naturalistic cause of the origin of life. During their time, there was no evidence to suggest one over the other. So it appears that the Darwins had a naturalistic or atheistic bias, as their hypothesis was not based on evidence but on the concept that "complexity starts with simplicity" which was more amenable to naturalism. This is a philosophical viewpoint on nature and not a scientific determination.

Chapter 9 – Closing statement

Evolutionary theory is more a question of history than science, as it is not amenable to scientific investigation. It is not observable, testable, reproducible or falsifiable. There is no direct or empirical evidence to support it, and each piece of evidence on its own requires a great degree of inference to suggest that the theory is correct. Some of the pieces of evidence do complement each other, but this appears largely due to circular reasoning.

Evolutionary theory seems very improbable, even if it is broken down into a multitude of stages. Pro-evolutionists argue that it is probable when you consider the length of time that it has been working for, and the fact that it is a step by step process with one change at a time. You may even hear of how an eye can develop from a flat retina in as little as 250,000 generations, which is a relatively tiny speck of time in the reportedly 3.8-billion-year history of life. However, we have shown how it is the actual changes that are improbable due to them being caused by random chance mutations. And the accumulation of these changes resulting in a significantly advanced structure, let alone a new species, just seems too far-fetched.

Evolutionary theory has been built on the premise that complexity starts with simplicity, but, as we have shown, there are no grounds for this premise, meaning that much of the theory is based on circular reasoning. There is simply no reason, scientific or otherwise, to presume that a complex organism or structure must have been preceded by a simpler one.

Complex structures, such as eyes, backbones and venom, are difficult to explain through an evolutionary model. So too are complex functions like seeing and flying. This is because a smooth gradation of increasing complexity coupled with increasing functionality seems highly improbable, and even impossible in functions which are "all or nothing", such as the use of an effective venom.

The concept of convergent evolution seems highly improbable. There is a contradiction here too, in that evolutionary theory is based on the premise that degree of similarity positively correlates to degree of relation, however, when an observation occurs which contradicts this premise, then the theory simply accommodates this by stating certain similarities are independent and not closely related. This is clearly a form of hindsight bias.

Many if not all species seem remarkably unique. Many functions and abilities seen in species are unique to that group of species. Intermediary functionality and redundant structures are generally not found in species, even though they should be expected in the evolutionary model.

It has been shown that there are many unanswered questions with evolutionary theory, and this seems to be because they are unanswerable. The uniqueness of the human is a point of significant curiosity, and one which goes against the model of evolutionary theory. In fact, when you think about it, this is probably the most eye-opening point for anyone investigating evolutionary theory. It is remarkable to think that you (as a member of the human species), in terms of your appearance, behaviour and functioning, are the most isolated and unique species in existence. No other species can read this. No other species can understand this. No other species can formulate an opinion on this. Of course, one of the 1.2 million species known to exist today has to be the most isolated and unique, but it is you that has this accolade. So the human species really is one in a million. Isn't it an irony that the most isolated and unique species on the planet is the only one capable of proposing evolutionary theory and critiquing it?

Without question, the human species is the most intellectually advanced species by far. It is also far more successful than any of its presumed ape-relatives. No other ape lives on every continent in the world. No other ape makes beautiful art and architecture. But humans ending up as the most isolated species should not be expected by the evolution model. Because, if evolutionary theory is correct, there would have to be other species with a modicum of the intelligence and ability that the human species displays – perhaps ones that could wear clothes, hunt with weapons, cook with fire or communicate through speech. But, bizarrely, there aren't. This degree of uniqueness would not be expected to exist in isolation if evolutionary theory is true, because intelligence is a great attribute for survival. Even lost tribes wear clothes, cook food, build shelters and hunt with weapons, so this level of intelligence and ability would appear to be unique and natural to the entirety of the human species.

Close relatives of the human don't exist when we would expect them to. Living ancestors of any species are lacking, yet we have shown that there is no plausible reason for this. Theoretically, ancestors should be able to coexist with their descendants. It seems logical to presume that some of members of a species can change or evolve while others remain the same. Evolutionary theory cannot offer a reasonable explanation for the lack of living ancestor species. The theory claims that all ancestors have evolved, but it cannot justify this in view of the observations and assertions that the theory itself makes. It cannot explain how ancient end-point species exist today but not similarly-aged, or even younger, transitional/ancestor species.

We really do not have an answer to the chicken and egg dilemma. Without an answer to this fundamental question, a significant part of evolutionary theory is missing. How sexual reproduction can arise from asexual reproduction is a conundrum that evolutionary theory cannot explain. For new sexual organs to arise from nothing seems illogical, and there cannot be an argument for their gradual evolution, as a steadily increasing gradation of improving functionality with increasing anatomical structure is unrealistic. It seems grossly speculative to suggest that a complex function like sexual reproduction can develop spontaneously.

The idea of one species evolving into another has severe theoretical problems. Species can be separated from each other by their inability to reproduce with each other. Evolutionary theory has an impossible task of identifying where this point arises on an evolutionary lineage. Differentiating species when one merges into another seems an impossible and contradictory task. Also, it seems a peculiar idea to suggest that the ability to reproduce reduces gradually with increasing divergence. Modern day observations suggest that reproduction is binary – either two animals can reproduce or they cannot. To suggest that prehistorically this may not have been the case requires evidence, otherwise it is just gross speculation.

The previous distribution of the human race just seems incompatible with evolutionary theory. It is evident that prior to the beginning of human records circa 6000 BCE, distinct racial groups did not coexist anywhere in the world, and such cohabitation only occurred very late in recorded human history. So up until only a few centuries ago, there was clear separation and segregation of all racial groups throughout the world. This seems incompatible with evolutionary theory's premise that all human groups evolved from one origin. Because, the idea of monogenism supposes that primitive groups crossed great geographical barriers tens of thousands of years ago, settled in one location, did not make subsequent migrations, lived in isolation until very recently, and had no knowledge of the outside world, from which they supposedly originated from. It also supposes that every region of the world was discovered and colonised by one group with no subsequent visitors until tens of thousands of years later.

There are many anti-evolutionists out there who question the suitability of the evidence used by evolutionary theory. They claim that the evidence does not support evolutionary theory in the way pro-evolutionists would have you believe. Different scientists interpret the evidence for evolutionary theory differently, and the same evidence is promoted one way by the pro-evolutionists and another way by the anti-evolutionists. But it is the same evidence, so what is the layperson supposed to do?

The evidence to support human evolution is very questionable. Firstly, is it reliable? Secondly, has it been interpreted correctly? And thirdly, does it actually add any weight to evolutionary theory? The first two questions are difficult to answer. The third question is not: the answer is no. Evolutionists go in search of human ancestors and cousins with the unproven premise that evolution and common descent are true. Then when they find a fossil which could fit the bill, they give it a place in the story of human evolution without considering alternative possibilities. It is classic example of observer bias.

Fossil DNA extraction and analysis over the last few years has added a new dimension to the study of evolution. But the question that has to be asked when analysing DNA of two similar life forms is, does the DNA actually suggest that they are distinct species? (That is to say *if* DNA can actually establish this in the first place). Even if DNA can establish that two similar life forms are distinct species, does it *prove* ancestry or relatedness? The answer to this question is invariably no. DNA cannot reveal the relationship between different species.

Regarding dinosaur denial and the view of evolutionary theory as a hoax, of course, it is not expected that you should take these views on board. But the views should be given consideration at least. They are viable whether you like them or not. We are not asking you to reach an opinion on them, but they have to be considered. The dinosaur deniers and conspiracists of evolutionary theory have put forward cases where they are able to demonstrate viable conspiracies with motive, means and opportunity. There is no way that you or I could know with any degree of certainty whether these conspiracies have any truth behind them or not. In essence, these conspiracy theories are similar to others, like the ones which suggest that climate change and the 1969 moon landings were a hoax. It will come down to your own intuition to establish whether there is any truth behind them or not. As mentioned however, these have only been provided for your reference, and they shouldn't really play a decisive role in establishing whether evolutionary theory has been proven to a reasonable degree.

What is not up for dispute, however, is the fact that there have been false pieces of evidence and hoaxes provided by pro-evolutionists to support their case. Some of these have been instrumental discoveries for evolutionary theory, only to be found later to be hoaxes. Now, of course, it would be wrong to demonise the whole of the evolution movement based on the wrong actions of what would appear to be just a few individuals, seemingly acting for personal interest rather than for a more sinister cause. But it is clear that the credibility of the pro-evolutionists as a collective group has been harmed by the actions of these few. It is like the boy who cried wolf. Once a deliberate lie has been made to promote the theory, and the lie has been supported by the wider pro-evolution community, then the credibility of the whole community comes into question, as well as the evidence that is being used to support the theory. It would seem that evolutionary theory has been involved with more hoaxes, false evidence and controversies than most other unproven theories, which itself may be of some relevance. It is hard to think of any other scientific theory that has been subject to anything like this. For us, it is not possible to know what evidence is real and what evidence is not real, and an element of faith is required.

You might argue that the reasoning used in chapter 6 suggests that anything can be explained away by assuming the existence of God, rendering scientific enquiry redundant. But remember, we are only offering a rebuttal to evolutionists' claim that there are observations in nature which cannot be explained though any means other than evolution. We have already established that certain scientific and non-scientific phenomena do not require alternative explanations, as they have met the burden of proof. The premise of our enquiry is that evolution has not met this burden of proof, hence the need to explore alternative theories. However, we are not *promoting* an alternative theory to evolution; we are simply seeing whether evolutionary theory stands up to the general requirements (scientific or non-scientific) of a good theory, which is one which should not be explainable by other means. There is nothing in evolutionary theory's case that could not be explained by God being the cause of it. Creationism can account for all of the inconsistencies described in Chapter 4, as the laws of nature are not applicable to God.

Creationism is not limited to the perspective of the monotheistic religions of the West. Almost every religion of the world has a supernatural intelligence as the cause of the world and life. Of course, there are different variants of how this was achieved. The exact method of causality is not required, as long as we are aware that a supernatural intelligence *is* a viable alternative to evolutionary theory. To say that it is not a viable alternative is an example of bias against creationism and towards naturalism. It seems likely that a strong denial of a supernatural entity could subconsciously determine the verdict on evolutionary theory, generally towards a supportive position.

We have shown that evolutionary theory driven by God guiding it step by step seems implausible, as this would appear to be too inefficient for such an intelligence. It would also create other problems, such as differentiating human beings from animals. However, even if you think that this is possible, the burden of proof for evolutionary theory would still have to be met.

As we have seen, there are a substantial number of people who accept both evolutionary theory and religion/God, and this is curious position to take. Theists technically accept supernatural processes in the universe, so for them to insist on explaining all life forms through naturalistic means is a bizarre paradox. Creationism is already a viable theory for theists.

While atheistic evolutionists believe that biodiversity has resulted from pure chance, theistic evolutionists are obliged to believe that biodiversity has resulted from God being mischievous. This unusual belief system could arise for various reasons. Perhaps a mixture of biases results in the inexplicable position of accepting both. Perhaps people are adopting a form of Pascal's Wager, while at the same time accepting evolutionary theory on other irrational grounds. Or perhaps they accept one or both to fit in for social reasons. Who knows?! Whatever, we have shown it is an unintelligible position to hold.

We have managed to give an explanation for why evolutionary theory is so popular despite the weak case for it. It is a strong weapon for atheism and it has been used as such. Widespread indoctrination of the theory has followed its proposal, and many experts and non-experts have jumped on the bandwagon of this growing movement for various reasons. A bias for atheism has been shown to be a significant factor in the acceptance of the theory. This explains why the theory extends to such dramatic claims, and why proponents of the theory also support a naturalistic model for the origin of life, which, in fact, has nothing to do with evolutionary theory. There is no correlation between evolutionary theory and the theory of the primordial soup. The fact that almost all people who believe in one believe in the other, suggests a high likelihood that there is an underlying bias resulting in their acceptance of both theories. As, both theories seem highly illogical and irrational.

It appears that there are multiple reasons why people accept evolutionary theory despite its lack of evidence and seeming illogicalness. These include the hard promotion of the theory, an underlying motive or bias, herd mentality or what could crudely be termed as intellectual laziness or blind faith, whereby they simply accept what they are told.

Interestingly, the United States of America would appear to be one of the only Western developed countries in the world that has had a difficult time promoting and teaching evolutionary theory as an academic subject, with 38% of Americans rejecting the theory. Many Western countries view the United States of America as being backwards on this subject – they see Americans as scientifically less educated and less informed. But this is an irony, as we have shown that a denial of evolutionary theory would actually appear to be a more intelligible position to adopt! So the Americans can boast that they are actually more scientifically smart than their comrades in the rest of the Western world. It is curious as to why this might be. Obviously, it is beyond the scope of this book to explore this, but it is interesting to note that the United States of America, unlike many other Western countries, has always had religious freedom with separation of religion and state. And the citizens of the country have never been victim to high levels of religious persecution and terror. Consequently, a bias against religion would appear less likely to develop in the United States of America. This could be one of the reasons why there is less of an inclination towards evolutionary theory there than in other Western developed countries.

In summary, there is no scientific case for evolutionary theory, and evolutionary theory is not a scientific question. Evolutionary theory seems highly illogical and highly improbable, and there are gross inconsistencies with the theory. Alternative theories have been proposed, and these have been shown to offer as plausible explanations as evolutionary theory does for the observations of the natural world. There are scientific groups that disagree with the theory and interpret the evidence in different ways. Conspiracy theories exist which claim that evolutionary theory is intentionally fraudulent, and it is a fact that forgeries and fraudulent information has been previously used to support evolutionary theory. Despite all of this, many people continue to support it. However, we have given you probable reasons for why this is so. We would not expect you to base your judgment on the opinions of others, even if those opinions belong to the majority.

We have conceded that evolutionary theory is a *possible* explanation for biodiversity. However, the convergence of all the circumstantial evidence does not seem to make a strong case for it. And when considering all the other information, such as the seeming illogicalness and improbability of the theory, the inconsistencies of the theory, and the alternative explanations, then the circumstantial case would appear too weak to be given serious consideration. But with the use of sophisticated terminology, along with probably an appeal to an atheistic attitude, pro-evolutionists have managed to impress and convince society into believing the theory. Their own belief would appear to be guided more by passion rather than intellect. Granted, the evidence used to support evolutionary theory does not contradict the theory. But it doesn't *prove* it ether. It is not good enough to suggest that the suspect *could* have killed the victim. We need strong evidence to suggest that the suspect *did* kill the victim.

The standard of evidence required to convict a suspect in a murder trial should be the same whether there is another suspect in the crime or not. But, as we often see in murder cases, external pressures to convict someone for a heinous crime can often lower the thresholds for the evidence required. It is not inconceivable that here too also a strong desire to find the cause of biodiversity on Earth has lowered the bar for the strength of evidence required to establish a plausible theory. However, we have to remember what's at stake here. If evolutionary theory is going to be taught as fact to children in schools, it must meet a threshold which puts it beyond reasonable doubt. The threshold for the burden of proof should not be lowered by disbelief of the alternative theories. You may think that God does not exist and aliens cannot be responsible for life on Earth, but that should not influence your judgment on whether evolutionary theory has been proven to a reasonable degree. You should not be drawn to evolutionary theory based on a desire to have an answer, any answer, to the mystery of life. Many mysteries go unsolved, and we cannot lower the burden of proof due to curiosity or a desire to have an answer.

With crimes there is often a motive, and it would seem reasonable to presume that there is a motive to promoting evolutionary theory against the evidence. We have shown possible motives for this, although admittedly intent is a little speculative. Of course, many crimes do not have a motive, such as manslaughter, and the promotion of evolutionary theory may be a case of unintentional misleading. The eminent scientists who promote the theory certainly seem to believe it to be true, and it seems excessive to accuse them of deliberately misleading people. It may simply be a case of misjudgement, mixed in with some subconscious denial and refusal to adjust for whatever reason. If it is a case of deliberate misleading, the obvious motive would be to promote atheism and demote the theory of creation and thus reduce the power, hold and authority of religious institutions. Although, it seems that the majority of eminent scientists do not strongly believe and promote the theory for this reason but due to ignorance and blind acceptance. Either way, it is not necessary for you to concern yourself with possible motives and intent for the purposes of making your judgment as, of course, the burden of proof is unchanged by this. We are trying to establish whether evolutionary theory is true, not whether it is corrupt or not. And besides, we have no direct evidence to establish intentional foul play.

Biology makes many fascinating observations about nature, but it seems to take these observations and apply magical processes to them for explanatory purposes. For example, it is fascinating to have discovered that an Australopithecus afarensis "species" *may* have existed many millions of years ago, but to claim that this species evolved into Homo sapiens through a series of random mutations is a presumption which is not based on scientific principles or logic. There is no actual evidence to support this presumption, and therefore it is nothing more than a dreamed-up process. It is no different to using a theory about aliens to explain crop circles. Ernst Chain, the German-born British biochemist who won the Nobel Prize for his work on Penicillin, called evolutionary theory *"a very feeble attempt to understand the development of life"*, and said *"I would rather believe in fairies than in such wild speculation."*

Remember, you cannot agree with parts of evolutionary theory. It is an all-or-nothing deal. You cannot agree with evolution of some species but not others, nor can you agree with evolution within animal classes but not between classes. Similarly, you cannot believe evolution occurs for all the animals except for humans, or that humans were made separately and specially. The theory states that *all* life arose from the one initial single-cell organism through the process of evolution, and that is what you are being asked to determine: the likelihood that your direct ancestor was so small in size that you would require a microscope in order to see it.

We have shown that evolutionary theory has not met the burden of proof and there appears to be more than reasonable doubt. The conclusion is that evolutionary theory has not been proven to a reasonable degree. It is unscientific and should be withdrawn from science classrooms in schools. It is a question of faith, and is no different to religious faith – the same mechanisms of thinking and rationality are used in both. Evolutionary theory is a *possible* cause of biodiversity, and it could still be taught in school to encourage free-thinking. However, it should be reserved for philosophy or theology classes, where it can be taught alongside creationism theories. Similarly, we are not advocating that creationism is taught in science lessons, as this too is not a scientific matter. What can continue to be taught in science classrooms are the processes of evolutionary theory which have been shown to be true, such as DNA replication, gene mutation and natural selection within a species. But the speculative presumption that the cumulative effect of these processes is evolution, which has not been shown to be true, should not be taught as scientific fact. Any scientist who thinks it should, needs to examine what science actually is.

For so long the public has been deceived into believing evolutionary theory is an unchallengeable fact. But now is the time to put an end to the evolution indoctrination that is plaguing the world. Let's face it – we've been misled. It's time to acknowledge this and put an end to it.

Evolutionary theory would appear to be the greatest mistake science has ever made. Whether it is also the greatest *deception* the scientific community has ever sold is left to your discretion...

"I myself am convinced that the theory of evolution, especially to the extent to which it has been applied, will be one of the greatest jokes in the history books of the future. Posterity will marvel that so very flimsy and dubious an hypothesis could be accepted with the incredible credulity it has."

Malcolm Muggeridge, The End of Christendom

Printed in Great Britain
by Amazon